BADGE 387

BADGE 387

The Story of Jim Simone,

America's Most Decorated Cop

Robert Sberna

For my aunt, Dr. Evelyn Maroon, in appreciation

of her love and inspiration.

—ROBERT SBERNA

To Dave Sumskis (1947–97), my partner, my friend,

and the best cop I ever worked with.

To my wife, Lynne, who has given me many years of love and support,

and our children, Stephanie, Michelle, Mary, Nick, and Steve.

—JIM SIMONE

Contents

Acknowledgments

The research, writing, and production of this book was helped by many people. The author thanks (in no particular order):

Tom O'Grady, Joe Simone, Tom Evans, Alex Zamblauskas, Eric Sandy, Mary Rose Oakar, Ed Kovacic, James E. Bond, James MacLachlan, Craig Caldwell, Jon Jakeway, Sherri Buck, Susan Zamblauskas, Carole Deighton, Carole Gentile, Andres Gonzalez, Daniel Chaplin, Dave Grossman, Ed Gallek, Ernestine Buckley, Michelle Pallo, Zach Pallo, Fred Yearsley, Joe Paskvan, Stephanie Simone-Berardinelli, Michelle Simone, Mary Simone, C. Ellen Connally, Dean Kavouras, Keith Sulzer, Ed Kovacic, Mansfield Frazier, Jill Kekic, Michael Jenovic, Michael Scott, Michael Roberts, Peter Moskos, Nick Szymanski, Steve Szymanski, Jodi Sours Grant, Rabbi Sruly Wolf, Robert Shores, Robert Ducatman, John Ferak, Jim Hollock, Laura Bozell, Greg Baeppler, Brian Miller, Margery Gerbec Slatkovsky, Kathleen Sutula, Chad Colley, John Thomas, Jenny O'Grady, John Graves, Jim Huser, Laura Paglin, Rita Workman, Carl Basa, Joe Ciacchi, Diane Giordano, Dean Ciacchi, Mary Sberna and Mary Adkins.

Introduction

I first became acquainted with Jim Simone in May 2013, shortly after the arrest of Ariel Castro, the Cleveland man who had imprisoned three women in his house for nearly a decade. Simone, while working as a traffic cop in 2008, had pulled over Castro for operating a motorcycle without a valid license plate.

After a short conversation that was recorded on Simone's dash cam, he issued citations to Castro and then released him. Simone, of course, didn't know that the mild-mannered, contrite Castro was holding Michelle Knight, Amanda Berry, and Gina DeJesus hostage.

When media outlets learned of Simone's dash-cam video, he was interviewed on several national news shows. I noticed that some of the commentators referred to Simone (pronounced Si-moan-ee) as "Supercop" and mentioned his history of deadly gun battles. In following months, police across the nation were involved in several high-profile shootings. The controversial deaths of civilians in Cleveland, Chicago, Baltimore, and Ferguson, Missouri, ignited a national debate on police use of force.

In the midst of an escalating wave of frustration and anger at police, I became interested in examining law enforcement protocol and the elements involved in a deadly force incident. I was seeking answers to weighty questions: What are the inciting factors that compel a police officer to take lethal action? Can civilians fairly judge a cop's split-second response to a perceived deadly situation? Is the media acting objectively in their second-guessing of police discretion, or is their criticism driven by agenda?

Simone, a forty-year police veteran involved in five fatal shootings, seemed to be an obvious interview source. Retired from the Cleveland Police, he was employed as a part-time patrol officer for two suburban police departments. He agreed to be interviewed and this book was born.

During eighteen months of conversations with Simone, he was straightforward, self-assured, and consistent—which, as I came to learn, was how he conducted himself as a police officer. The many cops and citizens I interviewed typically described Simone as an aggressive, no-nonsense officer who rarely cut breaks for anyone.

Ed Kovacic, who rose from patrol officer to Cleveland's chief of police, was known for holding his officers to a high ethical standard. Simone, said Kovacic, always met and exceeded that standard.

"He is the most ethical person I've ever known," said Kovacic, conceding that Simone's by-the-book mentality occasionally caused problems.

"One of the most difficult things in police work is to be 100 percent," Kovacic said. "If you're going to enforce the law for one person one way, you must enforce the law for all people the same way. Simone was 100 percent down the line. That's a difficult thing to do, and I admired him for it. He had the guts and courage to issue tickets to citizens and cops alike, even if that made his life difficult amongst his colleagues."

However, Simone's fellow cops always knew they could count on him to cover their backs, added Kovacic. "When things got out of hand, Simone would take charge," he said. "He would never let someone take a risk that he could take himself."

Kovacic, who was one of Cleveland's most respected and popular police chiefs, nevertheless said it wouldn't be practical to have an entire department of Simone types. "Jimmy is too rigid," Kovacic explained. "The citizenry would rebel if there were too many Simones on the police force. If Jimmy has a fault, it's that he's inflexible. At the same time, it's his strength. He's an absolute. Every department should have at least one Jim Simone to show other cops how good they can be, even though we know they will never come close to matching his accomplishments."

While Kovacic said that we are a safer community with diligent, pro-active officers like Jim Simone, he said this age of political correctness and "soft" policing makes it unlikely that we'll see another Simone on the police force again.

Simone has meticulously documented the highlights of his police career, storing news clippings and photographs in several large plastic bins. Included in the bins are hundreds and hundreds of plaques, medals, and letters of commendation for valor and professionalism. At one point, I attempted to determine how Simone stacked up against other U.S. police officers in terms of awards. After researching the police departments of major cities and posting queries on law enforcement Internet forums, it seemed very probable that Simone is America's most decorated active-duty cop. If my research is determined to be inaccurate, I apologize to the many dedicated police officers who serve our communities.

Along with the accumulation of decorations, Simone has become the subject of numerous urban legends and folklore. Nearly everyone who lives or travels through Cleveland's Second District has a Simone story. He made more than ten thousand arrests during his career, with many of those apprehensions involving a chase, a struggle, or a fight.

But the legacy of Simone is perhaps best characterized by his unseen, unheralded acts. A nighttime ride-along with Simone—taken just before his retirement from the Cleveland Police—revealed his paternalistic commitment to the residents of his beat.

During the ride-along, Simone turned his cruiser into a high-rise public housing project and headed toward the complex's unlit courtyard. Silhouetted figures huddled in the darkness. A match was lit, a muted shout, and then laughter seemed directed at Simone's car. He stopped and flipped on his car's spotlight. For a second, he aimed the powerful beam at the courtyard, illuminating its occupants in stiff poses. Then, training the light at the second-floor windows, he slowly drove along the entire length of the building.

"What are you looking for?" asked his passenger.

"I'm not looking for anything," Simone replied.

After a moment, he explained, "There are a lot of elderly people living on the second floor. I'm just letting them know that Simone is on patrol. They tell me they sleep better when they know I'm out here."

Then, with a smile, he added, "They say I'm better than Valium."

1 No Exit

The following is taken from a Cleveland Division of Police incident report dated November 16, 1983, at 8:24 A.M.:

> After Patrolman Simone was shot in the basement of the Christian and Missionary Alliance Church by Dennis David Workman, he was conveyed to Deaconess Hospital, where Dr. Feltoon states that Ptl. Simone sustained an entrance wound of the left cheek. *(Dr. Feltoon noted "no exit" on his report).*
>
> At the time that Ptl. Simone was shot, he was dressed in civilian clothes. The following clothing was confiscated by detectives in the Emergency Room at Deaconess and conveyed to the Homicide Office and entered into the property book as evidence. The clothing of Ptl. Simone consisted of a black leather jacket—waist length, blue jean trousers, brown belt, brown loafers, pair of blue socks, and brown clip-on inside the belt holster.
>
> Ptl. Simone's .38-caliber Smith & Wesson 5-shot snub-nose revolver, blue steel with brown wooden handles, was recovered by Lieutenant Greg Baeppler in the basement of the church and turned over to detectives.
>
> Ptl. Simone's personal property consisted of a key ring with seven keys, one notebook which was left in the upper pocket of Ptl. Simone's leather jacket, and one Cleveland Police badge, number 387.
>
> The investigation concerning the attempted aggravated murder of three police officers and the homicide of Dennis Workman actually begins with the aggravated robbery of Ernestine Buckley at Lincoln-West High School.
> Nov. 16, 1983, 7:15 A.M.

After spending two weeks in the hospital recovering from double pneumonia, fourteen-year-old Donald Buckley was happy to be returning to school. On most days, Donald walked the half-mile from his home on

Cleveland's Near West Side to Lincoln-West High School, even in chilly, rainy conditions such as this morning's. His mother, Ernestine, however, was nervous about exposing him to inclement weather so soon after his illness. So she bundled him into her 1976 Ford LTD and drove him to Lincoln-West.

Outside the school, Donald slid out of the passenger seat and joined the other students entering the building. Just as Ernestine was putting her car in gear to drive off, her door was yanked open.

A tall, bearded man was pointing a revolver at her. "Get out of the car and leave the keys in the ignition!" he shouted.

"Take it. Just don't shoot me," pleaded Ernestine as she scampered from the vehicle.

She watched her car speed away, then hurried into the school to call police. Inside, two teachers were comforting assistant principal Celia Marie Giganti, who was still trembling after her encounter with the gunman moments before he took Ernestine's car.

Giganti had noticed the man outside her office shortly after 7:00 A.M. He identified himself as Dennis Workman and told her that he needed to speak to the principal about an urgent matter. Workman then told Giganti that he was at the school to save the children from a bomb attack. Nuclear warheads, he said, were going to strike the school at 8:30 that morning.

"The world is coming to an end. We need to escort the children to the basement," he implored.

The thirty-one-year-old Workman, who had attended Lincoln-West in the late 1960s, gestured toward the stairwell leading to the basement. As his black leather jacket swung open, Giganti spotted a gun tucked in his belt.

A .38-caliber Titan-Tiger revolver, the gun belonged to his wife, Rita Workman. She had bought the firearm a month earlier at her husband's request. Because he had a felony conviction, he wasn't permitted to purchase or own a gun, or even reside in a home with an unsecured firearm. But he'd convinced Rita that they needed a gun for security.

Shortly after purchasing the gun, she had misgivings about having it in the house. Dennis had been a casual drug user ever since she'd known him. But recently his drug usage had become more frequent. On a daily basis, he was smoking pot laced with PCP (phencyclidine), a powerful anesthetic that can cause hallucinations and paranoia.

He'd told her that smoking "wet" (the street name for PCP-laced pot) calmed him, but Rita could see the drug was having the opposite effect. He wasn't sleeping and his behavior was becoming increasingly bizarre.

Several times a day, he'd jump up from the couch and peer through the window curtains. "They're going to hurt you to get to me," he'd tell Rita. When she asked who, specifically, was after him, he didn't answer.

"I was so confused," said Rita. "Was the PCP causing his paranoia or was he having a mental breakdown? Or were there really people who were out to get him, maybe because of a bad drug deal?"

Her distress over Dennis's behavior was complicated by other concerns she had about him and their marriage. She'd recently discovered that he'd been having an affair with a coworker at the factory that employed him. When she had confronted him about his girlfriend and threatened to leave him, he'd become angry. Throwing her on the couch, he'd held a hunting knife to her throat.

She had been frightened, but not completely surprised by his violent outburst. She'd seen flashes of anger during the ten years they'd been together. They'd met when she was seventeen and he was twenty-two. He was a friend of her older brother's and visited her family's house often. Rita's father, like Dennis's, had relocated his family from West Virginia to Cleveland seeking work in the area's auto plants.

Growing up in rural West Virginia, Dennis had played sports, hunted, and fished. In Cleveland, he initially had difficulty acclimating to city life. He committed several juvenile offenses and often skipped school. In 1969, he dropped out of high school and enlisted in the army. Returning to Cleveland after his discharge, he soon became known to police as a tough guy who hung out with biker gangs and occasionally sold drugs.

She'd heard enough stories about his barroom fights to know that he wasn't averse to hurting others. But he also had his charms, she rationalized, describing him as six foot two with brown eyes, dark brown curly hair, and an easy smile.

"I didn't like his lifestyle or that he had a lot of girlfriends. But then again, maybe that's the reason I was attracted to him," Rita said. "I was shy and didn't go out much. Dennis was a 'bad boy' who made my life interesting. One day he came to my family's house to see me instead of my brother. He brought me a box of fudge. I didn't even like fudge and I'm not sure how we became a couple, but he never left me after that. He came to see me every day."

In 1980, the couple married. "When it came time to say his vows, Dennis kept stumbling over the word 'faithful,'" recalled Rita. "That was a big red flag." Afterwards, they celebrated at a reception that featured a checkerboard wedding cake and a keg of beer.

Foregoing a honeymoon, they returned to their jobs. He had a well-paying position at a steel plant and she worked at the former Halle's department store downtown, selling scarves, gloves, and jewelry. But three months after they wed, Dennis had a dispute with the tenant of a rental property that he'd purchased with one of his brothers. Dennis fired a gun in the direction of the tenant, which resulted in his arrest and a six-month prison sentence. When he was released from prison, he found that his felony record prevented him from getting his job back.

The loss of his job was the start of a three-year downward spiral for Dennis. He eventually found work, but at a fraction of the wages he was making at the steel plant. In late 1981, Dennis discovered that his name had not been included on the deed to the rental property. The money he'd invested was gone. While discussing the situation with his mother, he became frustrated and angry. They began arguing and he slapped her across the face with a stack of envelopes.

"He was very ashamed of hitting his mother," Rita said. "The guilt really ate at him."

She recalled that his drug use seemed to escalate after the incident with his mother. "He began dealing drugs, mainly to support his habit," Rita said. "But he tried to keep that part of his life secret from me."

By October 1983, paranoia was consuming him. "He picked me up from work one day and began screaming about withdrawing our money from the bank and driving to Florida. He kept saying that there were people out to get us," said Rita.

At work, Dennis accused his coworkers of trying to kill him by putting poison in the office coffeepot. "I think you need some time off," his boss told him. Dennis locked himself up in the house after that, leaving only to buy more drugs.

He had been a heavy smoker, but stopped smoking because he was afraid that family members would try to contaminate his cigarettes. After he hadn't slept for a week, Rita convinced him to seek treatment at Cleveland's Veterans Administration hospital.

The doctor who examined him told Rita that Dennis seemed to be experiencing a psychotic reaction from his drug use. But Dennis refused to be admitted and since he wasn't an imminent threat to himself or others, they couldn't hold him.

"Well, what should I do if he does get violent?" she asked. The doctor shrugged and said, "Run."

That evening, Dennis told his brother-in-law that he wanted to die. "He told him that he'd messed his life up," Rita said. "He didn't think he had anything left to live for. He was overwhelmed by guilt over his drug use, the loss of his job, and his unfaithfulness towards me. It seemed like he just wanted to end his pain."

On the night of November 13, Dennis experienced hallucinations. He told Rita that he was hearing voices and he couldn't stay in the house because he was afraid that someone was going to break in and hurt him.

At 10:00 p.m., she took him to the emergency room of MetroHealth Hospital, where a physician diagnosed him as depressed and schizophrenic. Believing that he posed a substantial risk of physical harm to himself and others, the doctor wrote an order authorizing Dennis's transfer to the Cleveland Psychiatric Institute (CPI), which was across the street from MetroHealth.

A hospital orderly accompanied Dennis and Rita to the admissions desk at CPI. However, the on-duty physician told them that he was very busy and he wouldn't be able to examine Dennis until at least 3:00 a.m. Rita was emotionally and physically exhausted. She knew she wouldn't be able to keep Dennis, who had become increasingly agitated, sitting in the waiting room for several hours. They went home.

On Tuesday, November 15, Fred Yearsley, the pastor of the Christian and Missionary Alliance Church, received a phone call from Rita. She told Yearsley that Dennis wanted to meet with him. Pastor Yearsley drove to the Workman's home, where he prayed with Dennis for an hour. To Yearsley, Dennis did not appear to be rational.

"I couldn't get a feel for his problems, but I could see in his face that he wasn't all there," Yearsley recalled.

That evening, Rita and Dennis attended Pastor Yearsley's church service. Dennis, leaning forward in his seat, listened attentively to the sermon. To Yearsley, Dennis's mental condition seemed marginally improved from earlier in the day.

On November 16 at 7:00 a.m., Rita awoke to find that Dennis was gone. "I suddenly had an eerie premonition," she recalled. "I jumped out of bed and pulled open the bottom drawer of my chest, where I kept the revolver." It was gone.

At that moment, at Lincoln-West High School, Celia Giganti was frozen by the sight of the gun in Workman's belt. She fought back panic as he once again told her that the children were in danger. Abruptly, Workman then said that he needed a ride to church.

Regaining her composure, Giganti told him that she would gather the children up and take them to the church for safekeeping. "Go get the church ready," she told him. "I'll bring the kids there."

Workman agreed and then left. She watched him run from the school toward Ernestine Buckley's car. Then she called the police.

Cleveland Police officers John O'Brien and Vaso Milojevic arrived at the school and took reports from Giganti and Buckley. Then, with Buckley riding in the backseat of their cruiser, the officers drove around the neighborhood searching for the stolen LTD and Workman. At 7:55, they spotted the car in front of the Christian and Missionary Alliance Church at Broadview Road and West 28th Street.

After speaking with an employee at a dry cleaning business across the street from the church, the officers learned that a man matching Workman's description had pulled up in Buckley's car and entered the church.

While one officer radioed for backup, the other pulled a Remington pump shotgun from a rack in the cruiser's trunk. Buckley, still in the backseat, asked, "What am I supposed to do if he comes out shooting?"

"Lay down on the seat," she was told.

By 8:00 A.M., six police officers were at the church. Others were on their way.

Jim Simone, after spending most of his ten-year career working nights as a patrol officer in Cleveland's Second Police District, had recently been assigned to daytime shift in the Juvenile division. He was reviewing the previous evening's reports when he heard radio chatter about the Buckley carjacking.

Officers John Thomas and his partner Richie Auner were at a doughnut shop when they heard the broadcast. "We met every morning for coffee," recalled Thomas, who had joined the police department four years earlier. "Later that morning, I was supposed to visit my son's first-grade class as 'Officer Friendly,' but when we heard that the carjacker was at the church, we decided to head over to see if they needed help."

The officers who had gathered in the church lobby had limited information about Workman, except that he was an army veteran with a criminal history. Auner and Thomas began searching the main floor of the church, where they noticed that the pulpit on the altar had been knocked over.

When Simone arrived, he learned that the basement hadn't been searched yet. As he headed toward the stairwell, he was joined by Thomas and Brian Miller.

"I left Richie upstairs, which I didn't feel good about," said Thomas. "It was the first time that we had split up since we'd started working together. As partners, we were responsible for each other."

Simone, Thomas, and Miller descended into the unlit basement, fairly certain that Workman was hiding in one of the rooms. In the main area of the basement, a desk had been flipped on its side. They yelled for Workman to surrender, but there was no response.

"We didn't have much intel about Workman," said Thomas. "We didn't know what his mindset was. But we were starting to come to the conclusion that he was going to make a last stand in the basement. No matter what happened, we thought we were prepared. We had distance and cover."

Miller, a twenty-four-year-old former Marine, stood in front of a restroom that hadn't been checked yet. Gathering his nerve, he placed his boot against the door.

"I was about to enter a room that possibly held a felon with a gun," said Miller. "I admit that I was scared. It's difficult to explain that kind of fear. Unless you've actually been in fear for your life, you can't even imagine what it's like."

He kicked the door open. The restroom was empty.

They next checked the children's playroom, which was decorated with cardboard cutouts of turkeys and Thanksgiving scenes. In the darkness, they could see that the playroom was empty. But a supply closet needed to be checked. Simone, at age thirty-five, was the senior officer among the three. Fifteen years earlier, Simone had been a platoon sergeant in Vietnam. He'd led patrols through enemy territory, often walking point—the most exposed position.

Now, standing in front of the closet, there wasn't any question who would open the door. He motioned Thomas and Miller to move behind him. He then dropped to one knee. If Workman was in the closet and fired his weapon, the bullet would pass over his head, Simone reasoned.

He slowly turned the doorknob. From inside the closet, Workman suddenly kicked the door open. Simone saw a gun and jerked his head to the side just as the muzzle flashed.

The bullet ripped into Simone's left cheek an inch below his eye, then exited the back of his skull and hit Thomas's left thigh.

Simone was knocked backwards, his head slamming against the linoleum floor. Thomas also went down. His femoral artery and femoral vein were severed, spurting blood against the basement wall. A trained paramedic, Thomas realized he was in danger of quickly bleeding to death. He crawled for cover behind a half wall just outside the playroom and applied pressure to the wound.

Miller, who was directly behind Simone when he opened the closet door, heard him yell that Workman had a gun.

"Then I immediately heard the gunshot," Miller said. "Jimmy and John were in front of me, so I couldn't take a shot."

After firing again, Workman stepped back inside the closet, and then immediately reemerged.

"The next thing I knew, Workman was pointing his gun at me," said Miller. "He fired twice, but I didn't even hear the shots because I was so focused on him."

Miller, a left-handed shooter, was struck in the left forearm. He tried to return fire, but his arm was numb. He scrambled toward Thomas.

Simone was now alone in the playroom, sprawled on the floor. "I felt like I had been hit in the face by a baseball bat," he recalled. "I laid there feeling sorry for myself for a second. Then I thought to myself, 'Workman, you motherfucker, you just killed me.'"

Workman, who had earned a marksmanship medal while serving in the army, swung his gun toward Simone and took dead aim from 4 feet away. Simone could only watch helplessly. Dazed and in pain, he was unable to take any evasive action or even raise his own weapon. Workman fired twice at Simone, the bullets just missing his head and ricocheting off the floor.

"Now he was making me angry," said Simone. "I was dead, but he was still shooting at me. After a couple of seconds, I felt a surge of adrenaline. I came off the floor like a coiled snake. I couldn't see clearly because I had blood in my eyes from my wound, but I kept firing at him until my gun was empty."

Simone, firing from a kneeling position, wasn't sure if any of his five bullets had hit Workman. "I remember that he was staring at me as if he was surprised that I had shot at him."

Workman returned to the closet. *Most likely to reload his gun,* thought Simone.

"Then I heard him wheezing," Simone said. "I knew then that I got him."

Thomas, meanwhile, was bleeding profusely. "The pain was excruciating. I knew that I was in trouble," he said. "I couldn't see into the playroom from where I was, but I heard the gunshots and I realized that Workman was continuing to shoot at us. I knew I needed to do something. At that second, I had a vision of my daughter, Athena. I remember seeing her long brown hair. In my vision, Athena told me to get back up and shoot."

He pulled himself to a standing position. Using one hand to apply pressure to the gunshot wound in his thigh, he gripped his shotgun with the other hand and fired toward the closet.

Miller, shifting his gun to his uninjured right hand, also fired. Miller then yelled for help. But the officers upstairs couldn't hear him — most hadn't even heard the gunfire. The children's playroom had been sound-proofed with double sheets of drywall.

"I was the only who could walk, so I told Simone that I needed to get John help before he bled out," said Miller.

"Take him," Simone managed to say.

Miller wrapped his arm around Thomas's waist and helped him move toward the stairs.

Simone, pushing himself backwards on the floor, moved into a doorway to reload his revolver so that he could lie down covering fire for Miller and Thomas. He tried to push cartridges into the cylinder, but his hands were so slippery with blood that he kept dropping the gun.

Thomas and Miller began climbing the stairs. "I looked back at Jimmy and I could see that he was in a bad way," said Thomas. "But I knew that Richie Auner and the others would be down in seconds to help him."

Lt. Greg Baeppler, the Second District shift commander that day, recalled that he had been at work for an hour when he heard about the carjacking.

"I had been monitoring the radio and heard that one of our cars was hopscotching with a guy named Workman," said Baeppler. "We were familiar with that family name. They were tough hillbillies who we'd dealt with before. When I heard they had found the stolen car at the church, I told a sergeant that we'd better go over there."

Arriving at the scene two minutes after Simone, Baeppler saw that several officers had set up a perimeter around the church.

"So I told the others at the scene to do a total search of the building," he said. "A minute later, we heard yelling and gunshots. Then we saw Miller come upstairs with Thomas. Miller's hand was bloody and I could see that Thomas was bleeding badly from his femoral artery. I remembered thinking, 'that's not good.'"

Baeppler and Auner then ran downstairs, charging into the gunsmoke-filled playroom.

"It was dark down there, but I saw Jimmy on the floor in a small alcove," Baeppler said. "I could tell from his blood trail that he'd scooted there from the playroom. He had a gunshot wound in his face, which is never a good thing. It looked serious. At that point, I didn't know that the bullet had blown out the back of his head."

Baeppler could hear Workman moving around inside the supply closet.

"Simone was quickly going into shock. I told Auner to give me covering fire so I could get Simone to safety. For the rest of my life, I'll never forget Richie Auner putting shotgun rounds into that closet. In the darkness of that basement, the flashes of gunfire and the smell of gunpowder were surreal."

After pulling Simone to the stairway, Baeppler asked him how he was doing. "I'm dying," Simone told him. A divorced father of three daughters, Simone had one urgent thought: "I grabbed that pretty white shirt of his with my bloody hands and I said, "Tell my girls what happened down here. Tell them."

"I didn't want that responsibility," recalled Baeppler, "So I told him, 'You're going to have to do that yourself. Let's get out of here.'"

Two other officers took Simone from Baeppler. He then stepped back into the playroom. "I could still hear noise from the closet, so I knew Workman was still alive," he said.

Baeppler and another officer pushed open the closet door. Workman was lying on his back, with a 1-gallon paint can underneath him. He was in cardiac arrest and had a bullet wound in his chest. One of Simone's rounds had penetrated his heart.

With ambulances en route, Baeppler took a moment to de-stress and assess the shooting. *How had Workman put three of his officers down?* he wondered.

"As soon as my adrenaline stopped pumping and I knew the cavalry was on its way, I began to consider whether we could have handled the situation differently," he said. "In hindsight, we could have figured out ten different ways of avoiding a gunfight. But we didn't have a lot of facts at the time. We only knew that we were looking for a carjacker. We didn't know Workman's state of mind."

Baeppler, who had been involved in several shootings during his fourteen-year police career, noted that Workman had been at Lincoln-West and other two locations earlier that morning.

"We weren't sure whether he was using the church as a pass-through, or if he had decided to make a stand," he said. "If we had known his mental state, we could have done things differently."

Rita Workman received a telephone call from her mother at 8:30 A.M. Before her mother could tell her, Rita knew that her husband was dead.

"I was angry and confused when I first heard how he died," she said. "At that time, I remember wishing that the police hadn't needed to use deadly force. I wished there would have been a way to spare the man's life. Maybe they could have tried to talk him out the basement," Rita said. "In retrospect though, he had become so deranged that it probably wouldn't have mattered. He wouldn't have responded. As the years have passed, I've come to feel sorry for the three cops that he shot. They walked into a bad situation. They didn't know that Dennis was depressed and paranoid; that he had been smoking PCP for a week; and that he was suicidal."

She said it's likely that Dennis had been bent on self-destruction for several years, but lacked the nerve to actually kill himself. "He had once mentioned to his mother that he was feeling depressed and thinking of suicide. She was a Pentecostal Christian with strict religious views. She had gotten angry and told him that if he killed himself, he would be committing a sin and he would never get to heaven. I think that influenced his thinking. He told me once that he would 'die by the gun.' Since he couldn't do it himself, I think he had a plan to get someone else to do it."

Rita was surprised to learn that two of Dennis's shots had missed Simone from point-blank range. "He was a marksman, he'd hunted all his life, and he liked to go to the shooting range. I'd seen him hit squirrels on a branch from so far away that I couldn't see the squirrel. For him to miss, I don't know what to make of that," she said, her voice trailing off.

At 9:00 A.M., O'Brien and Milojevic returned to their cruiser, where Ernestine Buckley was patiently waiting. The officers, who were visibly shaken, told Buckley that three cops had been shot and two weren't expected to make it. Then they drove her to police headquarters in the Cuyahoga County Justice Center in downtown Cleveland, where she viewed mug shots of Dennis Workman to confirm he was the man who had stolen her car. Her son Donald was there when she arrived. After learning that she had been driven away from Lincoln-West in a police car, he had run two miles to the Justice Center to make sure she was okay. Buckley was interviewed by several teams of detectives, then she and her son rode a bus home.

Simone had been carried upstairs from the church basement and pushed into the backseat of a police cruiser. Two officers on their way into the church stopped to look at him. One of the officers, grimacing at the sight of Simone's gunshot wound, said to the other, "He's done."

It wasn't the first time that Jim Simone had been presumed dead.

2 Friendly Fire

Summer 1966. Jim Simone was recently graduated from high school in Lakewood, Ohio, a suburban Cleveland community that bordered Lake Erie. Life was simple at age eighteen. His future was a straight, bright line. He had landed a job installing phones for the telephone company. In the fall, he'd be attending college.

A good student, he'd been offered an academic scholarship to John Carroll University, a Jesuit Catholic institution in northeast Ohio. He planned to major in education and eventually teach history. Passionate about American history, Simone had acquired, from an early age, an indomitable sense of patriotism.

The seeds of his allegiance to nation and flag were sown by his father, stepfather, and uncles, who were all World War II veterans. They were proud of their service and often shared stories of battlefield courage and self-sacrifice with Jim and his brother, Joe. As Jim got older, he realized their stories were curiously bloodless and undoubtedly sanitized.

In 1966, the United States escalated its involvement in Vietnam's civil war. President Lyndon B. Johnson's decision to increase ground troops and begin B-52 bombing raids on North Vietnam had disenchanted a large segment of the American public. But among Simone's elders, the ideology and rationale of America's role in Vietnam was not at issue. Whether or not the war effort was misguided, ill-advised, or poorly executed, a line had been drawn: There were those who answered our country's call to arms and there were those who did not.

So Jim wasn't entirely surprised when his stepfather walked into his bedroom in mid-June and asked him, rhetorically, how old he was.

"Eighteen."

"There's a war going on."

"I know."

"Go enlist tomorrow."

In those few seconds, his life's trajectory had been rerouted. He took a moment to process the implications, but there was no question about what he was going to do.

"My brother Joe had already joined the army," Jim recalled. "I couldn't tell my dad—a decorated soldier—that I wasn't going. I couldn't tell my uncle—a paratrooper who had jumped on D-Day at Normandy—that I didn't think it was the right thing to do."

In the Simone family, the tradition of military service was so strong that refusing to enlist would have been nearly indistinguishable from the unpardonable sin of dodging the draft. In the Simone household, the word "Canada" was not spoken.

The next day, Jim visited an army recruiting station and signed the paperwork for a three-year hitch. Just a week later, his stepfather dropped him off at the induction center in downtown Cleveland. While some of Jim's high school friends had enrolled in college just to avoid the draft, he had traded keggers, Saturday afternoon football games, a history degree, and a teaching career for the rigor of boot camp and the not unlikely chance that he'd be wounded or killed in Vietnam.

"It was a matter of honor and duty for me to serve our country," Simone said. "It was my heritage. My uncles, father, and stepfather had always told me that you can never understand what the American flag means until you've fought in a war."

Three days after his induction, he boarded a troop train to Fort Campbell, Kentucky, for basic combat training. The intrepid Simone welcomed the challenge of boot camp. His hustle and leadership skills quickly impressed his commanding officers, who awarded him a private first-class stripe during the ten-week course.

"I wanted to excel; I wanted to be the guy," said Simone. "If that meant shining my boots better than anyone else, then that's what I did. That's how I was raised."

He was, in fact, well prepared for the psychological demands of army basic training. His mother, Zelma Faye, had always had high expectations for her two sons.

"Our mom was a very dominant personality. If she told us something, then that's the way it was," said Joe, who is two years older than Jim. "She was very strong woman and she maintained a very simple code of honor in our home. We didn't lie, steal, or cheat."

Zelma Faye Mills had grown up in Wayne, West Virginia, a town of fourteen hundred. Her father, grandfather, and many of her relatives worked in the deep mines of the Williamson Coalfield in the southwestern corner of the state. The region was known for its deposits of bituminous coal, a type of coal that releases dangerous amounts of firedamp, a highly combustible mixture of gases that can be ignited by flame or sparks. Firedamp explosions were not uncommon and nearly everyone in Wayne had lost a family member in a mine cave-in.

Not far from Wayne is Matewan, the site of a deadly shootout in 1920 between miners and detectives from the Baldwin-Felts Agency. The detectives had been hired by a coal operator to evict a group of union miners who were protesting the unsafe and dismal mine conditions. According to historical accounts of the incident, known as the Matewan Massacre, the angry miners fired on the detectives. Seven detectives and three townspeople lost their lives.

Every summer during their childhood, Jim and his brother would visit their Mills relatives in Wayne, where his uncle was mayor. "It was a typical town with a flag flying, a war monument, and two cannons in front of the courthouse," said Jim. "There always seemed to be a couple of older men playing checkers on the sidewalk. It looked like Hollywood's version of small-town America."

Wayne's cannons and war memorial, however, were hard-earned. During the Civil War, half of the surrounding Wayne County supported the North and the other half backed the South. The split loyalties led to the county being ravaged by both the Yankees and the Confederates over the course of the war.

World War II also took its toll on Wayne County. More than one hundred of its young men didn't return from battle. Shortly after the war, Zelma Faye moved to Cleveland seeking work. She met Anthony Simone, a truck driver whose parents had migrated from Italy to Cleveland. After a short courtship, Zelma and Anthony were married. They began their life together in an apartment above a five-and-dime store in the Superior-St. Clair neighborhood of Cleveland.

When Jim was eight years old, Anthony and Zelma divorced. She and her sons remained in the small apartment. The neighborhood, which had once been home to working-class families, was now plagued by crime. Rowdy teens clustered in front of neighborhood stores, blocking doorways and menacing passersby. Fights, muggings, armed robberies, and vandalism were on the rise.

"It was a rough neighborhood," said Joe. "Just walking home from school each day could lead to a fight. Groups of kids would intentionally bump into us as we tried to walk around them. Jim and I had to stick together."

He recalled an incident in which he was overpowered by a larger, older boy at a neighborhood gas station. "I was getting beat up pretty bad," said Joe. "From out of nowhere, Jim came running around the corner. He hit the kid with a gas pump to get him off of me."

Although thinner and shorter than other boys his age, Jim never backed down from a fight. "When we were young, our uncles would sit in chairs outside our grandfather's house and watch us fight our cousins," said Joe. "Jim was the smallest of all of us, but he would beat up everyone. He was totally fearless. He was junkyard tough; there was just no quit in him."

The Simone brothers had their own dustups too, said Joe, blaming their competitive natures. No matter what the contest, the boys were always trying to outshine each other.

"When we'd play pickup football, Jim would want us to play on opposite teams," said Joe. "He'd always play rough against me. On one particular day, when I was on the bottom of a pileup, I felt a sharp pain in my leg. It was Jim biting me."

"We grew up tough; we had to," said Joe. "But our mom made sure that we weren't bad boys. We didn't commit crimes. We didn't steal cars, break into places, or hurt people."

One of his most enduring memories occurred when he was age ten. He and Jim were hiding behind a trash barrel, throwing snowballs at the windows of passing buses. "We didn't realize that our mom was watching us. She snuck up behind us and banged our two heads together. It was the last time we threw snowballs at buses."

When the boys were just into their teens, Zelma remarried. Her husband, Frank Mraz, was a steelworker who had two sons, Frankie and Eddie. Anthony also remarried, to a woman who had three children of her own.

Their parents and stepparents all possessed a strong work ethic, which had a profound impact on the Simone brothers.

"Our father, Anthony, would always push us to spend our time productively," said Jim. "He'd say, 'If you can't eat, drink, spend, or make love to something, it's not worth pursuing.' He even discouraged us from watching professional sports games. 'It doesn't matter if they win or lose,' he'd say, 'It puts no money in your pocket.'"

Zelma, who worked as a cashier at a grocery store, exacted firm control over her household and didn't tolerate shirking.

"We had to have the house cleaned and dinner cooked by the time she came home from work," Jim recalled. "From a young age, we washed our own clothes. And each week, my brother and I were responsible for scrubbing the kitchen floor. We'd use a brush and soapy water. Then we'd dry the floor with a towel and wax it."

Frank, their stepfather, shared Zelma's industrious nature. He worked at the now-shuttered Jones & Laughlin Steel as an equipment operator on the hot strip mill. After leaving work each day, he went to his second job as a taxi driver.

"I felt very fortunate to have great parents and a great stepfather," Jim said. "I liked that both of my fathers worked hard and that my mom expected us to work hard also. Everything made sense back then. There was a right and a wrong; and they were clearly defined. When my mom told me to cut the grass, I did it because it was the right thing to do."

High on the Simone list of "right things to do" was military service. In 1965, eighteen-year-old Joe joined the army. He was stationed in Germany for three years, assigned to a motor pool on the Czech border.

When Jim enlisted a year later, Joe wasn't surprised that he chose the infantry. "That's where the action was," he said. "Everything he did was 100 percent."

Following basic training at Fort Campbell, Kentucky, Jim attended the army's three-week airborne school at Fort Benning, Georgia. He first practiced jumping from the back of a moving truck to simulate the shock of landing. He next jumped from a 34-foot zip-line tower and then from the 250-foot towers. And he ran. At jump school, running is a constant. Trainees run to meals, to classes, for physical training and as discipline.

For Simone, who had injured his knee during a high school wrestling match, running was uncomfortable at best, and often painful. The injury had occurred when his knee became trapped between two wrestling mats that had pulled part. He'd had surgery to repair torn cartilage. Several months later, while walking to school, a car struck his repaired knee, requiring additional surgery. He had downplayed the knee injury to an army medical officer at the time of his enlistment.

To pass airborne school, each soldier makes five jumps from 1,200 feet, with the last being a nighttime jump. Simone recalled being more excited than nervous on his first jump. "I didn't have enough sense to be afraid the first time," he said.

On the Saturday after their fifth jump, the newly qualified paratroopers marched to Fort Benning's parade ground for their graduation ceremony. A colonel congratulated the men and then pinned airborne wings on their khaki shirts.

The men were now officially airborne, but their initiation wouldn't be complete until they'd been blood pinned. Later that night, they were taken to a locker room and told to stand against a wall. A sergeant placed the ¼-inch-long spikes of the metal airborne wings into the fabric of their T-shirts and used the heel of his hand to pound the badges into their chests. The traditional rite, known as "blood wings," was later banned by the army, with one general calling it a "barbaric act."

Simone, waiting his turn, watched the pinned men grimace in pain, their T-shirts dotted with blood. "I was looking forward to it," he said. "It hurt like hell, but I was proud to be airborne."

During his military service, Simone would parachute thirty-five times. "And I was scared thirty-four times. The jumps got scarier because I knew what to expect. But I figured as long as the guy ahead of me could do it, then I could do it also."

As a paratrooper, Simone earned an extra $55 a month in jump pay. He then shipped to Fort Dix, New Jersey, where he trained for three months as a radio telephone operator (RTO). One of the army's more demanding military occupational specialties, RTOs were chosen for their map-reading skills, their ability to process information quickly, and their composure under pressure, which were all traits that Simone had exhibited throughout his basic training.

Carrying the bulky 25-pound PRC-25 radios on their backs, RTOs communicated information among their platoon leaders, the battalion TOC (Tactical Operations Center), artillery support, and other units. In a firefight or while patrolling enemy territory, RTOs would stick close to commanding officers. If the officer was injured or killed, the RTO would often temporarily assume command, with responsibility for calling in fire support and medevac helicopters.

Simone then returned to Fort Campbell as a member of C Company, one of five companies in the 3rd Battalion of the 187th Infantry Regiment (the 3/187). The storied 187th was the only airborne regiment to have served in all major wars since the inception of the U.S. airborne force in 1940.

The 187th Infantry Regiment was famously nicknamed Rakkasans during its tour in occupied Japan following World War II. Derived from the closest Japanese term for "parachutist," the word "rakkasans" was used by an interpreter as he attempted to explain to Japanese dignitaries what the unit was trained for. Not knowing the exact term for "airborne soldier," he settled on "rakkasan," which literally means "falling down umbrella man."

Since 1964, the 3/187 had been assigned to the 101st Airborne Division. First deployed to Vietnam in December 1967, the unit fought in twelve major campaigns, including the bloody battle for Dong Ap Bai, commonly known as Hamburger Hill. The 3/187 would emerge from the Vietnam War as our nation's most highly decorated airborne battalions.

At Fort Campbell, Simone underwent six months of advanced infantry training, where he was taught how to place trip flares and claymore mines, how to knock out enemy bunkers with grenades, and how to set up defensive perimeters. He learned the technique of assaulting hills by using leapfrogging fire teams, with one team laying down covering fire as the other team advanced.

Training was completed in November 1967. A month earlier, Simone had been promoted to sergeant. Typically, a soldier would need three years of military experience before promotion to sergeant. Simone had accomplished it in twelve months.

Simone's rapid rise through the enlisted ranks was testament to his leadership ability. "But there was also an urgent need for noncommissioned officers in Vietnam," he said. "The death toll for sergeants was high. They needed replacements."

Shortly after he was awarded his sergeant's stripes, Simone was named "Outstanding Paratrooper" of his training group. At a presentation ceremony, a colonel from the 101st Airborne Division called Simone to the stage to receive his pin. Simone, as was his custom, had starched his uniform so heavily that the colonel had difficulty pushing the prongs through his rigid shirt.

In December 1967, national news organizations reported that the 3rd Brigade Combat Team of the 101st Airborne Division would soon be deployed to Vietnam. Simone's mother, aware that the 3/187 was attached to the 3rd Brigade, immediately mailed a letter to Secretary of Defense Robert McNamara's office in Washington.

Two weeks after their deployment announcement, the men of the 3/187 were issued new jungle fatigues and instructed to mail their personal items home. In forty-eight hours, they would be on planes to Vietnam. That night, the barracks doors were locked and all civilian clothes were confiscated, just in case any soldiers had misgivings about their military commitment.

Within hours of his departure flight, Simone was called into a meeting with several officers. He was handed the letter written by his mother, in which she had informed McNamara that her son had incurred a serious knee injury in high school that made him unfit for duty.

"Sergeant Simone, is there any reason you shouldn't be on that airplane tonight?" he was asked.

Pocketing the letter, Simone said, "Gentlemen, this is just my mother's last-ditch effort to keep me out of combat. I fully expect to be on that plane with my men."

"You will be," he was told.

Simone and the 160 other members of C Company (Charlie Company in the military alphabet) boarded a C-141 Starlifter for the 10,000-mile journey to Southeast Asia. During a layover at Los Angeles International Airport, one of the men deserted, vanishing into the crowded terminal.

As they neared the end of their twenty-five-hour flight, the plane's public address system crackled. Capt. James Bond, the commanding officer of Charlie Company, announced to the already-jittery troops: "Men, we have entered Vietnamese airspace and you are now drawing combat pay."

After white-knuckling through a steep descent angle (to minimize exposure to enemy fire), the men landed at Bien Hoa Air Base. They stepped from the plane into South Vietnam's 100°F heat and oppressive humidity. Within seconds of deplaning, Viet Cong mortars and rockets began exploding around them. With their rifles and gear still in the plane's cargo hold, they were instructed to stay low and run toward bunkers beside the runway.

When the attack ended, they were trucked to Cu Chi for in-country indoctrination. A suburban district of Saigon (now Ho Chi Minh City), Cu Chi was notorious for its sprawling network of tunnels built by the Viet Cong as hiding spots and weapons caches.

Charlie Company was then transported north to Phuoc Vinh Base Camp, where Simone spent several months as Captain Bond's RTO.

"Bond took an immediate liking to Simone," said Lt. James MacLachlan, leader of Charlie Company's 2nd platoon. "As a communication chief, Jim was great. He was exceptional on the radio—talking to squad leaders, talking to the battalion commander and the artillery, making sure everyone was squared away."

Simone's confident bearing also attracted the attention of Lt. Craig Caldwell, who was seeking men for his platoon, which had been depleted by casualties.

Caldwell had noticed that Simone made a point of attending every religious service, regardless of denomination. On weekends, he would be present at the Catholic Mass as well as Protestant and Jewish services. "I'd take any opportunity I could to pray," Simone explained.

Caldwell was curious about Simone's religious inclusivity. He asked him what faith he was. Simone, a Catholic who served Mass and sang in the church choir while growing up, answered, "My grandfather always told me that we all have the same God. We just have different ways of worshipping him."

Simone, in turn, asked Caldwell what religion he followed. Smiling, Caldwell said, offhandedly, "I believe in the frog."

Several months after that incident, Caldwell and Simone were part of a patrol that was pinned down by heavy enemy fire. "I looked around and I saw a lot of scared soldiers praying," said Simone. "And there was Lieutenant Caldwell praying also. And I'm guessing it wasn't to the frog."

In Caldwell's view, Simone was a natural leader. "I could see that he was a sharp individual," he recalled. "He was one of those people who are on the edge of the bayonet; the very forward edge. In the field, platoon leaders liked to snap those people up and keep them close."

As Bond's RTO, Simone spent much of his time at base headquarters. Caldwell, however, knew that Simone was eager to get into the field.

"My unit was running around on patrols trying to find Viet Cong," he said. "I felt that Simone was ready to go outside the wire [of base camp], so I asked him to come out in the field with me."

Caldwell's judgment was quickly confirmed. While on a long-range patrol through a forested area, Caldwell's platoon unexpectedly found themselves at the edge of an open field. The men needed to cross the clearing, but Caldwell, a graduate of the Virginia Military Institute and Army Ranger School, understood the danger of exposing his men in an open area. If the clearing was covered by enemy machine-guns, the platoon would be caught in a deadly interlocking fire with no place to hide or escape.

Circumventing the clearing would have required hours of additional movement. "That wasn't an option, so I had my M60 machine-guns sight their weapons across the open area to provide covering fire, if needed," said Caldwell. "Then I asked Simone to take his squad across the field to the other side. If they made it, they would radio back that it was safe for the rest of the platoon to cross. And Simone was willing to do that."

Caldwell said the presence of the M60 machine-guns may have given Simone some measure of security. "Nevertheless, he followed orders and did what was necessary. We all did that for each other, over and over, every goddamn day. That's the bond that we had."

On August 30, 1968, Simone's bravery was again put to the test. On a morning patrol commanded by Captain Bond, two platoons were returning to base camp when they began taking enemy machine-gun fire.

"We were pinned down in the open with a rice paddy behind us," said Simone. "They were laying down heavy fire and we had no way out."

Bond told Simone to take two men and try to flank the enemy machine-gun nest. Hugging the ground, the three men began moving toward a tree line.

"We'd only gotten a short distance before they spotted us and started firing," said Simone. "We lost one of our guys immediately. I knew we were fucked, but I thought to myself, 'I'm not dying on my belly.' So I told the remaining guy to follow me. We ran across the clearing toward a clump of trees. Somehow we made it through the gunfire without being hit. We waited for a pause in the shooting, and then I said a prayer and we ran right at the machine-gun nest. I fully expected to get shot, but we were very lucky. At that second, the machine-gunners were in the process of reloading. I had my M16 rifle and the soldier who was with me had an M60 machine-gun. His gun jammed, so I flipped my rifle on full auto and took out the position."

Simone was awarded the Bronze Star with V device (for valor under fire) for his actions that day. A lieutenant told Simone later that his charge at the machine-gun nest was the bravest thing he'd ever seen. "Brave?" said Simone. "It was one of the dumbest things I've ever done."

Simone never considered his actions heroic. "I was just afraid," he said. "Fear is a powerful motivator."

During the Vietnam War, the *Cleveland Plain Dealer* regularly published updates about local service members in its military news section. In mid-1968, the *Plain Dealer* reported: "Army Sgt. James M. Simone, 20, has won the Bronze Star Medal for valor but has not told his parents what he did to win it. Simone's mother describes James as a very brave boy who complains more about the Vietnamese red ants than the enemy bullets. He has made 15 parachute jumps and is due home by Christmas. He corresponds mostly by means of tape recordings."

During a combat infantryman's tour in Vietnam, he had to survive ambush, firefights, mortar attacks, and booby traps. He also faced the very real risk of friendly fire. According to U.S. Army statistics, up to 14 percent of deaths in Vietnam were caused by our own bullets, bombs, and artillery shells.

During an intense battle, U.S. forces would routinely request artillery support, most often 105mm howitzer rounds. The high-explosive shells had a range of about 7 miles and would kill anyone within 30 yards of their blast. In a typical combat situation, a forward observer (FO) served as the eyes of the artillery, calling in map coordinates and then adjusting the first few shells on the target. Once the range was set, the FO gave the order to "fire for effect," essentially dropping enough rounds on the target to destroy it.

But in the fear and chaos of a battle situation, it wasn't uncommon for FOs, particularly if they were under fire, to misread maps or lose track of friendly troop movements. When the FOs got rattled and confused in the so-called "fog of war," the results could be disastrous.

Simone lost his best friend in Charlie Company, Kenny Kotyluk, in a friendly fire incident. The two had met at Fort Campbell during training, then shipped together to Vietnam.

Kotyluk, the company's medic, was a Sacramento native who carried a photo of his pretty blonde girlfriend and his Corvette in his wallet. "This is what I'm going back to," he boasted to Simone.

Like many medics in the 3/187, Kotyluk had covered up the large Red Cross symbol on his helmet to avoid being picked off by enemy riflemen. Instead, he stuffed cannabis leaves in his helmet netting as camouflage.

"What the hell are those?" Simone had asked when he saw the leaves. When Kotyluk realized that Simone, who had never used drugs, didn't recognize marijuana, he teased him endlessly about his lack of worldliness.

On April 21, 1968, Simone and Kotyluk had been part of a multicompany strike force near the Song Be River in Bien Hoa province. While walking through an abandoned rubber plantation, the group came under enemy fire.

Artillery support was requested. Moments later, the 105mm guns roared in the distance. The men heard the rounds coming their way, and quickly realized that they were going to drop directly on them. Amidst shouts of "Incoming!" they hugged the ground. The 105mm rounds hit, and kept coming, one after another.

When the explosions stopped, more than two dozen American soldiers lay wounded or dead. Simone, who was uninjured, requested medevacs. He then moved among the fallen men to provide assistance.

He found Kotyluk sprawled in a crater. "A large piece of shrapnel had ripped into his chest, but he was alive and conscious. When I got his first aid kit out and started pulling out bandages, Kenny said, 'Why are you doing that? I'm not going to make it. I'm a medic . . . I know how bad I'm hit.'"

Simone recalled the blood seeping between his fingers as he pressed his hand against Kotyluk's gaping wound.

"I felt numb and helpless," he said. "I asked Kenny what he wanted me to do. He said, 'Don't go. Let's have a cigarette.' I pulled a cigarette from my pack, but I was crying too hard to light it. Kenny said, 'Some day, tell my mother.' Then he put his head down and that was it. That day, I realized the utter finality of death. I became acutely aware that good people get killed too. Kenny only had three months left on his tour. At the end, he didn't want to die alone. No one does."

The cause of Kotyluk's death remains unclear. His inscription on the Vietnam Veterans Memorial Wall states that he died of "hostile small-arms fire." But several Charlie Company officers blamed a forward artillery observer for relaying inaccurate coordinates to the gunnery team. In the artillery commander's report, however, he attributed the incident to a "short round," military jargon for ordnance that is on-target but falls short.

3 Firebase Pope

Two months later after Kotyluk died, Simone was again taking cover from incoming rounds. On June 10, 1968, helicopters dropped his platoon in a hot landing zone. They were pinned down immediately by a barrage of enemy mortar fire. Two men screamed that they were hit.

"A round came in and landed in front of us," Simone said. "The second round came in and blew up behind us. So I knew they were bracketing us. I figured the next round would be on target. And it was. When the mortar exploded, I caught shrapnel in my back. I felt blood and then it started hurting. I crawled over to the two guys who had been hit and told them to hang in there. I got on the radio and ordered a medevac. Then I popped a red smoke grenade to let him know where to land."

Simone stayed at the firefight for another hour until a chopper picked him up and flew him to the surgical hospital in Long Binh. A doctor there told him that the shrapnel had missed his spinal cord by less than an inch. He was stitched up and sent back to base camp, where he was awarded a Purple Heart—the first of two he received in Vietnam.

While Simone was recuperating, a Western Union messenger knocked on the door of his parents' house as they were eating dinner. Joe, who had completed his army service, hurried to take the telegram. He knew immediately that Jim hadn't been killed—in the case of a soldier's death, the army typically sent two officers to break the news.

Sent by a major general, the telegram stated: "The Secretary of War has asked me to inform you that your son, Sgt. James Simone, was wounded in Vietnam as a result of hostile action. While on a combat operation, he received fragment wounds in the back. . . . Since the wounds are not life-threatening, no further reports will be furnished."

Despite Joe's assurances that Jim was only wounded, his parents were grief-stricken. When Jim learned of his parents' emotional reaction to the telegram, he requested that no future telegrams be sent home.

Three days after being wounded, Simone's commanding officer decided that his recuperation was over. He told him to remove his shirt and then he yanked his stitches out.

He was still very sore, but he knew that he was lucky to be alive. After seven months in-country, he had become very aware of the brevity of life. He missed the friends he'd lost and was saddened by their deaths, yet he somehow felt disconnected from his feelings. He'd become hardened to the human devastation he'd seen—and caused.

"The rules of life no longer applied in Vietnam," he said. "There were times when we were sent into free-fire zones with orders to kill anyone who moves. When we first got there, we weren't soldiers. We were just kids who went to war. It didn't take long for our perception of right and wrong to become twisted."

For some of the new guys, the reality of war was overwhelming. It wasn't uncommon for new soldiers to become paralyzed in battle; too frightened to shoot their rifles. On several occasions, Simone had seen noninjured soldiers attempt to flee the battlefield by jumping into helicopters that were removing casualties.

According to military psychologists, a major component of battlefield fear is the innate resistance to killing one's own species. During World War II, only 15–20 percent of individual riflemen fired their weapons at an exposed enemy soldier, noted Dave Grossman, a retired lieutenant colonel in the U.S. Army and a former psychology professor at the United States Military Academy at West Point.

Referencing studies by Brig. Gen. S. L. A. Marshall, a World War II historian and author of *Men Against Fire,* Grossman said, "Specialized weapons, such as a flame-thrower, usually were fired [at the enemy]. Crew-served weapons, such as a machine gun, almost always were fired. And firing would increase greatly if a nearby leader demanded that the soldier fire. But when left to their own devices, the great majority of individual combatants throughout history appear to have been unable or unwilling to kill."

Grossman, the author of several books on aggression and violence, said Marshall's anecdotal observations and a host of other military studies supports a fundamental conclusion that man is not, by nature, a killer.

"That is the reality of the battlefield," said Grossman. "Only a small percentage of soldiers are able and willing to participate. Men are willing to die; they are willing to sacrifice themselves for their nation; but they are not willing to kill."

Journalist Mike Roberts, who covered the Vietnam War as a reporter for the *Plain Dealer*, saw firsthand the performance of soldiers under fire.

"I was impressed by the guys who went over there to fight," said Roberts, who was in Vietnam during the Viet Cong's Tet Offensive in 1968.

Equating combat to an athletic contest, Roberts said, "It takes so much energy, skill, and effort to be a good soldier. Then you have the guys who are extraordinary; who have a gift to act on it. Most guys in a firefight would hit the deck and not return fire. But a few guys would carry the rest. It takes a lot of balls to shoot back when someone is shooting at you."

For Simone, fear in battle was a constant. "We were all scared. I was just as frightened as anyone else," he said. "We all think we're brave up until it's time to die, then we realize we're not that brave."

But then there was Lt. Ralph "Chad" Colley, an Army Ranger who arrived in Vietnam on Thanksgiving Day 1967. His father had been a career soldier, serving in World War II, Korea, and Vietnam. Colley, who had just married his college sweetheart, Betty Ann, was eager to begin his own military career.

Deployed initially as a platoon leader, he was quickly promoted to acting commander of the 150 men of Charlie Company, Simone's outfit.

On July 21, 1968, 3rd Battalion field headquarters received reports that U.S. soldiers were taking fire from a much larger Viet Cong force. A plan was quickly formulated to send several rifle companies, including Colley's, to surround the area under fire.

The companies were dropped down about a half-mile from the firefight. They advanced swiftly toward the fighting, with Colley in the rear of his company as they moved through an area of old garden plots that were bordered by hedgerows.

Suddenly, the men around Colley heard a click. A split-second later, Colley was thrown into the air. A booby trap, rigged to a 105mm artillery shell, had been remotely detonated under him. He landed in a 4-foot-wide crater caused by the explosion, with dirt and debris raining down on him. Both of his legs had been ripped off at the knees. His left arm was shredded, with most of his hand blown off.

Several of the men around him had been knocked to the ground by the explosion. They got to their feet, then watched in stunned horror as

Colley, seemingly unaware that his legs were gone, tried to stand. Unable to balance himself, he fell backwards and lay in the crater.

The company's medics were initially slow to treat him, frozen by the sight of his horrific injuries and certain that his death was imminent. After a moment, they rushed forward to apply tourniquets to what remained of his legs. The twenty-three-year-old Colley, with his blood pooling in the crater, not only fought off the onset of shock, but had the presence of mind to issue orders to his men.

After telling a radio operator to request a medevac, Colley added, "Tell them to bring oxygen—I'll need oxygen." He then reportedly called his senior platoon leader to his side and officially handed the company over to him.

Just before the medevac lifted off, Colley beckoned several of his men toward him. "Find my left hand," he said. "It has my wedding ring on it."

In 1967–68, the 3/187 suffered substantial casualties. Both Bravo Company and Charlie Company had twenty-eight men killed in action. Hit hardest was Alpha Company, with the death of fifty-eight men. The losses of noncommissioned officers—corporals and sergeants—were disproportionately high. Although it was common for officers and NCOs to remove rank insignia from uniforms to avoid being targeted by enemy soldiers, sergeants were easily discernible. In a fighting unit such as the Rakkasans, sergeants led by example. They were typically at the front of their squads, leading assaults and directing fire.

On a particularly deadly day in 1968, two sergeants and a corporal lost their lives in a firefight known as the Battle of Song Be. The fighting began when several companies of Americans walked into an ambush by members of an elite North Vietnamese Army (NVA) regiment. The enemy soldiers were dug-in, concealed in spider holes in front of a large bamboo thicket.

The Americans were taking heavy losses from AK-47 fire and RPGs (rocket-propelled grenades). The situation was becoming desperate. Ammo was running low and resupply would be tricky, if not impossible. Without being ordered to, Sgt. Fred Larsen charged a two-man spider hole, throwing a grenade in the pit. The NVA gunners shot Larsen before the grenade explosion killed them. Larsen fell, mortally wounded, 5 feet in front of the enemy line.

A minute later, Sgt. Gary Burnett and Cpl. Mike Langer yelled for covering fire and then made a grenade charge at a pair of spider holes near Larsen's body. In both cases, the men's grenades hit their marks. Burnett and Langer were killed, but their bold actions startled the NVA, spurring them into a retreat.

The 3/187 was now in short supply of platoon sergeants. Simone, who had been in Vietnam for eight months, was called to Captain Bond's office and promoted to acting platoon sergeant of Lieutenant MacLachlan's 2nd platoon.

"Bond was grooming Simone. He thought that he would eventually be good material for Officer Candidate School," said MacLachlan. "So he put him with Charlie Company's best rifle platoon, which happened to be mine. Bond told me to keep him close, show him the ropes, and take care of him."

Shortly after Simone was assigned to 2nd platoon, the outfit was deployed to Firebase Pope, a new encampment about 20 miles north of Phuoc Vinh.

One of many fire support bases (FSBs) in Vietnam, Pope's function was to provide artillery cover for infantry operating in areas beyond the normal range of fire support from their own base camps. Pope's artillery battery included 105mm howitzers and mortars of various sizes.

Typically, the FSBs had a platoon of engineers on-site for construction and maintenance projects, at least two landing pads for helicopters, a Tactical Operations Center (TOC), a first aid station, a communications bunker, a company of infantry serving as the defense garrison, and a cavalry troop that served as a reconnaissance and security force.

A standard feature of FSBs was the ubiquitous sandbag ("If I had a dollar for every sandbag I filled in Vietnam, I'd be wealthy," said Simone). Weighing about 60–75 pounds, depending on soil and moisture content, the sandbags were used as fortification for dug-in fixed fighting positions around the perimeter, and for walls and overhead cover of bunkers used as living areas.

The arrival of the 3/187 troopers was announced as a protective measure for FSB Pope, which had come under increasingly aggressive attacks by Viet Cong guerrillas since the launch of the Tet Offensive. Dug into an old rubber plantation, Pope had been built on a route used by enemy forces to transport men and supplies to antigovernment forces in Saigon.

Named for the Vietnamese New Year, the Tet Offensive encompassed a wave of surprise attacks against hundreds of South Vietnamese civilian centers and U.S. military targets. The U.S. and South Vietnamese armies were caught off-guard by the initiative, which was a well-coordinated effort by the NVA and Viet Cong insurgent forces.

While FSB Pope ostensibly existed to drop howitzer and mortar round on hostiles, several 3/187 officers suspected the encampment existed for reasons other than just fire support.

"We were basically bait for the enemy," said MacLachlan.

There were two regiments of Viet Cong in the area. They had been coming out of the jungle and attacking nearby villages, and then returning to their hideouts. When we first arrived, the base was just being built. Our orders were to give the impression during daylight hours that we were undisciplined soldiers, just lazing around the camp. Then at night, we got busy laying mines, stringing concertina wire around the perimeter, and setting up artillery. The thinking was that the Viet Cong and NVA would try to attack us before the base was hardened [fortified]. Our plan was to draw them into a battle.

But the 3/187, which was often used as a tactical strike force, wasn't content to play defense. On most nights, several platoons would slip outside of the camp to patrol the surrounding area and set ambushes. Among the patrol's objectives was luring the enemy into firefights, which held the possibility of catastrophe because the Viet Cong were skilled at masking the size of their units.

MacLachlan took pride in bringing his men back safely from operations. "We had a long run where nobody had gotten hurt, so it wasn't uncommon for guys from other outfits to want to join my platoon. I'd say, 'Go to your company commander and ask permission. But if he lets you go, I probably don't want you.' I couldn't afford to have a weak link in the chain. I didn't need a guy, for example, who was going to light up a cigarette while we were on a nighttime ambush."

The average age of the men in MacLachlan's platoon was nineteen. "Occasionally, I'd hear them grumble about orders I'd given them," he said. "They'd refer to me as 'the old man.' But I was only twenty-two years old. I had gone from being a fraternity rat in college and hustling girls to setting up ambushes and being in firefights with Viet Cong. As a platoon leader, I carried the burden of responsibility for my guys. I needed to make good decisions."

MacLachlan took Simone on several reconnaissance missions in the wooded area around the base in order to assess his abilities.

"After exchanging fire with hostiles on a couple of occasions, I could see that Simone was organized and disciplined," MacLachlan said. "He was a little overwhelmed at first. He was only twenty years old and had just been made platoon sergeant. Now he was responsible, with me, for the lives of thirty or so guys. But he didn't back down. As my platoon sergeant, it was expected that he lead by example. And he did."

In mid-September 1968, a 3/187 scout reported a large amount of enemy movement near FSB Pope. On the evening of September 16, 2nd platoon set up an ambush position about 2,600 feet west of the base.

"We had a tracker dog with us and it was clear from his alerts that there was enemy in the area," MacLachlan said. "I picked a likely ambush spot at the junction of three trails."

Because the Viet Cong units didn't typically have radio equipment, they would meet at prearranged locations after a firefight for debriefing and to get instructions from their commanders. MacLachlan suspected that the trail junction would be their meeting point.

He set up three ambush positions at the head of the junction. He put Sgt. Ron Rondo, a veteran of two Vietnam tours, at the top of the kill zone. Simone and medic Philip "Zeke" Zeleski were behind Rondo.

Zeleski, a conscientious objector, initially refused to carry a rifle, saying that he would never shoot it. MacLachlan, however, had persuaded him to carry a gun and one magazine of ammunition just in case he decided he needed it.

The men settled in for the night and waited for enemy soldiers. Shortly after midnight, MacLachlan heard explosions coming from the direction of Firebase Pope. From radio chatter, he learned that two battalions of North Vietnamese Army regulars, about four hundred men, had launched an attack on Pope. As the battle raged, the sky above the base was lit by crisscrossing red and green tracers and rocket fire. At times, the illumination from the flares and exploding artillery turned night into day.

The attack continued for several hours, with a human wave of enemy soldiers repeatedly charging the base, sometimes shoulder to shoulder. At 4:00 A.M. the fighting at Pope subsided. Nearly one-third of the enemy force—131 men—had been killed. Four Americans were dead, with forty-eight wounded.

Shortly before dawn, MacLachlan, still in his ambush position, looked back toward the base. In the dim light, he saw what appeared to be hundreds of trees bending in the wind. A second later, he realized that he was looking at a large mass of NVA soldiers returning from their attack on Pope. MacLachlan had been correct: The enemy troops were planning to use the trail junction as a rallying spot. That would put them directly in front of 2nd platoon's ambush position.

Simone had been dozing. MacLachlan tapped him on the shoulder and pointed out the hundreds of soldiers moving toward them. "Holy shit," whispered Simone. At that moment, a lead element of six NVA soldiers was approaching the kill zone. They were chatting among themselves, smoking cigarettes and carrying their weapons upside down, undoubtedly exhausted after a night of battle.

Simone and MacLachlan frantically tried to get Rondo's attention to warn him not to spring the ambush. It was too late. Rondo gave the command to open fire. The platoon triggered the claymore mines and unleashed two M60 machines guns. The lead element was quickly cut down.

The main force of NVA soldiers charged toward the gunfire. Within minutes, the thirty men of 2nd platoon were flanked on three sides. The Americans dug in against a barrage of AK-47 fire and RPGs.

MacLachlan radioed for reinforcements and artillery support, and then crawled from position to position, making certain that everyone was at their firing posts. "A day earlier, we had four new men join the platoon," he recalled. "I paid special attention to them to make sure they hadn't frozen."

The platoon's machine-gunners, and then the riflemen, soon began running low on ammo. Simone got on the radio to request more, although it seemed unlikely that resupplies would reach the men in time. He then redistributed the remaining ammo, even retrieving unspent M16 magazines from dead and wounded soldiers.

"It was clear that the enemy wanted our trail intersection and was intent on overrunning our position," said MacLachlan. "My platoon was now fighting on all fronts. During lulls in the shooting, I could hear screams from our side and theirs. Zeleski was seriously wounded, but kept moving about each position, saving lives. We were nearly out of ammo and they were still coming at us. I gave the command to fix bayonets."

If the enemy charged one more time, 2nd platoon would have been wiped out. But just as the last of their ammo was fired, artillery rounds from FSB Pope came crashing in. The first rounds landed 200 yards outside the platoon's perimeter. The enemy surged closer to 2nd platoon in an attempt to avoid the artillery's killing zone. MacLachlan radioed that he wanted the artillery adjusted tighter to their perimeter. He knew it was their only hope of survival.

"When I said that I wanted it closer than 200 yards, I was told that it would be dangerously close and would require my initials," said MacLachlan. "I yelled, 'Juliett Mike' (J.M. in the NATO phonetic alphabet), but get it going!"

As MacLachlan waited for the artillery team to recalibrate its fire, he heard the welcome noise of an AC-47 gunship overhead. The pilot dropped a parachute flare and then circled the perimeter, firing his General Electric miniguns at the now-illuminated NVA soldiers. The AC-47 was affectionately nicknamed "Puff the Magic Dragon" by U.S. soldiers for the growl of its engines and because it spewed a torrent of red phosphorous tracer rounds that, at night, looked like it was spitting fire at the ground.

The side-firing plane could fire eighteen thousand rounds per minute from its pilot-operated guns. Much more accurate than long-range artillery fire, the gunship pilots were able to "walk" their fire very close to U.S. defensive perimeters, which were marked by soldiers holding small strobe lights.

Just the sight of Puff was enough to trigger a retreat by enemy soldiers, who called the AC-47s "dragon ships."

The gunship fire gave MacLachlan time to do a quick assessment of his men. Rondo's position had taken a direct hit. Rondo, Zeke, and Sgt. Allen Burke all had fatal shrapnel wounds.

"I heard a groan and saw Simone a few yards from the others," he said.

He was bleeding very badly from a wound in his throat. The grass around him was turning red. I moved closer to check on him. I tried to talk to him to see if he could hang on, but he didn't seem conscious. I had to decide if I was going to treat him. All around me, men were dying and screaming for help. I had the rest of my platoon to look after. I had a whole bunch of bad guys trying to kill me. And I had to be on the radio. The artillery guys needed to talk to me, Captain Bond wanted to talk to me, gunships were trying to talk to me, the battalion commander and the operations major all were trying to talk to me, and I was trying to convince a resupply chopper to bring us ammo. I looked at Simone and thought, *That's a dead man and I need to get back to work.*

A moment later, Firebase Pope's mortars and the 105mm and 155mm howitzers began dropping rounds nearly on top of 2nd platoon's position. The concussions bounced the men off the ground, and shrapnel rang in the air. During the barrage, MacLachlan sustained shrapnel wounds in his ankle, chest, and back.

The artillery barrage worked. The enemy fire diminished. MacLachlan began to breathe again.

As the sun rose, he checked the surrounding area. He estimated that the VC/NVA force lost thirty-five to fifty men. Most of the bodies had been dragged away in the night by retreating soldiers, leaving bloody trails that led into the jungle.

The 2nd platoon returned to Pope with eleven of its original thirty-one men. The missing were either dead or had been medevaced to field hospitals. Only four members of the platoon weren't injured. Silver Stars would be awarded to MacLachlan and Zeleski (posthumously) for their gallantry.

"Every time we went into the field, we knew we could be killed," MacLachlan said. "Zeleski told me just before we went out that evening that he thought he was going to die. He used to wear his ring around his neck on a chain. He had asked me to make sure his mother got the ring."

MacLachlan didn't see Simone medevaced. "I felt bad about Jimmy. He'd only been with me for a month. He didn't have to go out in the field. He could have stayed in headquarters as Bond's RTO. Instead, he chose to do more. I had told Captain Bond that I would take care of him. But then I got him killed and left him in the weeds."

4 Homecoming

Simone, in fact, was clinging to life. He had been blown into the air by an RPG round. Landing on all fours, he was disoriented for a moment.

"Then I felt a terrible pain in my neck," he recalled. "Every time I took a breath, blood spurted from my throat. I figured an artery had been cut. My hand was all cut up—the bones were exposed. I was in bad shape."

He yelled for Zeke, but no answer. In the pitch blackness, he could see Zeke, Rondo, and Burke lying motionless, all killed by the RPG's razor-sharp shrapnel. As Simone's mind cleared, he recalled that just before the round hit, Rondo had been struck by rifle fire. Zeke had moved toward Rondo to help him. When the RPG had exploded, Zeke's body had absorbed most of the blast, shielding Simone. Simone then remembered that Rondo's tour was up the next day. One more wake-up and he would have been on his way home.

"It was a horrible feeling to realize that they were gone," Simone said. "There was a tremendous sense of loyalty and love among us. I knew that they would have given up their lives for me. And I would have done the same for them. I had to push aside my feelings and keep fighting."

The platoon was still taking heavy fire. Simone's left hand was barely usable and he was losing blood rapidly. His carotid artery and jugular vein were torn. He pushed his right forefinger into the hole in his neck to stop the bleeding.

Simone crawled toward the radio. He phoned Captain Bond for a medevac and ammo resupply. His requests were declined. Bond told him it was too hot for a chopper landing.

"Hang in there, be careful," Bond said.

"I'm already dying."

Bond offered to send help at first light. "We won't make it until then," Simone told him.

An unfamiliar voice then broke into the radio net. Lt. Bill Meacham, a helicopter pilot known as "Wild Bill," offered to bring ammo and remove casualties.

Meacham, who was assigned to Bravo Company, 101st Aviation Battalion, had achieved a legendary reputation for taking on high-risk missions. He and the other assault pilots in Bravo called themselves the "Kingsmen."

"What's your ground situation?" Meacham asked.

"Not stable," said Simone. Despite the dire situation, Simone wasn't willing to draw Meacham into what amounted to a suicide operation.

"Do you have criticals?"

"Yes, but I repeat: The situation is unstable."

Ignoring the warning, Meacham told Simone to hold a strobe light to mark his landing spot.

Simone clicked off the radio. He propped his M16 on a downed tree branch and shot into the darkness at the outlines of enemy soldiers. When his ammo was gone, he threw his remaining grenades. Then, with his hand pressed against his neck wound, he rolled onto his back.

He was terrified of being captured by the Viet Cong. During advanced infantry training at Fort Campbell, the instructors told the new soldiers that the Viet Cong rarely took prisoners. But when they did capture Americans, they were subjected to torture. On one of his first patrols, Simone had seen the mutilated corpse of an American soldier. And he'd heard grisly stories of prisoners having their hands hacked off to deter them from escaping.

"They'd tie tourniquets around their arms so they didn't bleed to death," he said. "Then they'd lead them through villages displaying them like trophies. Afterwards, they'd be killed. We had quickly learned that there were no rules in Vietnam, except the ones we made for ourselves. I had one rule: Never be taken prisoner."

Simone removed his Air Force survival knife from its sheath and stuck the blade in the ground. "I didn't think I was getting out of the situation alive, but I was going to take as many with me as I could. They were going to have to kill me—I wasn't going to be taken alive."

As he awaited death by an enemy bullet or bayonet, he thought of his mother, wondering who was going to tell her what happened.

Then he heard the faint *whomp-whomp* of approaching helicopter blades. He flipped on his strobe and pointed it at the sky, cupping it with his hands to avoid enemy detection.

Meacham spotted the blinking light. He planned to land with his running lights out, but he knew it wouldn't take long for the enemy to zero in on the noise of his chopper. As he descended on short approach, green tracer rounds flew past his windshield. During the Vietnam War, the Communist troops used green tracers, which were supplied, along with their weapons, by the Soviets and Chinese. The Americans used red tracer rounds.

Meacham landed and waited on the ground for several nerve-racking moments while ammo was quickly off-loaded and eight bloodied men were pushed into his cargo compartment.

Simone, the last to be taken aboard, has vague memories of lying face down in the mud, semiconscious, with the helicopter's prop wash rippling over him. "I heard a voice say, 'It's time to go, Sarge,' and then a big hillbilly kid picked me up and put me over his shoulder."

As he was pushed into the chopper, Simone felt liquid splash against his face. The propeller downdraft was spraying blood from the helicopter's cargo bay throughout the landing area.

Meacham, carrying a full load, struggled to get his bird off the ground. Once aloft, tracer rounds converged on him. The enemy fire intensified as Meacham slowly gained altitude. Five tense minutes later, he cleared the area. Amazingly, Meacham said later, the helicopter hadn't taken any direct hits.

He radioed the 12th Evacuation hospital in Cu Chi to alert them he was inbound with eight wounded. When he landed, medics were waiting to carry the soldiers into the Quonset hut that housed the hospital. A doctor quickly inspected Simone. "You've lost a lot of blood," he said.

A nurse cut off his jungle fatigues—he wasn't wearing underwear or socks because of the heat—and tossed them on a large pile of bloody clothes. When she cut his dog tags from the nylon cord around his neck and taped them to his wrist, he groaned. "I thought to myself, *You bitch, I know that's how you mark dead guys for Graves Registration*," he recalled.

The doctor returned and said, "We're going to take you to surgery, but I can't promise that you're going to make it." He then asked Simone's religion. When told, "Roman Catholic," he waved over a priest.

"The priest told me that I was hurt bad," Simone said.

I became very scared. He said he wanted to hear my confession. I tried, but after a few seconds, I said, "Father, I'm confused. I can't remember all my sins." He then granted me general absolution. He prayed over me and then said, "When you wake up, you'll be with God." At that instant, my fear dissipated. I remember feeling a tremendous sense of relief as if a 1,000 pounds had been lifted from my chest.

His arms were strapped down and he was wheeled into an operating room. A surgeon stood above him. He was covered in blood, except for his gloves and mask. As Simone went under, he heard the doctor say, "We'll do what we can do. No guarantees."

He woke up the next day, disoriented and unsure where he was. "I remember thinking for a split-second that I really was in heaven. And then I saw a nurse in a green army uniform and I thought, *Why is my angel wearing fatigues?*"

Simone was wheeled to an open ward full of wounded men. He lay there naked, his body covered in dried blood. The next day, Charlie Company's first sergeant, John Humphries, came to visit Simone. Humphries, a career soldier, had served in Korea and was now on his second tour in Vietnam. As first sergeant, he was the highest-ranking noncommissioned officer in the company. However, unlike the stereotypical gruff and outwardly intimidating "top kick," Humphries was more counselor than disciplinarian to his men. He gave Simone a pack of cigarettes and then he sponge-bathed him, cleaning the blood from his body.

Simone was moved out of the medical ward to a room. About a week after he arrived at Cu Chi, a colonel and Simone's executive officer from the 3/187 came to visit. They presented him with a Purple Heart—his second—and a Bronze Star—also his second.

"They wanted to get me back to the unit, but I told them I was done. Mentally, I was just spent. I had killed more people than I wanted to remember. I'd seen more atrocities than I could imagine. Captain Bond had recommended me for Officers Candidate School, but my army days were over."

From Cu Chi, he was transferred to an army hospital in Saigon. The doctor there examined his jagged scar, which stretched across his neck from ear to ear, and pronounced him extremely lucky. Simone had survived an injury that was usually 95 percent fatal.

"The helicopter pilot had saved my life," said Simon, who, until 2001, hadn't known that the pilot's name was Bill Meacham. "He landed in heavy fire and then somehow managed to get us out of there safely."

He was then flown to a military hospital in Japan. From there, he used a Red Cross telephone to call his mother. "I've got a little injury, Mom . . . just a bit of shrapnel in my hand," he said cheerily.

"You're missing an arm!" she screamed, crying throughout the entire telephone call.

Assuring her that he was intact, he told her he would soon be on his way to Walter Reed Army Medical Center in Bethesda, Maryland.

"She wanted to come right away to Walter Reed, but when I got there, I realized it was no place for her. There were so many nineteen-year-old and twenty-year-old kids there who were disfigured and missing limbs. There were double amputees in wheelchairs and guys with horrific head wounds. I only had a nasty scar on my throat. I was one of the lucky ones."

At Walter Reed, he was bored, lonely, and missed his mother. His spirits lifted, however, when he saw Jon Jakeway, a buddy from Charlie Company, walk through his ward. Jakeway had been convalescing at Walter Reed since being wounded nine months earlier.

Simone was surprised to see Jakeway alive. "His guts were hanging open when I had last seen him," said Simone. "He'd taken a direct blast from a grenade during a firefight. He kept trying to stand up. We had to hold him down until the medevac arrived."

For Jakeway, being rolled into Walter Reed was a sort of homecoming. Twenty years earlier, he'd been born there. His father, an Air Force officer, was then stationed in China. He and Jakeway's mother flew home to Walter Reed to have their baby.

Jakeway's arrival back in the United States wasn't the heroic return from war that he'd envisioned. Doctors had removed half of his colon and he was wearing a colostomy bag.
A machine-gunner, he recalled that he "didn't feel a thing" at first when he was wounded. "I remember being on the ground. Then, after a few seconds, I looked at my stomach and I saw blood and intestines coming out of it. I pressed my hands against my stomach to hold everything together and then I noticed that my left thumb was dangling off. When I saw the injury to my thumb, that's when the pain started."

A large piece of shrapnel had penetrated Jakeway's abdomen. At a medical facility in Long Binh, a doctor took a hurried look at his wound and pronounced, "He's not going to die right away." He then lay on a stretcher for eight hours until he was taken to surgery. Afterwards, he was flown to a hospital in Japan, and then to Walter Reed.

He'd been at Walter Reed for six months when he saw Simone. "It was great to talk to someone from Charlie Company," said Jakeway. "I felt like I had just vanished into thin air when I left Vietnam. It had always seemed strange to me that there was rarely a chance to say good-bye to each other when we were wounded and medevaced away or shipped out. We fought together; we were willing to die for each other; and then we were just gone."

Jakeway and Simone and the other members of Charlie Company had trained together at Fort Campbell and then flown as a unit to Vietnam. Jakeway had been in-country for four months when he was wounded in March 1968.

Simone brought Jakeway up to date on the casualties to Charlie Company. He then told him that he had decided not to return to Vietnam.

"Listening to Jim talk, I could see that he had seen enough death," Jakeway said. "When Kenny Kotyluk died in his arms, nothing else was the same for him. Kenny's death had a profound impact on Jim. Kenny was a fearless medic. He had patched a lot of us up in the field. His presence made us feel more secure on patrols. When Kenny was gone, that was a defining moment for Jim. It hit him hard."

Calling Simone a fine sergeant and a tough soldier, Jakeway said that he and many of the others in Charlie Company drew strength from him.

"He had balls as big as basketballs," Jakeway said.

He wasn't afraid, so guys liked to follow him. I remember a night patrol when we had built a small camp in the field. We were far from base camp and out of range of artillery support. In the middle of the night, we heard a noise. Everyone was on alert. Somebody had to go into that pitch-black darkness and investigate. Our lieutenant asked Jim if he was ready to go. And I could tell by Jim's eyes that he was ready.

Jakeway takes a charitable view toward soldiers who succumbed to fear.

We were all scared, not just the so-called cowards. Soldiers are made from people right off the street. You don't have a damn clue how you're going to react in a firefight until you're in it. There were not a lot of "Rambos" in Vietnam. Nothing could have prepared us for the terror of combat. But when you have someone in your unit like Simone, who didn't show fear, it helped us to overcome our own fears.

While anxiety was a constant in Vietnam, Jakeway said he was continually struck by the absurdities of war. Recalling a rocket explosion that threw a soldier 20 feet in the air, he said:

The guy, Anthony Nicholson, landed with a big piece of shrapnel stuck in his head. I called in a medevac. They thought he was dead, so they put him in a body bag and threw him in the chopper with the other body bags. The helicopter took off, but got shot down. The Viet Cong overran the ship and killed everyone who had survived the crash. But they didn't touch the body bags. While I was in Long Binh hospital waiting to be operated on for my injury, I saw Anthony Nicholson walk into my ward with that shrapnel in his head. He was walking like a zombie right toward me. I found out later that while he was in the morgue, he had sat up in his body bag. It scared everyone. But a morgue worker just opened the bag and pointed him toward the hospital. They didn't even escort him.

After four weeks at Walter Reed, Simone was granted a thirty-day convalescent leave. He was given a uniform with an extra-large shirt so that it didn't aggravate his neck wound. Because he'd left his medals and ribbons behind in Vietnam, he was supplied with replacements for his Bronze Stars, Purple Hearts, combat infantryman's badge, and other awards. He took a taxi to the airport and bought a first-class ticket home. He arranged for his father, Anthony, to pick him up at the Cleveland airport.

Once he landed in Cleveland, his father ran across the tarmac and locked him in a hug. "You're skinny," he said.

Jim laughed. "Well, yeah, Dad, it's hot in the jungle and we walk around a lot."

From the airport, they went to a nearby bar. After they'd had a few drinks, Jim looked at his father and asked, "Why didn't you tell me what war was really like?"

"Because you wouldn't have understood," he replied. "You can't understand until you feel the warm blood running through your fingers. Now we can talk about things that we couldn't discuss before."

At midnight, his father dropped him off at Zelma's house. "I knocked on her door and she came downstairs and started crying," Simone recalled. "I got down on my knees and I kissed her feet."

"Get up," she said. "What the hell are you doing?"

Mother and son then walked upstairs. "She called every living Simone to tell them I was home from the war, and then she cooked me a huge steak."

5 Transition

Released from Walter Reed in early 1969, Simone served out the remaining months of his military service at Fort Indiantown Gap in east-central Pennsylvania. An expert marksman, he served as a handgun instructor at the 19,000-acre military reservation.

Fort Indiantown Gap, commonly referred to as "The Gap," was originally constructed in the 1750s by the Commonwealth of Pennsylvania as fortification against neighboring Susquehannock Indians. The Indians launched their attacks on white settlers from a separation in the Blue Mountains, which gave Indiantown Gap its name.

The Gap, throughout much of its modern history, was a training site for the army and National Guard. During the Vietnam War era, the base served as a summer camp for the army's Reserve Officers' Training Corps.

Simone taught hundreds of ROTC cadets in the use of the .45 caliber M1911, the semiautomatic pistol that had been standard issue for the U.S. military since 1911. Based on a design by John Browning and originally manufactured by Colt, the sidearm was issued mainly to officers or those soldiers whose duties precluded them from carrying rifles, such as mortar men and machine-gunners.

For hours on end, he instructed classes in gun safety, operation, and combat tactics. Simone often used the firing range himself. Happy to be shooting at paper targets instead of enemy soldiers, Simone became, in his words, "a very, very good shot."

His time at Fort Indiantown Gap provided an insular environment in which he could decompress from the madness that was Vietnam. At The Gap, Simone was also sheltered from the civilian world, where public opinion had shifted hard against U.S. involvement in Southeast Asia.

Like so many returning soldiers, Simone had been disheartened by the antiveteran sentiment.

"We had suffered while college kids partied," Simone said. "They had no conception of the hell we went through. I went to war because I felt a personal sense of duty, but it was unbelievable how much I had given up during that ten months in Vietnam. I knew I would never get it back."

The conditions in Vietnam had been grueling. The temperature and the relative humidity were routinely over 100°F. Not only was it physically exhausting to trek through thick jungle vegetation while carrying 70 pounds of gear, but the threat of enemy ambushes, booby traps, and deadly snakes and spiders caused immense psychological stress.

Simone and the others in his unit were sleep-deprived throughout their tours. While on base, they slept in bunkers constructed of sandbags and timbers. The bunkers were oven-hot and perpetually soggy. At night, large rats, attracted by open food containers, would crawl over the sleeping men. Despite the threat of enemy snipers and fragmentary grenades, most men preferred to sleep on top of or beside their bunkers, rather than endure the sauna-like conditions and risk of rat bites inside.

On long patrols, they would typically sleep on bare, damp ground. Sleep was fitful, if it occurred, with the men taking turns at guard duty every two hours. In the inky blackness of a triple-canopy jungle, every broken twig or rustling palm frond could induce heart-stopping fear. All the while, they were tormented by a bewildering array of aggressive insects. Stinging ants, wasps, horseflies, ticks, and mosquitos inflicted painful bites, as did the blood-sucking leeches and lizards.

Despite their constant fatigue, the men knew they could never let their guard down. Patrolling through jungles and rainforests was tedious, monotonous work. At any moment, however, the enemy was liable to engage, most often through hit-and-run ambushes that were intended to obviate the effectiveness of American air and artillery superiority. The Viet Cong exploited the element of surprise and then ended their attacks quickly, escaping before Americans could call in helicopter gunships and fire support.

The enemy's guerrilla warfare tactics, combined with the danger of crippling booby traps and the inhospitable climate, demoralized the Americans. Adding to the soldiers' frustration was the challenge of fighting an indistinct enemy. The Viet Cong were essentially a Communist insurgency group residing in South Vietnam, interspersed among civilian populations. Because South Vietnamese villages and hamlets were sometimes used to harbor Viet Cong fighters and weapons, American soldiers could never fully distinguish between friendlies and enemy.

The seemingly blurred lines between South Vietnam's civilians and combatants fed a moral ambiguity among American troops, particularly when weapons caches and booby traps were discovered in villages. In those cases, American soldiers tended to act out their generalized frustration, anger, and fear toward villagers who may or may not have been willing to assist the enemy.

"The principles of civilized society weren't always observed in Vietnam," Simone said.

Especially after we'd realized that we could be killed in an instant. That was a frightening prospect. Up until that point in my life, my experience with death was limited to funeral homes and seeing someone's deceased grandfather in a nice suit or someone's grandmother in a pretty dress. That's not how it happened in Vietnam. Death was painful and horrible there. That's very tough to handle when you're a twenty-year-old platoon sergeant in charge of other twenty-year-olds whose lives are literally in your hands. I had to grow up fast. To lead men, you have to be a man. I couldn't show fear.

There were occasions when soldiers discovered the mutilated corpse of an American or learned of the mistreatment of a captured soldier. "We saw things that you can't imagine a person doing to another person," Simone said. "When you see the body of a soldier that had signs of torture, how do you stop your men from taking revenge on the enemy?"

Simone received his honorable discharge from the army on October 9, 1969. One month later, journalist Seymour Hersh's reporting of the massacre at My Lai sparked international outrage and intensified America's growing antiwar chorus.

William Calley, a twenty-four-year-old army lieutenant, led a company of American soldiers to My Lai on March 16, 1968, in search of elusive Viet Cong guerrillas. The My Lai hamlet, part of the village of Son My, was thought to be an enemy stronghold.

In the weeks before Calley's men descended on My Lai, several members of their team had been killed by the Viet Cong—one had been shot by a sniper, another was blown apart by a booby trap. The simmering pent-up rage and frustration of the men came to a boiling point during an emotional memorial service for the most recent victim just a day before the My Lai massacre.

At My Lai, they did not find any Viet Cong among the hamlet's women, elderly men, and children. Two soldiers, Pvt. Paul Meadlo and Pvt. Dennis Conti, would later state that they were standing among a group of villagers when Calley told them to "Take care of the people."

Calley then departed, leaving the men with the group. When Calley returned, he said, "I thought I told you to take care of them." Meadlo replied, "We are. We're watching them." Calley then said, "No, I mean kill them."

Over the next two hours, three hundred to five hundred villagers were rounded up, pushed into ditches, and mowed down with M16 fire. An army photographer attached to Calley's company, Ronald Haeberle, documented the carnage. Haeberle's photographs appeared first in the *Cleveland Plain Dealer* on November 20, 1969, and then in *Life Magazine.*

Calley was court-martialed, found guilty of premeditated murder, and sentenced to life imprisonment and hard labor in Fort Leavenworth. Calley's guilty verdict, however, provoked outrage among many Americans, who believed that he was merely following orders and was being used as a scapegoat. With the White House deluged with telegrams urging leniency for Calley, President Richard Nixon ordered him transferred from Fort Leavenworth to house arrest in Fort Benning, where Calley would serve a total of three years.

Nixon characterized the My Lai incident as an unfortunate aberration and an "isolated incident." Calley was lauded as a patriot and a hero by many. A song written in his honor (sung to the tune of "The Battle Hymn of the Republic") was recorded. More than two million copies were purchased.

Even so, for the nine million Americans who served in the military during the Vietnam War, particularly those in combat roles, the My Lai massacre left an indelible and pervasive stain. My Lai tainted the legacy of the many soldiers who fought courageously and honorably. Despite the general public's perception that Calley and his men were guilty of little more than excessive diligence in carrying out their orders, many Americans now questioned whether My Lai was truly an "isolated incident." How had we come to victimize the South Vietnamese people—the very same people we were putatively defending?

The Vietnam War had never been a popular cause, but now it was viewed by many as a regrettable and shameful mistake. With the U.S. war machine under fire, soldiers became an easy and convenient target of peace activists.

Although the widely circulated stories of military personnel being spat on in airports may have been apocryphal, there were reports of returning servicemen experiencing overt hostility from protestors. In general, the American public affected indifference toward servicemen who came home from the Vietnam War—in stark contrast to the return of soldiers from previous wars. There were very few hometown parades for Vietnam veterans. A man in a military uniform was more likely to receive an icy glare than a complimentary drink at the bar or even a "thanks for your service."

"My own sister-in-law referred to me as 'a killer of women and children,'" Simone recalled.

> That hurt me. I'm sure I have a screw loose from what I saw in Vietnam. I certainly have a better understanding of life and death. I became acutely aware that death is permanent. The problem with dying is that you're dead for so fucking long. But I also learned that you don't run away and hide from the danger—you go after it. When I was in a firefight, I was too scared to think. I relied on my training. We all did. After the fighting was over, we'd clean up our wounded and dead, and then we'd talk about the fear. But I always had the mindset that, "When the smoke clears, I'm going to be alive."

As an ex-soldier, Simone now was faced with the challenge of finding a job. Like many returning combat veterans, he realized that the skills he'd acquired and honed in the army would not transfer to civilian life.

James MacLachlan, Simone's platoon lieutenant, recalled his own departure from the army:

> The rules instantly changed. All of a sudden, I went from being a fighter to being an ordinary citizen. When it was time for me to be think about entering the civilian workforce, I contemplated the skills that I could list on my resumé. As a soldier, I had learned to shoot people, burn villages, and set ambushes. I had to stop and ask myself, "Is that really the kind of guy I am?" My answer was, "No, that's the guy that I became."

Simone moved in with his mother and stepfather and regained his job as an installer for the phone company. Back home with his family, across the world from Vietnam, he was able to finally resume a normal life. But he'd soon find out how difficult it would be to escape his memories.

"There's a saying among Vietnam combat vets," said Simone. "The saying is 'When was the last time you were in Vietnam?' The answer is always 'Last night.'"

He was tormented by a recurring mix of flashbacks, recollections, and nightmares. His brother Joe recalled an incident in which their mother once woke Jim by grabbing his arm. "Jim experienced some sort of flashback," Joe said. "He jumped out of bed, grabbed her by the throat, and threw her on the floor. That was very scary for all of us. From then on, she knew to wake him gradually while standing at the foot of the bed."

During the Vietnam War era, there were few government-sponsored counseling and reentry services available to returning servicemen. Veterans and their readjustment problems were seemingly swept under the rug. Those who sought help for psychological issues at Veterans Administration hospitals found themselves tangled in bureaucratic red tape and then waited for months to see doctors.

Veterans themselves became responsible for finding ways to reconcile their war experiences with their post-Vietnam lives. For many, readjustment was a difficult process. Jon Jakeway believed that he experienced a smoother readjustment than many other veterans, in part, because he had never lost sight of his humanity.

"In advanced infantry training, they taught us to be very brutal to the enemy," he said. "They built fake Viet Cong Villages that we destroyed. They used ethnic slurs when they referred to the Vietnamese in order to dehumanize them to us."

Despite six months of training, Jakeway said he never became a gung-ho soldier. "I didn't buy into the bravado; I didn't lead the charge. I was just a soldier doing my job. Somehow I managed to keep my cool in some very difficult circumstances."

Jakeway experienced a moral watershed moment, of sorts, during a search-and-destroy mission.

My defining point occurred when I actually had a prisoner in my hands for the first time. Just some poor guy in black pajamas, and I had my machine-gun pointed at his face. He kept looking at the gun barrel and then at me and trying to smile. I was feeling a sense of power for a few seconds. Then I had a complete turnaround. It began when I noticed his features—he had a few gray hairs and some wrinkles around his eyes. What I noticed most was that he was absolutely terrified that I was going to kill him. I could see the fear in his eyes. I thought to myself, *Would I ever stick a gun in someone's face back in the U.S.?* It then struck me that I was the cause of this guy's torment. I moved back a few feet and lowered the barrel of the gun toward his belly. That calmed him noticeably. Then I had him sit down and I tossed my water canteen to him. That situation made me realize that I had more humanity than the killer that they had trained me to be. But then the South Vietnamese came by helicopter to take custody of the prisoner. They may have killed him. From what I'd seen, they were very brutal to their North Vietnamese counterparts.

Simone didn't have a defined strategy of acclimating himself to civilian life. As a phone installer, he had an active and physical job that kept his demons in check and left little time for recollections.

In 1972, he was assigned to troubleshoot and repair a residential phone line in Brooklyn, a Cleveland suburb. The homeowners, Bob and Carole Deighton, lived in a housing development that had been built during World War II for workers in Cleveland's war industry plants.

When Simone arrived at the couple's home, he was told the job was a rush because Deighton, a Brooklyn police officer, relied on his home phone to communicate with his police department. At that time, Brooklyn's police cars were equipped with mobile radios, but its officers did not have portable radios.

The Deightons' house, like others in the development, included a small crawl space that was intended to double as a bomb shelter. The telephone wiring ran from the street through the crawl space and into the house. Simone spent three weeks at the Deighton house, with much of that time in the crawl space, running new wire and restoring the family's phone service. Since Bob Deighton worked evenings, he was often home when Jim was at the house.

"Jim was here so long that we got to know him well," said Carole Deighton. "Bob really took a liking to him. He was impressed by Jim's direct and straightforward manner. He would tell me 'that kid is honest.'"

Each morning, Simone would arrive at the Deighton house and shimmy into the crawl space to begin work. One day, he remarked that being in the crawl space reminded him of the enemy tunnels that he had searched in Vietnam.

"Until that point, we didn't know he was a veteran," Carole said. "Bob had been in the navy, so he was interested in hearing about Jim's Vietnam experiences. It seemed that Jim wanted to open up about what happened over there. He felt comfortable talking to Bob."

After emerging from the Deightons' crawl space one evening, Simone sat at the couple's kitchen table and told them about his bone-chilling experiences as an army "tunnel rat."

Back then, he was searching for enemy soldiers, weapons, and military documents. The hand-dug tunnels, which were centered in the province of Cu Chi, snaked throughout South Vietnam and were used by the Viet Cong as ammo dumps, bomb factories, sleeping quarters, and first aid stations.

Originally built in the 1940s during the Indochina War, the tunnels were just large enough to accommodate the slight frames of the Vietnamese.

Simone, who weighed 120 pounds while serving in Vietnam (he'd lost 40 pounds since arriving), was one of the few American soldiers who had been willing—and small enough—to burrow into the narrow tunnel openings, which were often heavily booby-trapped.

During the Tet Offensive, the Viet Cong had used the tunnels to covertly plan and launch large-scale attacks on American positions. Frustrated by mounting casualties, the U.S. military was under orders to search all tunnels for enemy soldiers whenever they were discovered.

When Charlie Company encountered a tunnel opening while on patrol, the commanding officer, however, found it difficult to order any of his men to enter what was potentially a death trap. Instead, he'd ask for volunteers, typically swiveling his eyes toward the wiry Simone.

"The tunnels were a tight squeeze for me, but if I took my shirt off, I could get in," Simone said. "I'd take my trusty .45 handgun and a flashlight and drop into the opening head first. Then I'd inch along, making sure I didn't trip any booby traps."

The Viet Cong typically protected their tunnels by an array of lethal means, including pits lined with razor-sharp bamboo spikes, grenades, and highly venomous snakes. A favored booby trap involved tethering deadly kraits and cobras to bamboo stakes that, when bumped, would drop the snakes onto the trespasser.

Despite the terrors that awaited the tunnel rats—as they were known—the men were under steadfast orders to thoroughly explore the entire length of underground passages. "When searching tunnels, our rule was that we couldn't exit the tunnel from the same opening that we entered," said Simone. "If a guy came out the same way that he went in, then we'd think that he probably just laid down in there for awhile instead of searching."

Rounding corners in tunnels was particularly nerve-racking and dangerous, he said. "There was always the possibility that somebody could be on the other side with a bayonet or gun. You're in a situation where your life could be terminated in a second. You had to be so extremely careful, not just of the Viet Cong, but also of the rats, poisonous centipedes, and the other hazards."

On one occasion, he heard what sounded like Vietnamese "chitter-chatter" on the other side of a bend in the tunnel.

I slowly edged forward and the chattering kept getting louder. I extended my arms and stuck my flashlight and my gun around the corner. I was so nervous that I could hear my heart beating. Then I poked my head around the corner. I was shocked to see hundreds of bats. They were making the racket that I'd heard. I got out of there as quickly as I could.

During another exploration, he discovered an underground compound that had apparently been abandoned. He crawled into what seemed to be a first aid room. Inside, he found empty medical supply boxes that had been shipped from the United States. "The boxes had either been stolen from us in the field or sent to North Vietnam by communist sympathizers in the U.S," Simone said. "The thought that Americans were helping our enemy was difficult for me to handle."

Carole recalled that Simone talked until well past midnight. The next day, he completed the Deightons' rewiring job. But he would continue to visit the family. He took on the role of big brother to the Deightons' daughters—Carole, Susan, and Sherri—grilling them about the boys in their lives. Occasionally, Jim would bring a new girlfriend to meet the family. "Probably to get our opinion about her," said Susan. "Girls liked Jim until they found out that he was all business. He just wanted to work."

Bob Deighton, who passed away in 2015, had urged Simone to consider becoming a police officer.

"He'd tell Jim stories about criminals he'd arrested," said Carole. "And he and Jim would listen to police calls on the radio in Bob's patrol car. After getting to know Jim, Bob firmly believed that he would make a good officer."

One afternoon in March 1973, Carole Deighton answered a knock at her door. Simone was standing on her front porch, wearing a Cleveland Police uniform.

"He surprised us," Carole said. "We had no idea he had decided to be a cop. But he'd done it. We were all proud of him."

6 Back on Patrol

A winter evening in 1973. Jim Simone, five years removed from Vietnam, was back in the field. He was now patrolling Cleveland's Glenville neighborhood, a predominantly black community that was struggling with racial unrest and high crime.

In Glenville, he didn't have 2nd platoon covering his back as he walked the tough streets around East 105th and Superior Avenue, where many residents viewed him as an intruder.

Fresh from the police academy, Simone's foot beat included blocks that were controlled by gangs and drug dealers. He learned quickly that his primary goal was self-survival.

On his first night at work, his supervisor had dropped him off on East 105th Street, telling him, "If you make it through your shift, I'll pick you up at midnight."

Simone carried only a flashlight and a .38 revolver. Cleveland police back then weren't equipped with body armor, Tasers, pepper spray, or even mobile radios.

"If I needed to request backup or check in with the precinct, I had to use a police call box or a pay phone," said Simone. "Since there was only one call box in the neighborhood, I kept a dime in the tip of my tie for any pay phone I could find."

The residents, in general, gave him an icy reception. Others questioned his judgment in walking alone on darkened streets that they shied away from. "Look at that crazy white guy," he overheard an older black man say one night.

One night, he noticed a car illegally parked in front of a bus stop. He walked into the only nearby business, a pool parlor, and announced to the wary crowd that he was towing the car if it wasn't moved.

"They all looked at me like I was nuts," Simone said. "One of my supervisors told me later that the pool parlor was a hangout for a militant black group. And here's me, 'supertrooper,' just wandering in. I was told by my superiors to avoid going in there again."

The Cleveland Police in those days boasted that its foot patrols were a sure sign that it was serious about improving relations between the police force and minority communities. "The best way to get to know a neighborhood is by walking it," a police captain told a news reporter.

Many Cleveland street cops, however, questioned whether the foot patrols were effective in stopping crime. Joe Paskvan, who walked a beat in a high-crime neighborhood when he first joined the Cleveland Police in 1973, conceded that foot patrolling helped him get to know the people on his beat. But he added that Cleveland's on-foot officers were probably more a budgetary necessity than a community policing technique.

"In the 1970s, when I got on the job, there weren't enough cars for all of the officers, so we had to walk," Paskvan said. "There wasn't a choice."

Simone, nevertheless, looked forward to his shifts (also called "tours"). He was eager to fight crime and serve the public. Foot patrol suited his nature. He liked to stay busy and he enjoyed being immersed in a challenging environment.

"I wasn't unhappy working for the phone company, but I had started to miss the rush of adrenaline and the sense of teamwork that I had experienced in Vietnam," he said. "After spending so much time discussing police work with Bob Deighton, I realized that law enforcement was probably a good career choice for me. The job had some excitement and I'd have the opportunity to help people."

Deighton had suggested that he apply to the Brooklyn Police Department. Simone opted instead for the big-city action of Cleveland. Back then, Cleveland, with 725,000 residents, was the tenth-largest city in the nation.

Simone fared very well on the police entrance examination, ranking fiftieth out of more than five thousand applicants. During the admissions process, however, he was nearly stymied by the department's height requirement. At 5 feet 7 inches, he was an inch short of the minimum. But the admissions officer took a second look at Simone's neatly pressed clothes and his squared-away manner. He wrote down "five foot eight" and waved him on.

Simone's family, however, didn't share his career ambition. "My mom and dad did not want me to become a cop," he said. "My mom, in particular, was angry about it. She said, 'You almost got killed in Vietnam. Why do you need to do this?'"

When he was sworn in as a police officer, only one family member, his Uncle Tom, attended the ceremony.

Simone's class at the police academy was filled with military veterans. In the 1960s and 1970s, it was common for ex-servicemen to receive preferential hiring at police departments.

"Back then, police recruiters were interested in aggressive former soldiers and Marines," Simone said. "They knew we were disciplined, physically fit, and could function under a chain-of-command."

Veterans, in general, also tend to possess an affinity for duty and justice, said Peter Moskos, a former Baltimore police officer and an associate professor at John Jay College of Criminal Justice in New York.

"They also have a sense of responsibility, they show up on time, they have a good work ethic, and they are not usually fuck-ups," Moskos said. But he added that veterans—and any other candidates for a police job—must temper aggressiveness with discretion.

"I sometimes worry about military veterans being cops because it's a different skill set," he said. "Police aren't soldiers. There's no collateral damage that's acceptable in a police department. They aren't fighting an enemy."

Moskos, whose book, *Cop in the Hood,* chronicled his year as a Baltimore police officer, said that many people drawn to policing view the profession as a calling.

"Sometimes it can sound hokey and it's often part of a greater conservative ideology, but there is the idea of making a sacrifice, especially for veterans," he explained. "There is a certain nobility to the law enforcement profession. People who become cops see themselves on the side of good."

Police work can burn out its practitioners, so balance is essential, he said.

You don't always want the type of individual who says, "Oh my God, I want to be a cop because there are bad people out there and I want to catch them." At some point, being a cop is just a job. On the other hand, you don't want someone who always treats it as just a job. A lot of people became cops because the post office isn't hiring. And that's not always a bad thing. Most cops go into the field for the right reasons: a combination of wanting to do good for people and also having a secure job. There are not many occupations where you have that kind of job stability and a pension.

A look at Simone's employment application to the Cleveland Division of Police reveals his eagerness to become a cop. He was apparently concerned that he might be disqualified by the near-fatal neck injury he suffered during the RPG blast. On the handwritten application, under the "Personal Injuries" section, he stated: "Sept. 16, 1968, Vietnam, small shrapnel wound."

Simone may have been pining for excitement, but he was admittedly naive about police work. "I had the illusion that I was the knight on the white stallion fighting for truth, justice, and the American Way. It didn't take long for my stallion to become a mule and my armor to get tarnished."

During his first week on the job, he was driving on Superior and a young kid called him a pig. I was shocked," said Simone.

> I remember thinking that he didn't even know me. He didn't care that I was there to help him. When you're a police officer in the inner city, you quickly find out that kids are told not to respect you. Adults tell children that cops are going to take them to jail. I was in my car at a stoplight when I noticed a young black man in the car next to me. He had a baby in the car with him. He took the baby's fingers and manipulated its fingers so that it was giving me the middle finger. I said to him, "Why would you do that?"

Simone soon developed a reputation among his peers for fearlessness. A couple of weeks after beginning his rookie assignment, the Sixth District police station received a call from an anonymous male who said he was going to kill the first cop that he saw on East 105th and Superior.

"So, of course I was the first cop to show up there," said Simone. "I've always been a curious person. In this case, I was curious about what this person was going to do."

Five years earlier, only ten blocks from that corner, seven people, including three police officers, were shot dead during a confrontation known as the Glenville Shootout. One of the deadliest nights in Cleveland's history, the incident was triggered on July 23, 1968, when gunfire was exchanged between Cleveland police and black nationalists led by Fred "Ahmed" Evans, who headed a group called the Republic of New Libya.

Although it's not clear who fired the first shot, Evans and his followers had been angered that two police cars had staked out his apartment, where he was thought to have a cache of weapons. According to news accounts of the episode, twenty to twenty-five black nationalists emerged from Evans's building without warning and opened fire on the police cars with shotguns and .30 caliber M1 carbines.

Remarkably, the officers inside the cars were not hit. Other police cars and officers on foot raced to the scene. As they arrived, they were fired on by snipers positioned on the upper floors of nearby houses. The shooting went on for ninety minutes. When it stopped, seven people were dead: three police officers, three suspected black nationalists, and one civilian who had attempted to help an injured policeman. In addition, fifteen people were wounded, with one police officer dying later of his wounds and another losing his leg.

The following day, Cleveland Mayor Carl Stokes made the controversial decision to remove all white police officers from Glenville, allowing only black police officers and community leaders in the neighborhood. Stokes, the first black mayor of a major U.S. city, theorized that the presence of white officers would only escalate tensions in the area. The move angered the police, who complained bitterly that Stokes was giving impression that they were the cause of the Glenville Shootout.

The rancor between Stokes and the police department deepened after the revelation that Fred Evans had bought guns for himself and his followers from funds given him by Stokes's Cleveland Now! program. The private-public program was intended to finance community rehabilitation programs. Evans, who had received $6,000 from Cleveland Now! to run a purported social club, openly admitted that he used the money to purchase the carbines that were used in the Glenville Shootout.

During the six days following the shootout, Glenville was ravaged by wholesale looting and arson. When order was finally was restored by the National Guard, sixty businesses were damaged with a total loss of $2.7 million. Fred Evans was arrested the next day. When Evans was informed that three of his followers had been killed, he said, "They died for a worthy cause." He then told the three white officers who arrested him that he would have killed them if his carbine hadn't jammed. According to one of the arresting officers, when Evans was asked what sparked his members to fire at police, he said, "You police have bothered us for too long."

Tension between Cleveland police and the city's black residents had been ratcheting up for years. In the mid-1960s—although Cleveland's population was more than one-third black—only 165 of the city's 2,200 police officers were black. That disparity, along with the belief among black residents that city officials were not responsive to their needs, fed a growing distrust of police that, according to many Clevelanders, continues to this day.

Two years before the Glenville violence, rioting erupted in the Hough neighborhood after a white café owner denied service to a black resident. The ensuing violence left four people dead, thirty people critically injured, and hundreds arrested. Many of the dead and injured had been caught in crossfire between police and snipers. More than 240 fires blazed during the week-long violence. Firefighters initially had difficulty getting their trucks through streets that were clogged with angry residents. Even when they had penetrated the crowds, they were pelted by rocks and their fire hoses were cut. Eventually, the fire crews were told to withdraw from the neighborhood and let the fires burn.

The racial strife in Cleveland was the outcome of many factors. The black community was angry and frustrated over perceived unfair treatment by police; growing unemployment due to the loss and contraction of the city's industrial base; and a shortage of housing. Along with the deterioration of the aging housing stock, many of the single-family homes were subdivided by landlords into small apartments with high monthly rents.

As the city's working-class whites and blacks migrated to suburbs, property values plummeted and services such as grocery stores and banks also left.

Mike Roberts covered the Hough Riots as a reporter for the *Plain Dealer*. He theorized that the city's black flight during the 1960s and 1970s may have caused more repercussions than the white exodus.

"In the early 1960s, there were very few African Americans in city jobs. Carl Stokes opened up those job opportunities," said Roberts. "Educational jobs also opened up for the black community. So over the next fifteen years, blacks had opportunities like never before. They got jobs in banking, schools, and city government. And then they moved out of the city."

The blacks who were left behind in the inner city felt a sense of social and economic abandonment that fed a simmering resentment and distrust of all aspects of the white establishment, including the police.

Ultimately, said Roberts, the Hough uprising was triggered by a combination of fear and backlash against long-standing racism.

"These were not new problems," said Roberts. "This country was built economically on slavery. It was our original sin. The slaves were used as cheap labor to pick the cotton that fed the textile mills in England and America. This was not news to us. But people of a certain mentality didn't want to deal with the problem. We had turned our backs on it for such a long time."

In the 1970s, the nation was beset by cynicism and disillusionment brought on, in large part, by the escalating Vietnam War. The negative sentiment was particularly acute in the black community, said Roberts, which saw disproportionate numbers of its young males drafted and sent to Vietnam as combat soldiers.

The anxiety and frustration felt by black draft-age men, along with limited job opportunities and the generalized hopelessness of the impoverished, fueled an increase in violence and drugs in the inner city. Which begat even more violence and shootings and drugs.

"It's a loop that never ends," said Roberts. "For cops who work in the inner city, it would be tough to be out there every day and dealing with it. It's a no-win situation for them. In a black-white situation, they are automatically going to be accused of discrimination. Most of them do a good job. That doesn't mean, of course, that they can't do better."

It's a job that's complicated, to a degree, by mutual mistrust and the hair-trigger nature of race as a trip wire. Race was also a flashpoint issue in Cleveland's segregated schools. In the Collinwood neighborhood, a heavily Italian American enclave on the East Side, trouble erupted when an increasing number of blacks moved into the area. In April 1970, a group of three hundred white students gathered outside of Collinwood High School and threw rocks at the school's windows, ostensibly to protest the presence of black students.

The teachers escorted the school's two hundred black students to a third-floor cafeteria for their protection. The white demonstrators entered the school and unsuccessfully attempted to gain access to the cafeteria. Police were called to the school to escort the black students to buses that took them home. Racial tensions continued at Collinwood, climaxing in the fall of 1974, when three black students were stabbed and another student was fatally shot by a white student.

Not only was Simone inserted into an environment that harbored long-standing resentment toward police, but Glenville's crime rate had skyrocketed, fueled by joblessness, an influx of drugs, and the inevitable bloody turf wars between gangs battling for control of the drug trade.

In 1972, the year before Simone joined the Cleveland Police, the city recorded 333 homicides, the most in its history. Ten years earlier, Cleveland had only fifty-nine killings.

"The early 1970s was the beginning of the drug era in Cleveland," said Simone. "It was a dangerous time. Even the most minor disputes could turn deadly. I learned very quickly that when people fought in the inner city, they didn't fight with their fists. They pulled out a gun and started shooting each other."

While on foot patrol, Simone was constantly on the move, writing parking tickets, checking vacant buildings for squatters and vandalism, and shining his flashlight down alleyways. He always made time to chat with residents, passersby, and business owners.

Many of the residents, particularly the elderly, found his presence comforting. So too would women who exited buses late at night. On many occasions, he would keep a lookout for them as they walked home.

By showing that he was more interested in interacting with the locals, rather than harassing them, Simone gleaned information that was immeasurably helpful in solving and preventing crimes.

In Simone's view, the key to developing a rapport with residents was to treat everyone fairly, consistently, and in a professional manner.

> As a police officer, you can't be too friendly, but you can't be too hard either. It's important to get along with the people on your patrol. From a law enforcement perspective, there's no better communication than the interaction between a neighborhood and a cop on the beat. When you can get people to see past their fear of "snitching," the community becomes a safer place. The problem with the inner city's "no-snitch policy" is that the people they are protecting are the people most likely to hurt them.

Initially an outsider in Glenville, Simone was able to gain the residents' respect and acclimated himself to the neighborhood's peculiarities. In a sense, working in Glenville was a homecoming for Simone. He had spent his early childhood only twenty blocks or so from the neighborhood's center.

Joe Simone recalled that "times were tough" for him and his brother when their parents divorced. "We were very poor for a couple of years," he said. "We'd put cardboard in our shoes to cover up the holes. We didn't even have a refrigerator in our apartment—we still had an old-fashioned ice box."

When their mother got remarried, to Frank Mraz, the family moved to Lakewood, a middle-class suburb that was "like a different world," said Joe.

> In our old neighborhood on Superior Avenue, we were one of the few white families, so we expected to get in fights. We had to act tough and be tough to survive. When we first moved to Lakewood, we were still wearing our pointy-toed shoes and greaser clothes. We looked like we were right out of "West Side Story," while everyone else was wearing penny loafers and khaki pants. We learned that it wasn't the survival of the fittest in Lakewood. Acting tough was kind of silly there. It was a relief to not worry about getting jumped every day after school.

Joe wasn't surprised that Jim pursued police work after his military service.

> He always had a call to duty, even as a boy. One night, when he was thirteen or fourteen, an elderly lady got her car stuck on the railroad tracks in Lakewood near our house. We were on our porch and we could see that she had gotten confused and made a turn onto the tracks, thinking she was turning onto a road that ran parallel to the tracks. The railroad crossing gates started to come down, so we knew there was a train coming. Jim ran down to the tracks with a flashlight and helped her out of her car just in time.

7 The Crooked Line

In the spring of 1973, Simone was assigned to Cleveland's Second District on the city's West Side. Now riding in a patrol car, he worked nights as a traffic officer.

Simone had transferred from the predominantly black Sixth District to an area populated by a fusion of cultures and ethnicities. One of five current police districts (the Sixth was merged into the Fourth and Fifth in 2008), the Second District is bordered by the Cuyahoga River on the east, Lake Erie on the north, Brookpark Road on the south, and West 85th Street on the west.

The winding path of the Cuyahoga River cuts a crooked line dividing Cleveland into a western half and eastern half. During the latter half of the twentieth century, the river and the ravine that it flows through have served as a de facto line of segregation between the city's white residents, mainly clustered on the west side, and its black residents, who are largely located on the east side.

Up until the past twenty years, the population distribution was so pronounced, in fact, that Clevelanders tended to self-identify as either "west siders" or "east siders," with the terms sometimes used as euphemisms for "white" and "black."

The Second District, which would become Simone's world for much of his career, encompasses a broad demography, including Hispanics—both newly arrived and established—blacks, Appalachians, Eastern Europeans, and two Italian American neighborhoods.

The district is also economically diverse, with sprawling public housing projects, middle-class homeowners in the Old Brooklyn neighborhood, and a cadre of pioneering gentrifiers who have renovated old Victorians and repurposed warehouse space into loft condos.

Just as he was becoming acclimated to the Second District, Simone suffered the unexpected loss of two family members.

On a June evening in 1973, Simone was at work when he received a frantic phone call from his then-wife. "Your mom's house is on fire," she told him. He sped to Lakewood and found his mother's street barricaded. He drove around the barricades and over the firehouses.

He jumped from the car and ran toward the smoking house. "A cop grabbed me by my collar and pulled me backwards," Simone recalled. "I yelled at him, 'Where's my mom?' He told me to get my kids and go to Lakewood Hospital. He didn't have to tell me she was dead; I could see it in his eyes."

At the hospital, the doctor came into the waiting room and asked who was going to identify Zelma Faye's body. Simone, who was surrounded by relatives, felt all eyes turn toward him.

"One of the problems of being a policeman and a military veteran is that people assume that we're more capable of handling life's horrors," he said. "They think we won't get freaked out. That's not always true. But I followed the doctor and did what a son was supposed to do. The condition of my mother was unimaginable. That day, I started life without her."

Fire investigators determined that a television set had caught fire in the back den of the house. She had died of smoke inhalation and severe burns. Zelma Faye was forty-six years old.

Just three weeks earlier, on May 10, 1973, heavyweight boxer Earnie Shavers was in Cleveland training for an upcoming match under the tutelage of his manager Don King, a native Clevelander. While on an early morning jog in Edgewater Park near Lakewood, Shavers saw a body hanging from a tree. Police identified the victim as Frank Mraz, one of Simone's four stepbrothers.

A Vietnam veteran, the twenty-five-year-old Mraz had difficulty readjusting to civilian life, said Joe Simone.

"He was different when he came home from the war," he said. "Before he went into the army, he was a nice kid. When he returned, he was very, very different. He grew his hair long; he wasn't able to hold a job; and he got involved in drugs. We think he got hooked on heroin while he was in Vietnam."

A Cleveland homicide detective notified Jim about his stepbrother's death. He and Joe then drove to the county morgue to identify the body. When the morgue drawer was pulled open, Jim rolled Frank's body on its side.

"Joe wanted to know what I was doing," said Jim. "I told him I was doing my job. I was checking to make sure there were no signs of foul play. When I saw the ligature marks on his neck, I cried. But I also realized that his death was a relief, in a sense, for my parents. Frank was a heroin addict. He was always in trouble. Now they didn't have to worry about him every night."

The death of Frank disturbed Jim, but he felt devastated by the loss of his mother.

"We were very close," he said.

Every evening, during my dinner hour, I would stop and see her. She'd have something cooked for me. When I had been in Vietnam, my mother had written me every single day. Even if she wrote the same thing two days in a row, she always made sure that I had a letter. She sent a cake to Vietnam for my birthday. By the time it got to me, it was all dried out. But we all ate it.

Joe also was deeply affected by the loss of Zelma. "It was like getting hit in the head by a mallet," he said.

Jimmy and I were both mama's boys. She was such a strong force in our life. We got our empathy and compassion from her. Without Mom to tell us to "knock off that shit," there didn't seem to be any rules anymore. Jimmy was stronger than me, even though he was a couple of years younger. Vietnam had made him hard. When Mom died, he became even harder. He threw himself into his work. When our mom was alive, we'd get together at her house. Now, he went his way and I went mine. I started to drink a bit. He became a policeman twenty-four hours a day.

Over the next several years, Simone delivered extraordinary results as a patrol officer in the Second District. Throughout the 1970s and 1980s, his misdemeanor and felony arrest rates were 500–600 percent higher than the department average.

"It became common for people I arrested to complain that I would even arrest my own mother," said Simone. "So I'd engage them in verbal judo. I'd say, 'If I said your mother was a prostitute, would you be mad?' When they said, 'Hell yes,' I'd say, 'So let's leave our mothers out of this.'"

Simone never arrested his mother, but he did take a family member into custody. Not long after beginning his career, while he was still living with his parents in Lakewood, a sibling visited. Simone was aware that he was wanted for felonious assault, so he put handcuffs on him and took him to the Lakewood police station.

"Good job. Where did you find him?" a police supervisor asked.

"At home," Simone said. "He's my stepbrother."

Later, Simone explained to his disconcerted family members that, "It was better for him to be arrested by me in the afternoon than to have the sheriff's department break through his door at 3:00 A.M. and scare his children."

Along with Simone's remarkable arrest statistics, he wrote parking tickets and moving violations at an even more impressive clip. On average, his annual production in those categories was 800–900 percent higher than his peers.

Simone's success at apprehending impaired drivers earned him recognition from Mothers Against Drunk Driving (MADD). He was perennially honored by the Cleveland chapter of MADD for his efforts in keeping streets safe.

"Anytime that I arrest a drunk driver, I'm taking a potential killer off the streets," he said at one of the award ceremonies. "Drunk drivers not only cause damage and pain to their victims, but their actions can change the lives of their victims' families."

As a patrol officer, Simone encountered a broad spectrum of impaired drivers, ranging from working people to professional sports figures, judges, and other police officers. He treated each offender in the same way, even arresting his own supervisor on one occasion.

It wasn't uncommon for police officers to become angered by Simone's refusal to bend rules for their relatives, friends, and themselves. From the beginning of his career, his steadfast by-the-book mindset would be a contentious issue, especially among detectives and the police executive ranks, where special treatment was an expectation.

In the early 1970s, the Cleveland Division of Police was plagued by pockets of corruption. The department's homicide detectives, in particular, were notoriously susceptible to bribes.

Ed Kovacic, Cleveland's police chief from 1990 to 1993, served a stint in Homicide during one of the unit's darkest periods.

"I didn't get along well in Homicide because I could see that many of the detectives were pretty corrupt and I wasn't," said Kovacic. "The guys didn't like me because I was honest. I wouldn't take a nickel."

Kovacic recalled arresting a man whose uncle was a Cleveland Police commander. "He had raped a twelve-year-old retarded girl. I built a strong case against him. Then an attorney came up to me and said, 'Ed, it's worth 250 bucks if you just sit and say nothing. The case will go away and you'll get paid.'"

After Kovacic declined the bribe, his rape case was torpedoed by higher-ups and the suspect was released.

"It drove me nuts," said Kovacic. "In Homicide, I had no control of what was going on around me. Strange things could happen to a case."

Simone also would encounter unchecked corruption among the detectives. While a relatively new officer, he had arrested a Cleveland man for a moving violation. During a pat down, he discovered the man was illegally carrying a concealed weapon. Because the man didn't have a permit to carry the gun, it was confiscated. Three months later, Simone arrested him again. He searched him and found the same gun he had impounded previously.

During the booking process, the man casually asked Simone how much it was going to cost him "this time?"

Simone's suspicions were aroused. He pulled the report from the first arrest and found that the case had been dismissed, instead of being sent to the Cuyahoga County grand jury for indictment. Now furious, he approached the detective who had signed off on the case and threatened to personally take it to the grand jury for indictment.

"Hang on, hang on," the detective implored. He pulled open a desk drawer, scooped cash out of it, and thrust the bills at Simone. "Here, this was supposed to go to you."

Refusing the money, Simone walked back to the arrested man and said, "Good news, it's not going to cost you anything this time." He then monitored each step of the man's case to ensure that he was indicted.

In the 1970s, corruption among Cleveland police was so widespread that cops in nearly all units could be enticed to accept or deliver a bribe.

Simone arrested a Cleveland City Council member in 1974 for drunk driving and leaving the scene of an accident. When he arrived in court for the suspect's hearing, a detective pulled him aside and said, "There is no case."

"There has to be a case," said Simone. "I arrested him."

"It never happened. Now go home." He then pushed an envelope at Simone. When Simone didn't take the envelope, the detective said, "Take the money; it's yours."

"I'm not taking it," Simone said

"You are an idiot, Simone."

"I'm still not taking it."

"Fine," the detective said. "I'll take it."

While Simone was not interested in crusading against police miscon-duct, he fought hard against anyone who tampered with his cases. He noted that both detectives retired from the Cleveland Police shortly after they had attempted to bribe him.

8 "You Never Get Away from 213A"

In the mid-1950s, the Cleveland Division of Police was the target of an infiltration by an enterprising news reporter. The undercover journalist attended the police academy, graduating near the top of his class. Then, using his badge number as his byline, he filed the first in a planned series of exposés in a Cleveland newspaper. In his initial article, the reporter lambasted the department's training procedures and policies, calling them outdated and ineffective. Although he was discovered before he could publish additional installments, the department was now on the lookout for copycat spies.

So in March 1974, when police brass received a report of a young patrolman audiotaping his encounters with civilians, the department's Intelligence unit was alerted. The task of confronting the suspected spy fell to Ed Kovacic, then a sergeant in Intelligence, a ten-person team that was mainly responsible for investigating organized crime activities in the city.

"But we would investigate anything, inside or outside of the department," said Kovacic. "I got the call from a captain who told me to check out an officer named Jim Simone to see what he was up to. The captain had heard that Simone was recording everything that was going on during his shift. "

Kovacic introduced himself to Simone and asked if it was true that he was recording his activities.

"Simone told me that he was indeed recording every contact he had with the general public," Kovacic said. "He said it was for his protection and theirs. I told him that sounded like a good idea, but I let him know that some people were afraid that he was also recording other police officers."

Kovacic was assured by Simone that he wasn't a news reporter and he wasn't recording his fellow officers. "I told Simone that he was right about what he was doing. And then I went back and told the captain that I was convinced that Simone was a good cop."

. . .

On October 17, 1977, Cleveland Police officer Norbert Berendsen responded to a silent burglar alarm at 4:30 A.M. at a furniture store on 6710 Detroit Avenue. Berendsen was met there by store security guard Frank Gregor. The men noticed that a board had been pried from a wall at the rear loading dock.

While Berendsen waited for backup, a man fired at him from inside the store. The bullet missed Berendsen by inches. The shooter, Harley Reeser Jr., then slid down an elevator shaft cable to the store's basement.

Reeser, age twenty-two, was a dishonorably discharged ex-Marine. Recently unemployed, he and his nineteen-year-old wife had been living in his 1969 Chevy Nova while her sister took care of their two children.

Simone and another officer rushed to the store after hearing a radio broadcast of shots fired. After police fired tear gas into the basement, Reeser ran up a stairway to the third floor and crawled through a trapdoor to the roof. With Simone in close pursuit, Reeser leaped across an 8-foot open space to the roof of another building, then dropped 10 feet to an adjoining roof.

Simone, who was carrying a 12-gauge shotgun, cornered him between a chimney and the edge of the roof. He urged Reeser to give up.

"There's no way off the roof," Simone told him.

As other officers took up positions on the roof, Reeser pulled a .25-caliber semiautomatic pistol from his waistband.

"I'm not going to prison." Reeser told Simone. "I will kill you if I have to."

"If you do shoot me," said Simone, "my partner has his revolver aimed at your right ear."

"I'm not going to prison!" Reeser screamed. He then pointed his pistol at Simone. Reacting instantly, Simone fired his shotgun, the blast echoing through the empty streets.

Other officers at the scene reported that Simone walked to the edge of the rooftop and vomited over the side. Upset that he'd needed to resort to deadly force, Simone said he felt "physically distraught."

Cleveland's police prosecutor, Almeta Johnson, quickly ruled the shooting justifiable, saying that Simone had fired in self-defense. To police on the scene, Reeser's death was clearly a case of "suicide by cop."

"Reeser knew that he would be going away for a long time because he had fired his gun at a cop," said Simone. "At one point, I thought I had a chance to grab his gun from him. But he started yelling and I knew that he was building up for his grand finale. I was sorry that it had turned out that way."

In the early morning hours of May 16, 1980, police arrived at a house on Woodbridge Avenue to arrest Terry Murray, a suspected arsonist. The officers learned from Murray's mother that he was hiding in a crawl space under a first-floor bedroom. The only access to the crawl-space was through a 12-inch-wide opening in the floor.

Murray, whose criminal past included charges of felonious assault and kidnapping, was described as "suicidal and desperate" by his family members. They warned police that he could be armed. After the officers were unsuccessful in their attempts to talk Murray out of the crawl space, the Cleveland Fire Department was called to the scene to enlarge the opening so that two men could go in together to capture Murray. But the firemen were able to add only a few inches to the opening due to structural limitations of the old frame house.

Because there were elderly residents and young children in the home, police ruled out the use of tear gas.

Simone arrived at the scene and shone his flashlight into the hole. He saw Murray huddled against a wall. "Someone will have to go in there and bring him out," Simone told his lieutenant. He then volunteered, noting that he was the smallest officer at the scene.

Because Murray possibly had a weapon, the lieutenant was reluctant to let Simone enter the crawl space. "It's not my first time," said Simone, removing his gun belt.

As he descended feet first through the bedroom floorboards, he felt the same nervousness that he'd experienced a decade earlier when he'd inched through enemy tunnels in Vietnam.

Inside the musty crawl space, Simone knelt on one knee. Terry Murray, holding a kitchen knife, sat across from him on a pile of old clothes.

After a couple of minutes of conversation, Simone convinced Murray to surrender. "I told him about my 'ATM' policy," Simone said, explaining that that during his encounters with wrongdoers, he always followed a sequence of actions: "Ask them. Tell them. Make them."

Murray, he said, had been given a choice of coming out the hard way or the easy way.

Murray's arrest garnered Simone several awards and a letter of commendation from the chief of police that noted his "devotion to duty and his bravery in going into a closed area after a known felon."

Professing modesty to newspaper reporters, Simone said, "I'm not particularly brave. It's just that I don't have a reverse gear. I'm always charging forward."

Four months later, Simone would charge again, this time into a burning house. On September 19, 1980, Simone and his partner at the time, Walter Skoropys, were on patrol at 1:30 A.M. when they heard a radio call about a house fire.

Speeding to the scene, Simone recognized the house because its residents had helped him crack an auto theft ring in the past. He also knew that children lived in the house. The fire department was en route, but Simone wasn't waiting. He was still grieving over the loss of his mother in a house fire five years earlier.

Simone and another officer kicked down the front door, while officer Dave Sumskis went to the rear of the house.

"I kept thinking about what my mother must have gone through," Simone said. "I had to make sure no one was in that house."

The *Plain Dealer* recounted Simone's actions that day: "Smoke was so thick in the front room that the policemen had to crawl on the floor to see. Simone shouted that he was going upstairs. He told Skoropys to go outside and throw rocks through the upper windows to release the smoke."

Inside the house, however, the superheated air and acrid smoke forced Simone to retreat. He started backing out of the house on his belly. Unable to breathe, he became confused and started to panic. Realizing that the fire was consuming oxygen and creating toxic gases at a rapid pace, Simone knew that he'd be dead of smoke inhalation within minutes.

Skoropys, after being forced out of the house by the smoke and heat, realized that Simone was still inside. He went back into the house, crawling blindly through the smoke until he found Simone, who was by then unconscious. Sumskis helped Skoropys drag Simone to safety.

Simone was transported to MetroHealth Hospital suffering from smoke inhalation and first-degree burns of the face, chest, and arms.

In dramatic fashion, the *Cleveland Press* reported Simone's rescue: "Patrolman James Simone, regarded as one of the most outstanding young policeman on the force, was rescued in the nick of time. He was given oxygen by firemen as he was rushed to a hospital burn unit for treatment. 'Another few minutes and he wouldn't have made it,' doctors said."

Later that day, while Simone was still in the hospital, Sumskis appeared at his bedside. He told Simone he had a tip on a murder suspect. "Get dressed," he told him. Since both men were off-duty, Sumskis drove them in his personal car to the suspect's apartment. Once there, they arrested a thirty-four-year-old man. A search turned up seven guns, including a machine-gun and two sawed-off shotguns.

The next day, Simone got a call from the Second District commander. "You dumb son-of-a-bitch," he said. "I go to the hospital to visit you and you're gone. It's a good thing you made the arrest or I'd have put you up on charges."

Shortly after his release from the hospital, Simone began partnering with Sumskis, a former Marine and a Vietnam veteran. With Sumskis, Simone had found not only a trusted partner, but a best friend.

At 5 feet 9 inches and 240 pounds, Sumskis was blocky, but quick on his feet. "I knew that no matter what happened, Dave would not leave me," Simone said. "He was fearless. If I was dead, he'd be dead next to me."

He recalled the night they strolled into a scruffy West 25th Street bar in search of a murder suspect. Sumskis stood at the door with his burly arms crossed, while Simone told the bartender to turn the jukebox off and the house lights on.

"The place was full of drug dealers, pimps, robbers, and bikers," Simone said. "One of the bikers, a tough guy, said, 'I smell bacon burning.'"

Simone swept his nightstick across the bar, scattering drink glasses and beer bottles. "I looked the biker in the eye and asked him if he had a problem. He didn't say a word." As they left the bar, Sumskis said to his partner, "Are you stupid?"

"I told Dave that I wasn't worried about the biker. He was just another guy with an alligator mouth and a hummingbird ass."

During the years they were partners, Sumskis and Simone were tireless crime fighters. One early Saturday morning, when both were off-duty, Sumskis, who lived near Simone, called him to his house. "See that car across the street," he said. "It's stolen."

Sumskis could have reported the stolen vehicle to the Auto Theft unit, but, like Simone, he enjoyed slapping handcuffs on bad guys. Sumskis had set two shotguns against a wall in his house—one for him and one for Simone. They watched as a man hopped in the car and drove away.

When he returned, he was with another man. Sumskis and Simone arrested both men and impounded the stolen car.

Humorously referring to themselves as "Crime Catchers, Inc," they had pens printed with their names and the slogan, "You never get away from 213A," a reference to their patrol car number. Drivers who were ticketed by the duo were told to "Keep the pen."

"Dave would take our police cruiser home and change the brake pads himself," Simone said. "He was always tinkering with it. We had the best car in the fleet."

Newspaper stories about 213A's exploits shared a common theme: Simone and Sumskis were incredibly productive. Statistically, their felony arrests dwarfed the volume of other patrol teams in the Second District. They were outliers who fed off each other's near-compulsive commitment to work. On weekends, on holidays, or with just a few moments left on their shift, they policed 24/7.

While driving past a convenience store late one night, Simone and Sumskis didn't see the clerk in her usual spot. That irregularity prompted them to stop their cruiser. When they spotted a car parked near the store with its engine running and its lights out, they split up, covering the front and rear.

A gunman wearing a ski mask attempted to flee out the back door of the store but saw Simone. He turned and ran toward the front, fleeing past Sumskis. The officers gave chase, trading gunfire with the robber. They captured him when he attempted to hide under a car. When they returned to the store, they found the clerk in a back room. She tearfully told them that the robber had threatened to kill her, but had run away when he saw the police cruiser in front of the store. Police linked the robber to several other convenience store robberies in which clerks were shot, one fatally.

On another night, Simone and Sumskis were only minutes away from the end of their shift when they noticed two men in an oncoming car without its lights on. They flashed their lights at the vehicle, but it didn't respond.

Operating on instinct, the officers decided to pursue the car. After a brief chase, they stopped the vehicle and arrested the occupants, two brothers in their early twenties. They soon learned that the men were in a stolen car taken from a woman who had been raped the day before. After speaking with the victim, Simone realized that knives found in the car had been used during the rape. The woman, age twenty-four, told Simone she had left classes at Cuyahoga Community College at 10:00 P.M. when she was abducted by the brothers. She was taken to a park and assaulted. A computer check revealed the brothers were wanted on numerous warrants for violent crimes.

Simone's news clipping folder includes a handwritten letter from the rape victim. Addressed to William Hanton, then the chief of police, the letter states:

> I am writing this letter of thanks to the officers of Cleveland's police force. Officers James Simone and Dave Sumskis were responsible for the capture and arrest of the two men who attacked me, stole my car, and raped me. Officer Simone, I don't understand what caused you to believe the men were suspicious and stop them for questioning, but I thank you for your alertness and your concern.

Simone, who is discerning with his praise and not prone to hyperbole, called Sumskis "a truly good policeman and probably the bravest guy I ever knew." Sumskis would die on September 15, 1997, after undergoing heart surgery. The doctors were unable to restart his heart after the procedure.

At the end of 1980, in recognition of his dash into the burning house, Simone was named Cleveland's Patrol Officer of the Year. He also received the City of Cleveland's Medal of Heroism and the Rotary Club's Medal of Valor.

In a letter recommending him for Patrol Officer of the Year, Simone's supervisor wrote: "The officer displayed courage and bravery above and beyond the call of duty by entering the blazing inferno in search of human life, an act which in itself placed his very life in extreme jeopardy."

9 Split-Second

Opened in 1980, Club Synergy was a few beats late for the disco era. Nevertheless, the nightspot was a popular hangout for the hardscrabble Clark Avenue crowd. Formerly a shot-and-beer joint, the bar seemingly reinvented itself overnight as a discotheque, chiefly through the addition of black lights, a mirrored ceiling ball, and an illuminated dance floor installed in a space previously occupied by two battered pool tables.

The bar's facelift, however, hadn't extended to its clientele—scrappy men who were more likely to brawl than boogie, and feisty women who were typically at the root of the fights.

On February 26, 1981, Eugene Szejpcher, thirty-two, had been involved in a late-night altercation at Club Synergy. He stormed out and got his car, pulling it in front of the bar to pick up his girlfriend. She was followed out of the bar by the two men Szejpcher had fought with. In an attempt to get to Szejpcher, the men dragged his girlfriend from the passenger seat of his car.

Szejpcher got out of his car and announced that he was going home to get his gun and "take care of this matter." He then left the vehicle in a no-parking spot in front of the bar.

Several moments later, Simone and Sumskis drove past Club Synergy and noticed the illegally parked car. They stopped and Simone radioed Second District to request a tow truck.

During the call, the dispatcher told Simone that a woman had just phoned police to report that a man carrying a shotgun was walking on Clark Avenue toward him and Sumskis.

The partners got out of their car and waited for the armed man, who turned out to be Szejpcher on his way back to Synergy.

When Szejpcher, an ex-convict, saw the two police officers, he ran. Simone and Sumskis gave chase, splitting up in an attempt to corner him.

Szejpcher ran down an alley and threw his double-barreled shotgun into a trash dumpster, then hid behind the container.

When Simone entered the alley, Szejpcher jumped out and started running again. Reaching the end of the alley, he found himself trapped by a fence. He then spun around and pulled a chrome-plated revolver from his waistband. He pointed the gun at Simone's gut. Simone fired four times. Szejpcher died at the scene.

"I only noticed the revolver because a street light reflected off its chrome finish," said Simone. "If he had drawn a typical dark, blue-steel gun, there wouldn't have been a reflection and I probably wouldn't be alive today."

A police sergeant at the scene told news reporters that the officers were grateful to the unidentified woman who warned them that Szejpcher was on Clark Avenue with a gun.

"There's no telling what could have happened if Szejpcher had been surprised by the appearance of the two police officers, or if he had been able to take them by surprise," he said. "We could have had one or two police officers shot down this morning."

Simone's supervisor, arriving shortly after the shooting, offered a curiously cynical opinion. After taking a cursory glance at Szejpcher and then looking at his gun, a Colt .357 Magnum, he said, "Well, we know this was a good shooting."

Puzzled by the snap assessment, Simone asked, "How do you know that? You haven't even asked me what happened."

"Because no cop would throw away an expensive gun like that," the supervisor replied, suggesting the possibility that Szejpcher had been unarmed and Simone had planted the gun on him.

Cleveland prosecutor Jose Feliciano ruled that the shooting of Szejpcher was justifiable. "He tried to shoot the officer and that is that," Feliciano said. "The officer shot out of fear for his life."

Simone was relieved to learn of the prosecutor's ruling, but was shaken by the episode. "It was a traumatic experience," he said. "I never want to hurt anyone. A shooting happens in a matter of seconds. There's just no time to think. It's draw, shoot, and hope to God that when the smoke clears, you aren't wounded or dead."

In his two deadly shootings, Simone said he had no alternative. "Either they were going to die or I was going to die. When those situations occur, I'll be damned if it's going to be me. I have three daughters to support. I plan on coming home every night."

Simone, now thirty-four, was divorced. The marriage had crumbled for a number of reasons, including the chronic stress of police work, Simone's rotating shifts, and his enthusiasm for working overtime. His ex-wife had custody of their three daughters, with Simone seeing the girls as often as he could manage.

The day after the shooting, test results showed that Szejpcher's blood alcohol content was .28 percent, nearly three times Ohio's legal limit for intoxication at that time.

"Because of a drunken argument in the bar, he got a shotgun and was coming back with it," said Simone. While he was convinced that Szejpcher had left him little choice but to fire, Simone felt a sense of duty to telephone his family and notify them of his death.

"You're the guy who killed him?" asked the father.

"Yes," replied Simone. "I had no other choice."

"My son had just gotten out of jail. He was a no-good son of a bitch."

Simone told him when Eugene's body would be released so that burial arrangements could be made.

"You killed him; you bury him," said the father, hanging up.

"I cried when he said that," recalled Simone. "I felt horrible that I had to take someone's life. What kind of person would not feel remorseful over that? But to hear a father say that about his son was very sad."

Despite the prosecutor's ruling, Simone's actions were questioned by Szejpcher's girlfriend. In a television interview, she wondered whether Simone had been too quick to pull his trigger, particularly because Szejpcher was drunk.

"After a fatal shooting, it's routine for some people to say they would have handled the situation differently," said Simone. "But if they weren't present when the incident occurred, they can't know what they would have actually done."

In an armed confrontation, the bad guy will ultimately have the advantage, he explained. "Because he knows whether he's going to shoot. Police can only react to the threat. By the time a cop becomes involved in the confrontation, the suspect has already made a series of bad decisions. They've decided to rob a store with a gun or they've taken a gun into a bar. In a lot of cases, they've brought the gun along as a fear factor. To them, it's a tool to scare someone. But that's not going to work on me."

Simone bemoaned the general public's unrealistic perception of police work, blaming movies and TV police dramas.

"Television has ruined our job," he said. "Because of cop shows, everyone thinks they know how to do my job better than me. On TV, police officers always have time to tell a suspect to 'drop the gun.' But that rarely happens in the real world. We only have one-eighth of a second to decide if a guy is going to shoot. His actions determine our actions, even if he's drunk or high on drugs."

He also debunked the Hollywood-perpetuated myth that police officers can shoot a gun out of a person's hand or aim to "wound instead of kill." Simone explained that it's not practical to shoot at a knee or arm because those targets are too small to hit with any reliable accuracy, especially under stress and in the typical low-light conditions of a confrontation. Shooting a person in a limb would also not necessarily stop an attack, he added. Not to mention that a bullet strike to the leg, for example, could cause lethal bleeding or even travel in the body and strike a vital organ.

When officers make the split-second decision to shoot, they aim for the torso (known as center mass) because it's the largest target. And they are trained to continue firing until the threat is neutralized. That's not to say that police shoot to kill. They shoot to stop.

Most use-of-force law today stems from the 1989 U.S. Supreme Court case of *Graham v. Connor*, where the court ruled unanimously that "the reasonableness of a particular use of force must be judged from the perspective of a reasonable officer on the scene. . . ."

In *Graham v. Connor*, the Supreme Court also cautioned that the "reasonableness" of a particular use of force must be judged from the perspective of a reasonable officer on the scene, rather than with the advantage of 20/20 hindsight.

"Even the people you work with are going to question your decision," Simone said.

When I killed Harley Reeser on the rooftop, a lieutenant asked me later if I really had to shoot him. But it all happens in the blink of an eye. While I was in the situation, I was reacting. Later, I realized what happened and I experienced the fear.

Television doesn't show the after-burn of a shooting. You have many hours of reports to prepare. You undergo questioning by homicide detectives and the team that investigates the shooting. You have to deal with the media and the possibility of lawsuits by the victim's family. Then you have to live with the memory of what happened. Whatever a victim says or does just before they die will stay with you forever. It's not pretty.

Simone has succinct advice for police officers who are thrust into a shoot/don't shoot situation: "If you have time to think about whether to shoot someone, don't do it. If you shoot instantaneously out of fear, you're generally okay. But if you have time to think, you have another option."

Up until the early 1980s, the Cleveland Police did not offer its police officers a formal counseling or recovery process to help them cope with the trauma of killing someone in the line of duty. Although in some cases, the officers were reassigned to desk duty for a short period of time or reassigned to a different division.

"When we shot someone, we'd usually be back at work the next day," said Joe Paskvan, who was involved in several controversial shootings over the course of his career. Prosecutors ruled that Paskvan was justified in each shooting.

In 1983, Cleveland instituted a program for officers involved in deadly force incidents. The officers were assigned to the police gymnasium for up to ninety days and required to meet with a counselor once a week. The gym duty provided a cooling-off period that insulated the officers from media attention and also relieved them of the pressure of police work while their case was investigated.

By 1982, both Paskvan and Simone had been involved in a similar number of deadly force incidents: Paskvan had shot eight people, killing two; Simone had wounded seven and killed two. In all cases, the actions of the two officers were deemed appropriate. Both men also racked up misdemeanor and felony arrest statistics that were consistently higher than the department average.

News articles about Simone's shootings were generally favorable, with reporters citing his bravery in chasing the armed Szejpcher down a dark alley and Harley Reeser across rooftops. Decisive and direct, always ready with a pithy quote, Simone was fast becoming the media's go-to cop.

Paskvan's experience with Cleveland's news media was very different.

Simone's use of deadly force was rarely second-guessed, while Paskvan's was spotlighted and criticized. The disparate treatment could have stemmed from the men's differing personalities: Simone was engaging and seemed to enjoy discussing police procedure and philosophy, while the phlegmatic Paskvan seemed aloof to reporters.

But mainly, said Paskvan, it's because Simone's victims were all white and his were all minorities. "I certainly didn't plan it that way," Paskvan said. "It just worked out like that."

Paskvan and his supporters believed that he had become the poster boy for minority groups looking to push an agenda and reporters interested in sensationalizing stories.

Paskvan's first fatal shooting occurred in March 1978. He was driving past an apartment building when he noticed a police officer fighting with a black male, later identified as Darrell Parks.

"I saw the officer go down and I saw the male shooting at him, so I slammed my brakes on and bailed out of the car," Paskvan said.

The officer had been attempting to arrest the twenty-year-old Parks. The men struggled and Parks wrestled away the officer's service revolver and fired at him, missing. Parks then ran, heading directly toward Paskvan and several other officers.

"He saw us standing there and he raised his gun at us," Paskvan said. "I shot him six times and my partner shot him twice. The homicide detectives investigated the shooting, and the city prosecutor, Almeta Johnson, ruled on it the next morning. She said I was justified and I was back on the job."

In 1984, Cleveland established a Civilian Police Review Board to oversee investigations of deadly force incidents and allegations of police misconduct. That same year, Cleveland's mayor was granted the right to appoint the top fourteen police executives, stripping civil service protection from district commanders and heads of major units. The police department was now politicized.

The formation of the Civilian Police Review Board, which was generally opposed by the police department, occurred, in part, as a reaction to Paskvan's 1982 shooting of Michael Woods.

Paskvan said he shot Woods, who was black, because he pointed a revolver at him while both men were stopped in their cars at a traffic light.

"I was sitting in my car, a Volkswagen Rabbit, minding my own business," said Paskvan, who was off-duty at the time and driving to a police union meeting. "I looked at the car to my right and saw that a guy was aiming a gun at me out of his driver's side window. So I grabbed my own gun and shot him."

Woods's car coasted forward and hit a curb, then sheared off a telephone pole before rolling over. Woods, who was twenty-four, had been driving to downtown Cleveland to get a birthday cake for his one-year-old son.

Paskvan offered a possible theory on why Woods brandished his gun: "Another driver said that I had cut him off in traffic."

Howard Rudolph, then the lieutenant in charge of the Homicide unit (he would later become Cleveland chief of police), investigated the shooting. Rudolph determined that Paskvan had not violated any police department regulations.

Cleveland prosecutor Jose Feliciano ruled that there was no probable cause to charge Paskvan in Woods's death.

The decision angered Cleveland's black community as well as several local journalists, who noted that in all of Paskvan's eight shooting incidents, the victims were minorities.

Roldo Bartimole, editor of the Cleveland newsletter, *Point of View*, complained that Paskvan, who had remained on active duty after the Woods shooting, was reassigned from patrol to the Homicide unit—the same division that was tasked with investigating the shooting.

"In other words," noted Bartimole, "A witness calling in information on the Woods case might have spoken to Paskvan himself."

As an advocate of the Civilian Police Review Board, Bartimole said that such boards are essential to maintaining the public's confidence in justice when police are involved in crimes against citizens. In the March 12, 1983, *Point of View*, he wrote: "The police handling of the Michael Woods shooting and killing can be termed as sloppy and incompetent at best, corrupt at worst. Doctors don't expose other doctors, lawyers don't expose other lawyers, journalists don't expose other journalists. And police can't be expected to expose other police."

Paskvan said he learned to shrug off newspaper stories that second-guessed his shootings. "You can't win arguments against people who buy their ink by the barrel," he said, paraphrasing Mark Twain.

But if the press could put us out of business, we would have all been collecting unemployment checks a long time ago. There will always be "Monday morning quarterbacks." But those people weren't there when the shootings occurred. Of course I felt fear when I was in those situations. I didn't feel I had any other option but to shoot. Some people will never be convinced of that. And there's no point in trying to convince them.

Like Simone, Paskvan came from a large family of military veterans. He enlisted in the Marines and was sent to Vietnam. His tour ended early when he was injured in a helicopter crash and returned to the United

States for facial reconstruction surgery. Paskvan doesn't talk much about his Vietnam experience, except to say it was "long ago and another world. I did my duty and came home."

Home was Lorain, Ohio, and a job at a steel mill. The pay was good, but the work was monotonous and he was required to rotate shifts every five days. A self-described action junkie, Paskvan took entrance tests for both the Cleveland Fire Department and the Cleveland Division of Police.

"I scored higher on the fire department test, but the police called me," he said. "I found out that I liked police work. I was a hunter. I enjoyed adventure. A lot of patrolmen would take thirty minutes for their lunch break. My partner and I would skip lunch and go hunt for bad guys."

Paskvan particularly enjoyed traffic stops, which are considered one of the riskiest aspects of police work. Pulling over a traffic offender is a sort of Russian roulette in the sense that the officer has little knowledge of the character and motivations of the car's occupants, and whether they are armed.

"I was always prepared," said Paskvan. "I liked busting car thieves and finding guns. From 1973 to 1982, my partner and I confiscated 498 guns. Those were guns that could have been used against me or other cops, or innocent civilians."

With his focus on hunting felony-level prey, Paskvan conceded that he was sometimes lenient with minor offenses.

> If we pulled someone over for a traffic violation and they didn't have a gun or drugs, or if they had a very small amount of drugs, we'd give them a warning instead of a ticket. One of the great things about being a street cop back then was being able to use our discretion and judgment. Good judgment comes from experience. Everybody, including cops, make mistakes. And we learn from those mistakes. But nowadays, cops aren't allowed to use the judgment they've gained from their experience.

Paskvan received several police department honors during his career. In 1980, he was awarded the Rotary Club's Medal of Valor for apprehending the leaders of a crime ring that had robbed a dozen bars.

Paskvan's final deadly shooting occurred on April 10, 1985. The incident began as he and his partner were staking out a Cleveland bar waiting for a robbery suspect to exit.

The two officers were sitting in an unmarked police car when they noticed a male carrying what looked like a sawed-off shotgun. Paskvan immediately radioed for uniformed officers to respond to the scene. The male, later identified as twenty-two-year-old Marcos Luciano Jr., then got in a car and pulled up behind their unmarked car.

The uniformed officers then drove up and unknowingly stopped their patrol car next to Luciano's car. Paskvan and his partner yelled at the officers that they were beside the suspected gunman. They then exited their vehicles to alert the uniformed officers that they had put themselves in a potentially deadly position.

Paskvan watched as Luciano raised his weapon and pointed it at one of the uniformed officers. Although Paskvan yelled at him to drop the weapon, Luciano seemed oblivious to his presence. Paskvan, believing that he had only a split-second to act, fired three shots from his Smith & Wesson .357 Magnum. Two of the shots struck Luciano in his torso.

Luciano dropped his gun. Paskvan kicked it away, noticing that a BB fell from it. "I figured a shotgun shell had opened up and the BB came from that," he recalled. "However, it turned out that Luciano was carrying a pellet gun."

Luciano, who was Puerto Rican, was reportedly taking the gun to a female friend's house. Earlier, a man had threatened her and Luciano was bringing the pellet gun to defend her.

The shooting was investigated by Lt. Howard Rudolph, who determined that Paskvan did not violate any police department regulations. William Hanton, then the chief of police, concurred. Police prosecutor Patrick Roache ruled the shooting justifiable.

Leaders of Cleveland's minority communities objected. A black Cleveland City Council member urged Hanton to put Paskvan on desk duty, claiming that many citizens were concerned with Paskvan's involvement in "eight questionable shootings." A group of protestors marched to police headquarters, holding signs that called Paskvan a murderer, a racist, and "Kleveland's Killer Kop." They were joined by Luciano's twenty-year-old widow, who told reporters that she would fight the rest of her life to get Paskvan off the streets

Luciano's family filed a $21.8 million lawsuit against Paskvan. The plaintiff's star witness stated that she had been walking around the corner just before the shooting and arrived in time to see Paskvan shoot Luciano as his hands were raised in surrender. She added that she remembered the time of the shooting as 7:30 P.M. because she had just heard bells toll from a nearby church. However, her credibility was derailed when defense attorneys pointed out that the church bells only rang at noon and 6:00 P.M.

The autopsy results supported Paskvan. According to the coroner, Luciano's bullet wounds indicated that his arms had been in a position of pointing the weapon at the officers.

Paskvan won the lawsuit. But he had become a political liability to city administrators and police brass, who were feeling heat from black and Hispanic leaders in Cleveland. The minority groups were demanding Paskvan's dismissal from the police force, while newspaper columnists were urging that he undergo psychiatric testing.

Police executives—having no basis to fire him and unwilling to put him back on the street—decided to warehouse him in the gym. He would stay there for nineteen months, mainly occupying his time by reading books. Eager to leave the gym, Paskvan requested arbitration, per the collective bargaining agreement between the police union and the City of Cleveland. The arbitrator found in Paskvan's favor, cautioning that the city was acting in an arbitrary and discriminatory manner toward him.

He was returned to his previous position in the Auto Theft unit. But even then, Howard Rudolph, who had become the police chief, ordered that Paskvan not be allowed to perform work duties outside the police headquarters building unless he was accompanied by a supervisor.

In June 1987, Paskvan took the Cleveland Civil Service examination for promotion to police sergeant. He ranked third out of more than a hundred candidates. However, he was repeatedly passed over for promotion. Over time, forty-nine officers who scored lower than Paskvan on the sergeant's test were promoted.

He then sued Cleveland's Civil Service Commission, arguing that he was being discriminated against because he was white. In 1994, a jury ruled in Paskvan's favor. The city appealed the decision. The appellate court affirmed the original ruling, noting that the trial jury could reasonably infer from the evidence that "because he is white, Paskvan was offered as the sacrificial lamb to appease the protesting minority organizations."

Paskvan was finally promoted to sergeant, eight years after taking the test. He was also awarded compensation for the higher income he would have received as a sergeant. He used $60,000 of his payout to repay Cleveland's police union for its legal support, although he wasn't required to do so.

Paskvan would retire from the Cleveland police force in 1999. A pragmatist, Paskvan doesn't hold a grudge toward the city or the police department. But he sounded a cautionary note for police administrators and elected officials who allow political pressure and fear of a vocal few to trump community safety.

"Political correctness is killing this country," he said.

During my career, the people at the top of the police department were cowards. They are politically appointed to their jobs so they toe the party line or they get replaced. If you're a good, aggressive cop, you're fighting the system. In many cases, the good cops are the subjects of citizen complaints because they are highly active and making arrests. I could have just been a slug, put my time in, and got my pension. But that's not who I am. I always thought, "If there aren't cops like me out there to stop the bad guys, who will stop them?"

With 1.1 million local and state law enforcement professionals in the United States, there will be occasional lapses in training and procedure, incidents of negligence, and errors in judgment that lead to tragic consequences. The bad apples and the rogues, when identified, should be rooted out, said author Dave Grossman.

But if our nation's cops are made to feel that they no longer have the moral right to proactively hunt down bad guys, the "very fabric of our civilization is threatened," he warned.

In Grossman's view, the media-driven public opinion has become dangerously skewed, with cops increasingly being demonized while criminals are admired and even celebrated in video games and music.

"We cry out for the true heroes who uphold law and order, like Simone and Paskvan, and then we make them the villains," Grossman said. "It takes moral and physical courage to face danger and be shot and possibly die. To possess that combination of courage is rare and precious. Many cops are given the badge, but won't do the job."

Grossman, who frequently lectures at universities and at law enforcement gatherings, is acquainted with both Simone and Paskvan.

"Cops who are willing to take action are the ones who are actively trolling for bad guys and are the first to respond to calls for backup," he said.

Every other cop should learn from the Jim Simones of the world and lean forward in the saddle, answer calls for backup, and go hunt down criminals. But we now have a whole dynamic of political correctness. Not only does it take great moral courage for a cop to do his or her job, it also takes moral courage for a news reporter to transcend the cultural dynamics and present a realistic view of crime. Unfortunately, we now have reporters who will condemn and attack cops, and we have editors who will kill stories that are positive to cops.

According to Paskvan, when cops become oversensitized to negative media coverage and are fearful of being vilified by their communities, they are more likely to avoid situations that could lead to use-of-force incidents.

"It's called 'depolicing,'" said Simone. "Cops will become glorified report-takers. They will sit in the parking lot of the police station until they get a radio assignment. They will go take a report of a crime, then return to the parking lot. There won't be active patrolling."

That scenario played out in Baltimore with disastrous results in May 2015 when police there seemingly staged a work slowdown to protest the indictment of six officers in connection with the death of Freddie Gray. A twenty-five-year-old black male, Gray was arrested on April 12, 2015, by Baltimore police for possessing what was allegedly an illegal switchblade. While being transported in a police van, Gray fell into a coma and was taken to a trauma center. He died a week later, with his death blamed on a grave injury to his spinal cord.

Gray's death sparked protests and accusations of police brutality, although it was unclear how Gray suffered the lethal injury. The subsequent rioting in Baltimore caused an estimated $2 million in damages.

Residents said the riots were indicative of the long-simmering animosity between Baltimore's black community and its police force. An investigation by the *Baltimore Sun* found that the city had paid out $5.7 million since 2011 in settlements and judgments related to allegations of police brutality. Most of the victims were black.

After the six police officers—three white and three black—were arrested and indicted, arrests fell sharply across the city and shootings skyrocketed. In the month of May, there were more than forty-three homicides, the deadliest month in forty years. Statistics also show that police made only 1,177 arrests in May 2015, as compared to 3,801 in May 2014.

While police denied that an organized stand-down was in effect, a police representative said some officers are "hesitant to make arrests, out of concern that they could be prosecuted if a suspect is injured."

In a statement to the media, Baltimore police union president Gene Ryan said, "The criminals are taking advantage of the situation in Baltimore since the unrest. Criminals feel empowered now. There is no respect. Police are under siege in every quarter. They are more afraid of going to jail for doing their jobs properly than they are of getting shot on duty."

Without a strong police presence, the breakdown in social order experienced in Baltimore could happen in Cleveland and any other city in the United States, said Paskvan. "It will be like watching the rise and fall of the Roman Empire. If you're a resident of a high-crime neighborhood, you'd better make friends with your local criminals. Because if there aren't cops like me out there to stop the violent criminals, people will learn that they have to take care of themselves."

And in the longer term, he asked, "How are we going to attract good people to the field of law enforcement if they are afraid to do their jobs?"

Paskvan was dogged by negative news coverage during the 1970s and 1980s, perhaps more than any other Cleveland cop. Claiming that he didn't pay attention to bad press, he said, "It upset my wife and children more than it did me."

He noted that during that time period, cops, in general, went from being viewed as good guys in the eyes of journalists to being viewed as bad guys. "It's possible that I had something to do with that," he said, with a chuckle. "Even my own mother once said to me that there isn't enough holy water in Rome to wash the blood off my hands."

Simone, however, seemed immune from media barbs. He was the hero to Paskvan's goat. Simone's kid-glove treatment from reporters became a sore point with many of his fellow police officers.

"There might have been a little resentment about that, but there were also a lot of cops who didn't like Jimmy because he did such a good job," Paskvan said.

He made the slackers look bad. Jimmy was one of the 5 percent who did 95 percent of the work. I used to say that Jimmy Simone was the only cop better than me. If every police officer was as dedicated as him, there would be a zero crime rate. He was a leader. And he's proof that when you allow a cop to be a leader, even at the patrol level, he can influence others by example.

By the early 1980s, both Paskvan and Simone found themselves burdened with nicknames that they respectively disdained. Paskvan was called "Orkin Man Joe" by a few of his fellow officers, ostensibly for his efforts at exterminating society's rodents and parasites.

Simone was known to local reporters as "Supercop," a weighty handle that provoked a range of reactions from his colleagues. Some cops responded with good-natured ribbing, while others were resentful and even jealous.

However, the nickname quickly gained traction among the general public, despite Simone's attempts to disabuse the notion that he was superior to other officers.

"I'm no superhero; I'm not the bravest cop," he'd say, which only fueled his media-stoked *heroic, yet humble* image.

"But I'm also not a coward," he added. "I'm a hard worker and I'm always going to try to do the right thing."

10   **Homicide**

In the wake of Simone's second deadly force incident, he was removed from patrol duty and temporarily deployed as a detective in the Homicide unit. Although he was cleared of wrongdoing, the reassignment provided a de-stressing period—both for Simone and also any revenge-minded associates of Eugene Szejpcher, the shooting victim.

In nearly any police department, assignments to the Homicide unit are prized. Homicide detectives receive a bump in pay, a gold badge, and usually wear a suit and tie. The professional attire is thought to be less intimidating than a uniform, which can be helpful when interviewing suspects and speaking with families of victims.

Despite the perks of the new assignment, Simone wasn't happy that he was leaving the nonstop activity of nighttime patrol for the slower pace of detective work.

But the hiatus from street policing is a crucial step in postshooting adjustment, said Michael S. Scott, the director of the Center for Problem-Oriented Policing, a nonprofit organization that helps police devise strategies for handling a broad range of crimes and disorders.

"We know that deadly force incidents are very traumatic incidents for police officers and their families," Scott said.

It's a very profound thing for someone to take a human life. And when you find that an officer has been in multiple fatal shootings, irrespective of justified or not, that is a tremendous psychological burden. Although the public thinks that soldiers and police officers are immune to the psychological effects—that they feel no remorse and that they are just doing their job—it's not true. Most cops who have to take a life find it to be an enormously traumatizing incident. Many of them don't last much longer as cops because of that trauma.

Scott, a former police officer and administrator who is currently a professor at the University of Wisconsin Law School, said he's mindful of what a police department does to help its officers.

At the time of the Szejpcher shooting, Cleveland was still two years away from establishing a formalized counseling program for officers involved in deadly force incidents.

"The worst departments tell the officer, 'Take the rest of the shift off, but we expect you back at work tomorrow,'" Scott said. "And there's no counseling or time off. Where that has happened, there is a lot of evidence that it compounds the trauma to the officer. You often find that in departments where there is no care for the shooting officer, there is also very little care given to other officers who were at the scene. And no critique or analysis of the incident to try and prevent other deadly force incidents."

In the best-case scenario, all officers involved in the shooting are put on paid leave of absence pending the investigation. "But they are also given as much time as they need to recover psychologically from the incident," said Scott. "And the officers are required to attend at least one psychological counseling session."

Scott said that the law enforcement profession may want to give serious consideration to limiting a police officer to one fatal shooting during his or her career.

"I'm not saying we should terminate the officer, but maybe provide the officer with paid police work that doesn't allow the opportunity for another deadly force incident," said Scott, explaining, "The hypothesis is that an officer who has been involved in a shooting might be quicker to protect themselves in a future deadly force situation. They could be quicker to shoot."

Simone, not surprisingly, would not be in favor of a blanket proposal to shelve officers for, in his words, just doing their jobs.

The use of force is a part of the reality that every street cop has to face eventually, he said.

Sooner or later, every cop is going to hurt someone, sometimes fatally. I've seen cops shoot people and I've seen cops get shot. The younger guys at a shooting scene are usually the most upset. I tell them, "What did you think was going to happen? You can't go your whole career without this happening. If you think you can do this job and never hurt anyone, you're not really doing your job." Because we're dealing with violent people, we sometimes are left with no choice but to use violence in return.

Simone's military experience honed his fighting response ("you don't run away and hide; you go after the threat"). Surviving a dozen harrowing firefights in Vietnam also taught him the critical importance of staying calm in tense situations.

Noting that a gunfight is a last-resort scenario, particularly if there's a backdrop of people and there's a chance of hitting an innocent party, Simone said, "So many people depend on a police officer to make the correct decision in a life-or-death situation. None of us knows how we'll react in that situation. But I learned in Vietnam that if you don't react, you're dead."

The stakes are high for police officers who aren't willing to accept the significant risks and responsibilities of the job. According to Scott, those individuals who won't go into dangerous situations and perform the tasks that are required are potential liabilities to themselves, their partners, and civilians.

"They shouldn't be police officers," he said. "When those people are identified, they need to be weeded out. A cop can't be afraid. It takes courage to pull a trigger and it takes courage to not pull a trigger. The same amount of courage that is required to use force, when necessary, is required to use restraint."

Simone, by all accounts, is an aggressive, proactive police officer. But it would be a mistake to assume that he is more likely to be involved in a use-of-force incident than a more passive cop, said Thomas Evans, a psychology professor at John Carroll University and a longtime friend of Simone's.

Evans, a former Marine and a police psychologist for a dozen cities in northeast Ohio, said it's sometimes the nonaggressive types, particularly those who have less experience in confrontational situations, who lose their nerve and are unable to restrain themselves from overreaction.

"When cops become involved in a true life-or-death situation for the first time in their career, very few are equipped to handle it, especially if it's the first time they have ever drawn their weapon," said Evans, who has conducted extensive research on the neurophysiology of stress.

"The fight-or-flee response kicks in," he said. "Cops experience the same fear as anyone else. The most rational response to danger is to disengage—to flee. But cops can't leave. We don't want our cops running away from danger. We also don't want them resorting inappropriately to terminal force."

The best cops, and best candidates to become cops, are those individuals who are able to focus on their adrenaline rush and not let it override their decision-making process, said Evans. He explained that people who have some level of combat experience or a background in boxing, wrestling, or martial arts are often better able to modulate their emotions appropriately to a threatening situation.

Should Evans ever find himself in a dangerous spot, Simone would be his first call for backup—and not just because he's physically tough.

"Jim has been through the wars; he's seen all the bad guys and he's been in life-or-death situations," Evans said. "He has learned to control his fear. He is able to read the subtle cues that indicate whether a bad guy is bluffing or is a threat. He can then respond appropriately and also anticipate correctly what the consequences are going to be."

And if the bad guy is an actual threat, Simone, a former firearms instructor in the army, is a dead shot. Evans noted that most cops' experience with firearms involves little more than shooting twenty-five rounds at the firing range once a year. "Jim, however, is a very good shot and he has the ability to shoot under pressure. In any situation, I would know that we would come out okay."

By the early 1980s, articles about Simone's exploits had become a staple of the *Cleveland Press* and the *Plain Dealer,* the city's daily newspapers. Always accessible to police-beat reporters and always quotable, Simone was a favorite source of both papers, as well as the city's three network affiliate TV stations. Yet, with a nickname like Supercop, it was only a matter of time before his ascendance from the police blotter to the front page.

His star turn occurred by happenstance. A *Plain Dealer* reporter, James Neff, was stopped for a traffic violation by a Cleveland patrolman, Ronald Tomasch.

Ignoring Neff's pleas, Tomasch wrote him a citation, explaining, "You heard of Jimmy Simone, the No. 1 cop? Well, I'm No. 2 behind him in arrests. I need every one I can get."

Neff's curiosity about Cleveland's "No. 1 cop" sparked an introduction to Simone and then a lengthy and flattering profile in a Sunday edition of the *Plain Dealer.* The article, Simone's springboard to local stardom, was an anodyne portrait of an American Hero—the former altar boy who grew up in a rough inner-city neighborhood; the Vietnam War veteran who nearly lost his life in service to his country; the handsome single dad; the tough, duty-bound cop patrolling Cleveland's mean streets, saving lives at the risk of his own.

Stock Hollywood material, perhaps, but rooted in truth. Neff's article was signally interesting for its depiction of Simone's clearly defined code of ethics and his ferocious work output. While on traffic patrol, Simone would issue up to forty citations in an eight-hour shift, whereas some traffic cops wrote so few citations that they sometimes didn't bother carrying a ticket book in their car.

"A lot of guys wouldn't work with me because I worked so hard," Simone said.

I didn't slack. I made rules for myself and I abided by my own rules. I was first one to work and the last one to leave. I was consistent. I did the same thing repeatedly, over and over and over. My statistics for arrests and citations were off the charts. Other cops resented me, especially if their statistics were near the bottom. To them, I was a cowboy.

A city councilwoman once complained to Simone that her constituents were angry about Simone's zealous patrolling and ticket-writing. "Could you stop writing so many traffic citations?" the councilwoman asked. "Sure, if you'll write me a note asking me to please stop enforcing the law," Simone countered. He didn't hear back from her.

Simone's history of deadly gun battles was also cited in Neff's article. In just under ten years as a cop, he had killed two people and wounded seven. The shootings had become an integral aspect of the Supercop legend.

Simone, however, pointed to numerous situations in which he was able to resolve a confrontation or arrest a suspect without the use of deadly force.

Not long after joining the police department, Simone and his partner were called to a home where a man was threatening his family with a knife. When they arrived, the man confronted them in the front yard with a butcher knife in one hand and a paring knife in the other. He threatened the officers, and then turned to enter the house.

Simone knew he couldn't allow the man back inside the house with his terrified wife and children. He grabbed the man from behind and tried to wrestle him to the ground. During the struggle, Simone suffered two deep knife wounds to his arm. But he managed to hold onto the man until two other patrolmen arrived to help subdue him.

On another domestic call, he and several officers were in the process of arresting a man at his mother's house. The man began resisting, swinging wildly at the police officers. As they attempted to subdue him, his mother drew a gun from her bathrobe and fired at Simone from a few feet away. The heat from the muzzle blast seared his face.

He and the other cops pulled their weapons. "Drop the gun!" Simone screamed. The woman complied and was arrested with her son.

Shortly afterwards, while Simone and the other officers decompressed from the incident, he told the *Plain Dealer* that the woman was fortunate that she wasn't shot.

"She fired at me," he said. "But instead of shooting her, we disarmed her. See that kind of thing? If I had shot that woman, it would have been a front-page story. We were able to take her without shooting her, which is what we are getting paid to do."

James Neff's profile and subsequent newspaper features fueled Simone's public recognition. With his growing celebrity came attention from women. Darkly featured, with piercing brown eyes and relentless self-confidence, Simone had always attracted feminine interest. But now, flirtatious women slipped him their phone numbers during traffic stops and mailed letters to him at the Second District police station.

Simone, however, had his eye on someone. Lynne Stachowiak, a pretty brunette with a lively personality, was a Sixth District dispatcher. He'd noticed her at police social events and, since they worked the same (platoon) shift, he'd heard her occasionally on the police radio.

Lynne, however, had a fiancé—a landscaper who sported a ponytail and an easygoing manner.

"We'd been together for almost two years," she said. "He was a good guy. He was somewhat shy, though. I had taken him to a few of the police parties and tried to integrate him into our group, but he seemed uncomfortable in a room full of cops."

On a summer afternoon in 1982, Lynne was watching television with her fiancé. On the screen, Jim Simone was one of several police officers being interviewed by reporter Geraldo Rivera about police procedures.

"I was a fairly new employee, so I'd never met Jim or even heard of him," said Lynne. "But I guess I was looking too intently at the TV because my fiancé got a little jealous and said, 'I bet that cop comes up to visit you in the dispatch room.'"

Several weeks later, Lynne, then twenty-two, met Simone at a police picnic. "The platoon was like family back then. We'd get together after work or on the weekend, so I kept seeing Jim around. We'd always chat. It became clear to me that he was interested."

Despite his friendliness, Lynne was wary.

"He had a reputation as a ladies' man," she said. "I'd heard that he was divorced and that he'd dated a lot of the dispatchers and the lady police officers. I thought Jim was very good looking, but he was twelve years older than me and he seemed like trouble. I figured he was just trying to date the new girl. Besides, I was engaged. I just wasn't in the market."

Simone was not easily dissuaded. "She was attractive and I could tell she had a big heart," he said. "She was the whole package. I felt like we just hit it off."

At a bowling party, Lynne and her fiancé were having a drink at the bar when Simone suddenly appeared beside them. "He knew I was with my guy," she said. "We all got along fine, but Jim was persevering."

In August 1982, Lynne and one of her sisters attended a concert and then stopped by a Second District party in Cleveland's Brookside Park.

Jim was there and he was obviously glad to see me. We started talking and we kept talking until the sun came up. We discussed everything—our families, religion, our upbringing. We just clicked. I told him about my life and he told me about his. He told me that he wanted to introduce me to his family. I told him that he didn't even know me. "I know you," he said.

A first date followed. Then she invited Jim to join her and a group of her friends at a dance club. Jim, who doesn't dance or drink, was game. At the end of the night, Lynne was walked to her car and kissed.

"He came up to see me in the dispatch room on my birthday," she said. "He dropped off a striped black bag with a jewelry box inside. He'd gotten me diamond and pearl earrings. That was definitely a statement."

It was time for Lynne to have a talk with her fiancé.

"Jim had wooed me and won me," said Lynne. "On paper, we seemed different: I was a vegetarian and he ate steak; I was a hippie chick and he was a war hero; he smoked back then and I didn't. But he was very good to me. And the fact that he was a police officer was very comfortable for me."

The couple spent most of their free time together, usually at Jim's house, which was only a few blocks from the Second District station house. Lynne, who lived with her mother in Cleveland's Slavic Village neighborhood, would typically leave Jim's house late at night to drive home.

"It bothered him when I would leave in the middle of the night. He worried about me driving at that hour," she said. "I had a drawer of my own at his house. Gradually, I started moving my things in. Eventually, I had half of his closet. Then I moved his stuff into another room and I had the whole closet. It went from me leaving in the middle of the night to me never leaving."

For Lynne, the decision to move into Jim's house wasn't made lightly. Her parents had divorced when she was young. Following the divorce, her mother struggled with depression and other emotional issues. Lynne, the fifth of seven children, looked after her mother and siblings and shouldered many of the household responsibilities. Now, with her mother essentially a semirecluse, Lynne was reluctant to leave her.

"My mother was dysfunctional for many years," said Lynne. "I like to say that my father worked as an auto body technician and my mother worked on us."

She also had other, more personal reservations about sharing Simone's home. Although she lived with her mother, she enjoyed a level of independence. And she had always been fiercely self-reliant, even taking a job at age fourteen as a cook in a bowling alley. In her late teens, before meeting her fiancé, she had become ensnared in an abusive relationship. Afterwards, she had resolved to never again lose sight of her own identity.

"I made it clear early on with Jim that I had to be me," she said. "I needed to keep my identity without injuring his identity, especially considering who he was."

Simone, as a consequence of his media-driven persona, unquestionably brought baggage to the relationship. He was under the spotlight of the fickle press. He also had a growing number of detractors, mostly people he'd arrested, but also a few cops who objected to his unwillingness to break rules and ignore transgressions.

Early in his relationship with Lynne, Simone cautioned her and her siblings to be discreet when discussing him. "People either love me or hate me," he'd said. "If they hate me, they might hurt you."

Most people who knew Jim liked him, said Lynne. But he had occasional antagonists, and she sometimes became a target of their displaced ire.

I'd generally respond by saying, "If I have to defend him to you, then you don't really know him." But there was a time when I happened to be sitting next to a narcotics detective at a bar. Knowing that I was involved with Jim, he started to bad-rap him. He was talking the usual smack, calling Jim a glory hound and complaining that he would arrest his own mother. I finally stopped him and said, "You're a big boy and Jim's a big boy. Why don't you take this up with him instead of little me?" He never said a word to Jim.

As housemates, Jim and Lynne fell into an easy rhythm, adapting quickly to each other's idiosyncrasies. Jim's sleeping patterns, however, could be unpredictable and unnerving. He was plagued by nightmares related to his Vietnam combat experiences.

Lynne once shook him awake during a particularly traumatic nightmare. He jumped from the bed as if he was going to attack her. She learned to never startle him when he was asleep. If she needed to wake him, she would jiggle his toe.

"He told me the story about his mother trying to wake him up from a nightmare after he first returned from Vietnam. He reached his hands out and began choking her. When he woke up, he was terrified to realize what he was doing."

Lynne was curious about his Vietnam experiences, but she was reluctant to pry. "I was a twenty-three-year-old peacenik," she said. "I was just a kid during the Vietnam War. I probably would have protested the war if I had been older. I had no idea what had happened over there. I decided to wait until he was ready to talk."

On an afternoon in April, while they were cleaning their house, Jim finally opened up to her.

"It was a beautiful day, about 70 degrees and there was a really nice spring rain falling," recalled Lynne. "I had the windows wide open. He was working in the kitchen and I was in the living room. I was sitting on the couch just watching the rain coming in off Lake Erie. He walked into the room and looked out the window. He said the rain reminded him of the monsoon season in Vietnam. And then he just started talking. We sat there for two hours. I didn't say a word. I didn't want to stop him."

The monsoon's heavy rains would last for weeks, he told her. His platoon had to go out on patrol during the rainstorms, soaking wet beneath their ponchos. Often, they'd have to cross rice paddies, precariously balancing themselves on the narrow dikes made of compacted mud.

On the dikes, the men were exposed to snipers, and each step could potentially trip a land mine. But they preferred walking on the dikes instead of slogging through armpit-high water in the paddies, where they took the risk of stepping on poisonous punji sticks. On long patrols, they'd sleep on the dikes, taking turns dozing for an hour or two at most, while others stood guard. In the morning, they'd inevitably find leeches on their bodies, which they removed with mercurochrome or burned off with lit cigarettes.

While in the field, the men packed light. They carried only enough food to last until their resupply chopper arrived, which was typically three to five days. When resupplies were delayed, they foraged for food. Jim told her that his platoon had once gone a week without eating. They became so hungry that they made soup by boiling grass and water in their helmets. As a fuel source, they burned small pieces of C4 explosive.

Simone had lost so much weight in Vietnam that his brother Joe didn't recognize a photo of him in *Stars and Stripes,* the military newspaper. Joe had picked up the newspaper in April 1968 while he was stationed at an army base in Germany. "There was a story inside about Jim getting stuck in quicksand while on patrol," he said. "It took his platoon a couple of hours to extricate him. It was cool reading about my brother, but I was shocked at how skinny he was. The heat, stress, lack of sleep, and bad food had taken a toll."

Lynne sat spellbound as Jim described harrowing firefights. In broad strokes, he painted scenes of inexplicable bravery and paralyzing fear. He recalled the helplessness he felt when saw his friends die, and the psychological pressure of fighting an unseen enemy. She learned for the first time that he had planned on going to college. Ever the patriot, he didn't regret his time in Vietnam, but he recognized the futility of the war.

"He was purging," Lynne said. "It was horrifying and it was wonderful at the same time. He probably spared me a lot of the stories, but what he told me was amazing. It was the first time in my life that I'd heard stories of battle. It was bad, bad stuff. I remember thinking that I was glad I was a girl and I'm sorry that guys have to go through that."

In the weeks following, Simone continued to open up to Lynne and reveal himself. "I found out that he was very much like me in a lot of ways," Lynne said. "He has a big heart, he's compassionate, and he's loyal. Once he lets you in, you're always in."

Despite Simone's reputation as a "Robocop" who polices with machine-like efficiency, he is unashamed to express his empathy for society's unfortunates. On a daily basis, he encounters well-meaning, law-abiding people who have been derailed by bad circumstances.

"An example would be a woman who is a victim of domestic violence," he said.

People who aren't in an abusive situation don't understand the dynamics. It's not always easy for a battered woman to leave her husband or boyfriend, especially if she is tied through financial dependence, children, or even sex. The woman tries to make the relationship work, but realizes she needs to get out. What if she has nowhere to go? What if she has no job and her family has given up on her? If the abuse is so bad that she has to leave, she may end up on the street.

Any form of abuse or mistreatment of children also arouses fierce passion in Simone. On a child welfare call, Simone discovered young children home alone sleeping on a bare, filthy mattress. The home's toilet didn't work, so the children were using the bathtub to relieve themselves.

"Mom was drinking at the bar, so I arrested her for child endangerment," Simone said. "She was released, but I arrested her again after her boyfriend's pit bull chewed up one of the children."

The woman and her boyfriend were indicted for negligence in connection with the pit bull attack. Simone testified at the trial, but the judge forbade any mention of the previous child endangerment case.

As Simone was leaving the witness stand, the boyfriend whispered to him, "Go fuck yourself."

Simone quickly replied, "That's okay. I'll keep arresting mom for child endangerment, just like I did last time."

Because he mentioned the woman's prior acts, Simone was arrested for contempt of court and threatened with jail time. Later, in the judge's chambers, he explained, "Judge, to you, this case is about the law—it's black and white. But to me, it's personal. I see the damage done to the children."

Simone made over ten thousand arrests in his career, a number that far surpasses any other officer in the modern history of the Cleveland Police. A few of those arrests were of a benevolent nature.

On the coldest days of winter, there are always a few homeless people who elect to take their chances outside rather than check into a shelter. Their reasons are varied: Some are afraid of being robbed or assaulted in the shelters, while others prefer to stay on the streets where they can drink unimpeded.

When temperatures dipped to single digits, Simone kept an eye out for street people, offering them rides to city shelters. Those who declined would sometimes be arrested for innocuous offenses.

"I'd arrest them for their own good," he explained. "In some cases, they were so drunk they didn't realize how cold it was. I'd get them off the street so they didn't freeze to death."

While booking and processing an elderly homeless man, Simone made a surprising discovery while inventorying his clothing. The name "Simone" was printed in magic marker inside the man's coat.

"I realized it was my coat," Simone said. "I printed my name in all my clothing. It was a habit from my army days. I'd bought that coat a year earlier. One day, it went missing. I just figured that it had never come back from the dry cleaners."

At home, the next day, he told Lynne about his surprising discovery. When he described the homeless man and told her where he'd found him, she confessed her role in the mystery. She explained that she saw the same man sleeping on a sidewalk grate every night when she left work.

"I told Jim that I was worried that he was going to freeze," she said. "So one morning when the weather report called for bitter cold, I went up to Jim's closet and dug out a nice fluffy down coat. I had another dispatcher go with me after work and we gave the man the coat."

Jokingly, Jim told her to quit giving his clothes away to people he might arrest. But he was touched by her compassion. If he had any doubts about his feelings for Lynne, they had just been put to rest.

11 Dimple, Lola, and Curly

As a patrol officer, Simone moved about his assigned beat with unfettered freedom, guided by his intuition and experience. His interactions with the public were often substantial and personally gratifying, whether providing service and counsel to a crime victim or putting handcuffs on a perpetrator.

But in Homicide, much of his time was spent in the office—reviewing forensic evidence, searching criminal databases, interviewing witnesses and suspects, and tracking leads. An arrest was typically the culmination of a lengthy investigation and the execution of a warrant.

Once Simone acclimated to the slower, more deliberate tempo of the Homicide unit, he found that he enjoyed the investigative aspect of detective work. While working patrol, Simone saw the bare facts of murder cases—the identities of victims and the manner of death. Now, he was responsible for discovering not only the killers but the reasons for the murders. Sometimes those discoveries could be deeply disheartening, even to a veteran cop.

Shortly after joining Homicide, he helped crack a high-profile murder case that involved a disparate group of conspirators, including the victim's wife, his stepdaughter, a member of Cleveland's Mafia family, and two associates of the Hells Angels Motorcycle Club.

The case was set in motion in January 1981, when Henry Podborny, a wealthy Chicagoan, was reported missing after boarding a flight to Cleveland.

Two months after his disappearance, Simone learned that someone had tried to cash a traveler's check at a northeast Ohio bank by using Podborny's identification and forging his name. The interstate check activity triggered the FBI's involvement in the case.

Working with FBI agents, Simone traced the traveler's check to a Cleveland man. Within minutes of speaking with Simone, the man blurted, "Okay, you got me on the check, but you're not getting me for the murder."

Aware now that Podborny had been killed, Simone obtained information that led him to a decomposed body lying in a garbage-strewn lot on Cleveland's East Side. Dental records revealed that the body, which had been wrapped in a plastic pool table cover, was Podborny's. An autopsy showed that Podborny had been beaten on his legs and head with a blunt object, perhaps an iron pipe, and had suffered multiple compound fractures of his skull. He had also been shot in the forehead.

Further investigation led Simone and fellow detectives to a storefront bar near East 110th and Superior Avenue. During a search of the bar, which was undergoing renovation, detectives found small pieces of a pool table cover that seemed to match the material that covered Podborny's body.

While examining the premises, Simone paid special attention to the walls and ceiling. If Podborny had been killed in the bar, he reasoned, the force of the blows and Podborny's bullet wound would have likely left blood spatter. He noticed that the bar's walls and floor had recently been cleaned, but he also saw what appeared to be dried blood high on the walls.

"The walls had been wiped clean, but only to a height of seven feet or so," Simone said. "It was obvious that whoever had cleaned had only cleaned as high as he could reach."

As Simone suspected, the blood was the same type as Podborny's. Piecing together details of Podborny's life, he learned that he had been in the midst of marital problems with his wife, Dimple.

Podborny, a U.S. Military Academy graduate and a former army major, owned a large pallet company in Chicago that had an estimated value of $2.5 million. He had met Dimple, a native Clevelander, while she was working as a nurse's aide caring for his mother during a hospital stay in Chicago. Podborny's mother had been so impressed by Dimple that she had hired her as a private duty nurse after her stay in the hospital. In 1969, Podborny and Dimple married and settled in his fashionable home in Berwyn, a Chicago suburb.

In 1980, Dimple, sixty, filed for divorce. After Podborny, fifty-eight, was unable to change her mind, he cancelled her credit cards and hid his money in different bank accounts to keep it away from her. Dimple, who had relocated to Cleveland, was living with her son from a previous marriage and his wife, Lola Gail Toney. Upset that Podborny had cut her off from his money, Dimple hatched a plot with Lola to kill him. Dimple gave Lola $24,000 to arrange for Podborny's murder.

For help in setting up the hit, Lola turned to Robert O'Neal, the owner of the storefront bar that Simone had examined. Lola was O'Neal's part-time bookkeeper and also his mistress.

The conspirators decided to lure Podborny to Cleveland on the pretext of reconciling with Dimple. Podborny, who was desperate to regain Dimple's affections, readily agreed. He gave a house key to one of his employees and asked him to tend to his dogs. "I have to go to Cleveland," Podborny told him. "Everything I have in my life is at stake."

Podborny was picked up at Cleveland Hopkins International Airport on January 21 by Lola. She drove him to O'Neal's bar, telling him to go inside and wait for Dimple while she parked the car.

Inside the bar, Podborny was robbed and bludgeoned by O'Neal and several other men, including two Hells Angels associates, one of whom was Lola's brother. O'Neal left the bar and handed Lola $1,400 and several credit cards from Podborny's wallet.

Lola knew that Podborny had $50,000 in cash in his house. In addition, Lola and Dimple had drained $600,000 from Podborny's bank accounts and stashed it in a safety deposit box in Indiana.

In one of the case's several double-crosses, Lola concocted a scheme to extort the money from Dimple. The plan hinged on Dimple believing that Podborny was still alive and would be seeking retribution against her for the attempted murder. In return for Dimple's payments, Lola would arrange to have someone provide "protection" to Dimple.

Again relying on the contacts of her boyfriend O'Neal, Lola was introduced to John "Curly" Montana, one of the few remaining members of Cleveland's Mafia. The city's once-powerful underworld had diminished since the 1950s when up to sixty made (formally inducted) men ran its loan-sharking, gambling, and union rackets.

By the early 1980s, the Cleveland family had dwindled to a handful of members, primarily because longtime boss John Scalish had shown little interest in recruiting new soldiers. Scalish and his successors didn't have a pressing need to build the family's ranks. They had a solid and lucrative hold on the city's criminal enterprises. They also had a steady revenue stream from their investments in Las Vegas casinos, made primarily through Mafia-influenced loans from the Teamsters Central States Pension Fund. Each month, the Cleveland mob and other Midwestern Mafia families received up to $10,000 each in money skimmed from the casinos.

Scalish, who ruled the Cleveland mob from 1944 until his death in 1976, passed without grooming a replacement. The leadership void sparked a power struggle between heir apparent James "Jack White" Licavoli and Irish gangster Danny Greene, a brash former longshoreman who was backed by John Nardi, a Mafia associate.

The war between Licavoli and Greene led to nearly forty car bombings in the Cleveland area. National media dubbed Cleveland "Bomb City, U.S.A." and the Bureau of Alcohol, Tobacco, Firearms, and Explosives tripled its staffing in northeast Ohio in order to handle the bomb investigations.

No direct attempts were made on Licavoli's life, but many of his associates were killed. Nardi lost his life in May 1977, when he was blown up by a car bomb placed by Curly Montana and an associate.

The Licavoli faction tried to kill Greene on at least eight occasions. After each unsuccessful attempt, Greene became increasingly emboldened.

Ed Kovacic headed the Cleveland Police Intelligence unit in the 1970s. His investigations into mob activities became a concern for both the Licavoli and Greene camps.

"I had quite a few people threaten me, but I was never afraid," said Kovacic. "Danny Greene put out the word that he was going to blow up my car. So I started putting scotch-tape on the doors, hood, and trunk. I would check the tape every morning before I got in the car. And I never let my kids start their cars. I did it for them."

One day, Greene sent an emissary to tell Kovacic that there hadn't been a contract on his life. "The guy told me that Danny wasn't really upset with me and that they would never harm a cop. But I still put tape on my car just as a precaution. Later that week, I was driving my car and I noticed the scotch-tape was flapping. I had a second of panic. Then I thought, 'You son of a bitch, Greene, you got me. Where is the bomb? Will it go off when I reach a certain speed?'"

Kovacic then remembered that he had taken his car to a mechanic that morning to have the oil changed. He eventually developed a working relationship with Greene, even admitting to an amused respect for the cocksure Irishman.

Greene's luck ran out October 6, 1977, after a visit to his dentist. As he approached his Lincoln Continental, he was ripped apart by a remote-detonated bomb that had been placed in a car next to his. A police report noted that Greene's left arm was torn off and thrown 100 feet from his body.

In the aftermath of Greene's death, several higher-ups in the Cleveland mob were incarcerated, including Licavoli. The Cleveland family was left in disarray and facing extinction. Nevertheless, the power and prestige of the Mafia brand impressed Lola Toney. She decided to place her trust in Curly Montana.

She filled him in on her plan to extort Dimple, enlisting him as Dimple's ersatz bodyguard. She then arranged for him to travel to Chicago, telling him that money was hidden in Podborny's house and that she could provide keys and a map of the residence. Lola also told him that a large sum of money was kept in a safe at Podborny's business along with documents that concerned the illegal activities of a member of Congress. When she told Montana about the $600,000 that she and Dimple had placed in the safety deposit box, he convinced her to drop her extortion scheme.

Montana had a different idea. He suggested that they travel to Indiana and withdraw the $600,000. Then Lola would permit Montana to "rob" her of the money. The purpose of the robbery, Montana explained, was to cut Dimple out of her share of the money. Lola immediately agreed and offered Montana and her boyfriend $100,000 for their participation.

In the meantime, Lola and others raided Podborny's assets. Simone had obtained a search warrant for a safety deposit box belonging to Lola. Inside, he found jewelry, a clock, calculator, and personal effects of Podborny's.

Prior to the discovery of Podborny's body on April 24, 1981, Lola visited Podborny's home in Chicago and the safety deposit box in Indiana. She discovered the money had been removed. Investigators theorized that Montana had managed to loot the house and safety deposit box before Lola's arrival.

Six people were indicted for their involvement in the Podborny murder. Lola and Dimple accused each other of hatching the plot, with Lola cooperating with prosecutors and testifying against the others. At Montana's trial, however, she abruptly changed her mind and refused to testify against him. Five of the conspirators were sentenced to life in prison, including Lola and Dimple. Montana received a five-year sentence.

During Lola's trial, her husband James Toney sat in the courtroom in support of her. He also attended the trial of his mother, Dimple. He made few comments about the case, except to say, "I don't know why they had to kill Henry for money. He was such a nice guy. All you ever had to do if you needed money was to ask him."

Simone said the Podborny case, which he termed the most memorable of his career, was fueled by greed so overwhelming that the conspirators plotted and squealed against each other. The case also sustained his contention that "most criminals aren't very smart." Several of the conspirators provided an easily followed trail of clues and evidence.

Along with their clumsy attempts to cash Podborny's traveler's checks, they left damning evidence at the scene of the murder. Simone noted that the killers only halfheartedly cleaned Podborny's blood spatter from the walls. "They were apparently too lazy or dumb to climb a ladder to wipe the blood from the upper part of the walls, where it was clearly visible," he said.

Simone also recalled the competition and culture clash that sometimes occurs between federal authorities and local law enforcement. In the Podborny case, the FBI was sometimes slow to share material information with Cleveland detectives. The feds also insisted on paying an individual $10,000 for information about the whereabouts of Podborny's body. Simone, however, objected to the payment on moral principles as well as professional pride. He preferred to obtain the information through investigative means.

During the lengthy investigation of Podborny's disappearance and murder, which at times involved thirty detectives, the Cleveland Police and FBI agents jointly arrested several suspects. The arrests of the Hells Angels associates were executed with guns drawn as a safety precaution, although both men surrendered peacefully.

Shortly after the arrests, Simone overheard an FBI agent on a phone call with his wife. He chuckled when he heard the agent excitedly say, "Honey, I had my gun out today."

In spring of 1983, Simone's father, Anthony, was hospitalized with severe emphysema. During a visit, he asked Jim to wheel him down the hall so they could smoke.

"Smoke? You have lung disease," Jim protested.

"Son, don't you understand?" his father barked. "I'm never coming out of here. Now let's go have a cigarette."

Several months before he had entered the hospital, Anthony had proposed that he and Jim fly to California to visit Jim's brother, Joe. "A father spending time with his two sons," Anthony had said.

"I told him that I couldn't take off work—too busy," Jim said. "My father had known that he was dying, but he hadn't told me. I wish that he had."

Jim received a call at work one night telling him that Anthony's kidneys had shut down and he'd slipped into a coma.

"The doctors told me that they could keep him alive on a machine," said Jim, who had recently learned that his father had wanted him to make all decisions regarding life support. "But when I walked into his room and saw the IVs, the oxygen, and the feeding tube, I realized I couldn't do that to him. I held his hand and said, 'Dad, I'm sorry, but I don't think you want to live like this. If I'm wrong, you can yell at me when you see me.'"

He sat with father until he passed. The next day, Jim quit smoking.

In Homicide, Simone's large caseload included a mix of new and old murders. At any given time, he could be working on twenty cases. But he didn't restrict his investigations to just murders. If he observed a strange occurrence in the Second District or received a tip about suspected criminal activities, he would check it out, sometimes during his off-duty hours.

A random comment by a teenaged girl piqued his interest in Stephen Jones, a self-proclaimed minister. The girl mentioned to Simone that she and her friends frequently visited Jones's home on Cleveland's West Side.

The fifty-three-year-old Jones, who called himself the head of the First Church of God's Children, was described by neighbors as very cordial and well liked. But Simone sensed there was a dark side to the long-haired, bearded minister. Over a six-week period, he watched Jones's residence, observing the comings and goings of numerous young girls, some of whom he recognized as troubled runaways.

Simone spoke with several of the girls, learning that Jones had befriended them and offered snacks, money, advice, and a place to hang out when they wanted to skip school or hide from their parents. One of the girls showed him a card that included Jones's address and the message: "People! Need Help? Call or Stop By. Rev. Steve Jones."

Although none of the girls accused Jones of inappropriate behavior, Simone decided to obtain a search warrant.

Accompanied by a Vice Squad detective, Simone raided Jones's house, finding sex magazines and movies, vibrators, leather whips, masks, a chastity belt, and hundreds of photos of girls as young as nine in sexually explicit poses. In some of the pictures, the girls were dressed in lewd harem costumes.

Simone learned that Jones was sexually involved with dozens of girls from his neighborhood. Typically, he would give money to the girls and when they couldn't repay him, he would coerce them into nude photos and sexual activity. When word traveled that Jones was offering money and a place to hide out during the day, runaway girls from all over northeast Ohio visited his house.

Jones also sent girls to his friends for sex, including a sixty-seven-year-old man and the fifty-eight-year-old owner of a neighborhood shoe repair store. A third man who was accused of having sex with the minor girls committed suicide shortly after the case broke. Simone said none of the girls complained to police because they feared that Jones would make their nude photographs public.

"They also had a real attachment to him," said Simone. "The girls felt unloved at home. Jones was a father figure to them. He made them feel like he cared about them. In fact, after we arrested Jones, some of the girls were more upset with me than him."

Jones contended his actions with the girls were not improper. "They kept coming back," he said at his trial. He was sentenced to thirty-one years in prison.

As a detective, Simone often visited the Justice Center for court hearings and administrative functions. There, he encountered many citizens whom he had ticketed while working as a patrol officer.

He managed to shrug off the glares he received, regarding the rancor as an expected consequence of being a diligent cop. At times, he even poked fun at himself by wearing a Cleveland Fire Department hat in the Justice Center cafeteria, joking that, "Everyone likes firemen."

But the anti-Simone sentiment among his fellow cops stung. "A lot of people disliked me intensely," he said.

The enmity was powered, in part, by envy and resentment. His extraordinary volume of ticket-writing and arrests had led to numerous court appearances—and numerous overtime hours. Simone's annual compensation was consistently higher than that of his fellow patrol officers.

"A lot of cops were jealous of the overtime," said Simone. "I remember walking past someone's desk one day and hearing him say, 'I wish I had Simone's money.' I told him he could make just as much money as me. All he had to do was grab a set of keys for a patrol car and then go be a police officer instead of a paper-pusher."

But Simone conceded that his personal code of ethics sometimes placed him at odds with his colleagues.

Simone, hardwired for egalitarianism, explained, "I treated everyone, whether they were cops or civilians, the same way because that's how the law is written. No one should be exempt from the law, not even police officers."

His admittedly unorthodox perspective—a brazen defiance of professional courtesy, fraternalism, and workplace conviviality—became problematic.

"It's very difficult when you correctly do your job and arrest a cop or fireman and then you see your name written above every urinal in the Justice Center," he said.

> From the first time I arrested a cop—the first time I crossed that line—I was a marked man. There were times when I couldn't take a leak without seeing, "Simone is a prick" or "Simone sucks" on the wall in front of me.
>
> The hardest part of being a cop is doing the right thing every single time. It is tempting to cut someone a break, but that's not the right thing. If I do the right thing, I get ostracized by other cops. But I can't do it any other way. I can't undo who I am.

A year before his deployment to Homicide, he had arrested a drunk driver who was a relative of several Second District police officers. The next day, Simone found an anonymous note on his locker that read: "You think you're a smart guy. You could have let him go and driven him home. Someday you'll get yours."

Simone was angered by the threatening nature of the handwritten note. Determined to find the identity of the writer, he took the note home along with a stack of duty reports, which had been signed by each officer who worked that day in the Second District.

"I went through every report, probably a couple of hundred, until I found the officer's handwriting that matched the note," he said. "I then confronted the officer in the locker room. He was a younger guy. He denied writing the note until I showed him the similar handwriting on the duty report. I then told him to talk to me directly if he had a problem, rather than leaving notes. When I invited him to settle the matter in the police garage, he didn't have a word to say."

Simone's sergeant later reprimanded him for challenging the younger officer to a fight. "The sergeant's exact words were, 'The draconian days of fighting in the garage are over,'" recalled Simone.

Even as a detective, Simone occasionally collared inebriated drivers. In October 1983, he arrested the wife of a prominent attorney. The couple, angered at Simone, reached out to a police captain.

"Her case gets dropped now," the captain told Simone.

Simone refused. The next day, he was transferred from Homicide to the Juvenile division. His days would now be spent chasing truants and investigating misdemeanor offenses by teens.

"I was being punished for not fixing a drunk driving case for a lawyer's wife," said Simone. Whether he was being disingenuous or not, he had once again become sand in the gears of a machine driven by favoritism and patronage. Yet, in Simone's rule-bound world, personal moral code would always trump political expediency.

Although perturbed by his reassignment, Simone attacked his new responsibilities with the same measure of enthusiasm and vigor that he had shown as a patrol officer and Homicide detective.

Simone, in fact, found satisfaction in speaking with the mothers and fathers of offenders. He even devised the following list of rules for successfully raising children, which he would recite to parents:

- Give children a religious background
- Give them the best education you can afford
- Discipline your children—let them know there are consequences for their actions
- Teach your children morals

"I would tell parents that if they did those four things," said Simone, "there would be a good chance that their kids wouldn't end up in the backseat of a police car."

12 Through and Through

In the early morning of November 16, 1983, Simone was in his office at the Second District police station reviewing reports and preparing for a court appearance.

"I had the police monitor on so that I could hear what was happening. I heard a report that a woman had been carjacked by a guy with a gun. They found the woman's car in a church parking lot."

Simone immediately told his partner—who was eating a bowl of oatmeal—that he was going to the church to see if the cops there needed help.

"I didn't need to go," said Simone. "I was assigned to Juvenile and I was due in court in an hour. My partner told me to go ahead. He stayed and finished his breakfast."

On the short drive to the church, Simone recalled being in a good mood, despite the drizzly rain. "I wasn't particularly worried about the church situation," he said. "There weren't a lot of shootings on the day shift. Besides, it was 8:00 A.M. Nobody gets shot at 8:00 in the morning."

A half-hour earlier, Ernestine Buckley had reported to Cleveland police that an armed man had stolen her car at Lincoln-West High School. Two officers in zone car 222 spotted Buckley's Ford LTD in front of the Christian and Missionary Alliance Church on Broadview Road. The suspected carjacker, Dennis Workman, was believed to be in the church.

At 7:54 A.M., zone car 222 requested backup to the church, transmitting over police channel two, the Second District's frequency. The following is a transcript of the Second District's radio traffic that morning:

UNIT 222 (O'Brien and Milojevic): "Can you have another car meet us on Broadview?

DISPATCHER: "Alright, whereabouts on Broadview?"

UNIT 222: "We're across from a drycleaner. The [stolen] car is parked out in front of the church. We'll see if he [Workman] is inside. We'll wait for another car . . . 28th and Broadview."

UNIT 245 (John Thomas and Richie Auner): "We are coming up there."

UNIT 221 (Cornely): "We are going to head up that way also."

DISPATCHER: "7:56 . . . All cars up on Broadview, if you get that Workman, he's got a traffic warrant on him."

UNIT 222: "Thank you. Shut off the sirens, okay. We're over here."

UNIT 222: "Can you get ahold of Pastor Yearsley at (*unintelligible*) and see if he lives inside the church. If so, open up. All the doors are locked up . . . sometimes they have residency inside."

DISPATCHER: "Do you need anybody else up there? Is there a boss up there?"

UNIT 220 (Scheuermann): "We'll get a boss up there."

UNIT 220: "Who is going to respond from the district?"

UNIT 222: "We're going inside."

UNIT 221 (Stanczyk): "To the cars inside . . . if you can, guys, keep us posted, please."

UNIT 245: "Could you send us a couple more cars, please?"

DISPATCHER: "How about 233 . . . 28th and Broadview . . . assist those other cars at the church."

UNIT 233: "233 is on the way to West 28th and Broadview."

UNIT 232: "232 is on its way . . . (*unintelligible*) . . . we're almost there."

DISPATCHER: "Alright, 232 at 8:10. Any other cars disregard until we hear further."

UNIT 221: "245, where do you want 232 when they get here?"

UNIT 222: "Get the perimeter."

UNIT 214 (Todt): "To the other cars, where do you want us?"

UNIT 221: "I don't know. There's a couple teams inside . . . there's about five coppers inside . . . if you want, you can swing around to the back . . . maybe secure the back."

UNIT 214: "Okay, thank you."

UNIT 221: "221 to those cars inside . . . guys . . . keep us posted where you're at . . . in case something happens . . . upstairs, downstairs."

Twenty-three minutes had elapsed since the first unit arrived. There were now twelve police officers at the church.

UNIT 221: "To those cars inside, Simone is coming in plainclothes. He is going to be coming in behind you."

DISPATCHER: "8:17."

UNIT 221: "To the inside cars, you have a couple of supervisors coming in behind you . . . keep us posted where you're at . . . upstairs . . . downstairs."

At 8:20, Workman fired his first shot, striking Jim Simone and John Thomas.

JOHN THOMAS, on his portable radio: "Get us some help in the basement . . . Richie . . .

Thirty seconds later, BRIAN MILLER, on his portable: " . . . (*unintelligible*) . . . we have an officer shot, we need help . . . get C-Med ambulance fast."

DISPATCHER: "Alright, alright."

UNIDENTIFIED: "What part of the building?"

UNIT 230 (Sgt. Whitner): "230. Get ambulance to 28th and Broadview."

DISPATCHER: "They have been ordered sir. They are on the way."

DISPATCHER: "Is 277 on the air?"

UNIT 214: "214. Notify Deaconess Hospital, we are taking a male to Deaconess Hospital."

DISPATCHER: "Alright."

UNIT 230: "230 to radio . . . 230 to radio."

DISPATCHER: "230 go ahead."

UNIT 230: "Call Deaconess, tell them we've got two policemen . . . (*unintelligible*) . . . right up."

DISPATCHER: "Alright."

BRIAN MILLER: "Tell Deaconess we've got two officers shot . . . get their trauma unit ready."

UNIDENTIFIED: "Radio, be advised there is another policeman shot there supposedly."

Dispatch learns that Brian Miller has also been shot.

UNIT 230: "I'm taking another one to Deaconess . . . notify 'em . . . tell 'em we need a wheelchair."

At 8:24, Lieutenant Greg Baeppler (Unit 253) tells dispatch to notify the police chief's office and activate the Shooting Team (the CPD unit that investigates officer-involved shootings). "The whole ball of wax . . . we need another ambulance here also."

UNIT 210 (Sgt. Beranek): "210 on the air, dispatch, responding to the shooting scene."

DISPATCHER: "8:29."

DISPATCHER: "S.I.U. car on this channel . . . 277."

UNIT 277 (Scientific Investigation Unit): "We're at (*unintelligible*) . . . call you in a couple of minutes."

UNIT 253: "I want you to check where all the police victims are at. I also want to know if the shooting team has been notified."

DISPATCHER: "Sir, the shooting team has been notified and as far as we know, they are all at Deaconess."

UNIT 253: "Could you check on that? I have an understanding that one might be at Metro [MetroHealth Hospital]."

DISPATCHER: "Alright sir, will do."

UNIT 250 (Second District Commander Ed Rossman): "Greg, what is the exact location of this thing?"

UNIT 253: "West 28th and Broadview."

UNIT 250: "Alright."

DISPATCHER: "Okay 253, Deaconess has three gunshot wounds . . . two are officers. C-Med says they are on the scene with a victim in full cardiac arrest."

UNIT 253: "Okay, the third person that's shot is a plainclothes officer and we're here with the victim here.

DISPATCHER: "Alright, is there a suspect in custody on that?"

UNIT 253: "Correct, that's the full cardiac arrest at the church."

UNIT 11 (Deputy Inspector Richard Kazmir): "Car 11 to 253. Is there any need for my assistance out there or is the situation controlled relative to the suspect?"

UNIT 253: "We now have the suspect and it's a singular suspect. There is no need for SWAT. We just need the shooting team and that's about it."

UNIT 210 (Sgt. Beranek): "Do you want me there or at Deaconess Hospital?"

UNIT 253: "Sarge, I want you to go to Deaconess. I want you to put the situation there in control. We've got too many policemen over there . . . get all the information . . . get the policemen we don't need in the back out."

In the police dispatch center, which was located in the Cuyahoga County Justice Center, Lynne Stachowiak was unaware that a shooting had occurred in the Second District.

Lynne, who was then twenty-four, handled Sixth District calls. "But I sat next to the Second District dispatcher, so I knew there was some kind of activity going on," she said. "Then, at 8:30, the Second District dispatcher threw off his headset and switched to the loudspeaker so everyone in the room could hear what was happening. We heard police supervisors yelling for ambulances and Homicide detectives. Like everyone else in the room, my heart was in my throat. But I had to stay focused on the officers in my district."

Lynne never considered that Simone, a Second District officer and her boyfriend of two years, was involved.

"Jim was working as a detective in the Juvenile unit," she said. "And he had a court hearing to attend that morning. There wouldn't have been any reason for him to be at that church."

At 8:40, her supervisor tapped her on the shoulder and told her that it was time for her to take her break. When Lynne said she wasn't ready for a break, he told her to grab her purse and coat.

"I started getting irritated with him. It wasn't clicking for me that this wasn't about a break," she said. "I told him I was busy, so he told me then that Jim was shot. I was stunned. His words literally took my breath away."

After being told that she wouldn't be returning to work that day, a chief dispatcher drove her to Deaconess Hospital.

"I was freaking out, but nobody would tell me Jim's condition or where he had been shot," she said. "The chief dispatcher who was driving me kept telling me to keep calm and don't get in anyone's way at the hospital. He was coaching me to not overreact."

At the hospital, TV news vans and dozens of police cars were parked askew near the entrance, and on sidewalks and the lawn.

The dispatcher opened the hospital door for me. Just as I walked in, he said, "Lynne, Jim is shot in the face." Then he pushed me through the door and I was on my own. I walked through the atrium and into a corridor that was filled with about fifty cops. None of them would make eye contact with me. They were crying and they didn't want me to get upset. Suddenly, I felt like everything was moving in slow motion. I remember seeing Kelly Stillman, a brand-new cop. I kept staring at his shoes, noticing they were very shiny. I moved through the corridor like I was on a conveyor belt. Jeff Stanczyk handed me the gold chain and medal that Jim was wearing when he was shot. I walked to the triage room, where Jim and the other wounded officers were. Somebody asked me if I was ready to go in. I wasn't. I didn't know what to expect.

Stepping inside triage, Lynne was startled by Simone's appearance. "The left side of his face, where he'd been shot, was grotesquely swollen. His cheek was badly burned from the muzzle flash and he couldn't see out of his left eye."

Just as surprising to her was his demeanor. "Not only was he alive after being shot in the head, but he was talking," Lynne said. "Although

I could tell that he was in a lot of pain. They had prescribed a narcotic painkiller, but he didn't want to take it. He was afraid that if he fell asleep, he would never wake up."

Simone, Miller, and Thomas were hooked to medical devices, intravenous gear, and blood bags, with each attended by a huddle of nurses.

A series of neurologists, emergency room physicians, and residents examined Simone, with all marveling at his improbable survival. The .38-caliber bullet had punched a hole in his cheekbone and ripped through his skull, missing major blood vessels and vital brain structures by millimeters. Just as remarkably, neither the bullet nor his cheekbone had fragmented upon impact, which could have driven tiny splinters of metal and bone into his brain.

According to the initial medical consensus, he was alive through a combination of sheer luck and because he had reflexively turned his head away just as Workman fired his gun.

Greg Baeppler, however, wasn't willing to chalk up Simone's survival to mere chance.

"He survived because of his training and experience," said Baeppler, who rose to the rank of district commander before retiring. "Whether it was his military or police training, Simone reacted the way he had been taught. Most people who take the job of street cop are 'doers' and Type-A personalities anyhow. They have a survival gene that kicks in. They know how to respond."

Miller, Thomas, and Simone were all tactically good officers, Baeppler said. "They all had a strong work ethic. Simone worked very hard, which is why he got into so much trouble in his career. If you're going to go hard for eight hours a day in high-crime neighborhoods, like he did, you're going to be in some altercations."

Simone had been at Deaconess for three hours, yet none of his attending doctors had noticed that he had an exit wound. He had been placed in a partially seated position in bed. When he complained that he was feeling faint and that his back seemed wet, a nurse bent him forward and discovered his mattress was blood-soaked. The bullet, which had mushroomed when it hit his cheekbone, had left a dime-sized exit hole at the base of his skull. Blood was running down his back to his buttocks.

"Doctor, are you aware this is a through-and-through?" the nurse asked, directing the question to a neurosurgeon and other physicians conferring just outside Simone's room.

After another series of X-rays and examinations, the exit wound was cleaned and bandaged. At noon, Lynne requested a bite to eat for him, but was told that wouldn't be possible because he was being prepped for surgery.

"We were surprised by that news," she said. "So I tracked down his doctors and found out that a neurosurgeon was planning to do exploratory surgery on him. He wanted to cut Jim's skull open. When I asked why, the doctors told me that they wanted to see the path that the bullet had traveled. Basically, they were just curious to learn how he had survived."

"No, he will not be having surgery. It's not necessary," Lynne told the doctors. "Now feed him. He's hungry."

In the early afternoon, Lynne was taken to a guarded family waiting room after police heard rumors that Workman's relatives, some of whom had criminal histories, had issued a death threat against Simone. He was moved to a private room, where Lynne and other family members were required to use a security password to be admitted.

Several police officers visited Simone, including Dave Sumskis, his former partner. As Sumskis prepared to leave, he slipped a 9mm pistol under Simone's sheet. "Just in case they get past the guards," he said.

Sumskis, who worked with Simone for four years, was briefly interviewed by reporters in the hospital lobby. "Jimmy is by far the best policeman in the city," he told the *Plain Dealer*. "Even though a lot of people disagree with the way he works because he pushes, pushes, pushes."

Bob Deighton, the Brooklyn patrolman who persuaded Simone to become a police officer, also stopped by. The two friends had started a security firm together, providing protective services to a chain of retail clothing stores. At one point, they had sixty officers on their payroll.

The firm was profitable, but the partners decided to shut down after a disagreement over the direction of the business. When the two men formed the company, they had made a deal that they would break it up if they ever argued over money. The men agreed that their friendship was too important to let money come between them.

Shortly after Deighton left, Simone's ex-wife appeared at his bedside. During their stormy marriage, she'd often chided him about his career as a police officer, urging him to find a safer line of work.

Now, standing over him, she hissed, "I always told you this was going to happen."

She and their two oldest daughters had been picked up at home by a police officer and brought to the hospital.

"As they were getting out of the patrol car, a TV reporter stuck a microphone in my twelve-year-old daughter's face and asked, 'How do you feel about your father being shot?'" recalled Simone. "She hadn't even been told yet. She started crying."

In his room, the girls were frightened by his appearance. "My face must have looked pretty bad," Simone said. "My daughters didn't even want to touch me."

Finally, he sent everyone home and tried to rest. "I was physically and emotionally drained. Lynne told me later that her hand was bruised from me holding it so tight."

Police officers, some he knew and others who just wanted to meet him, continued to visit. A new officer nervously asked him what it felt like to be shot. "It's a terrible experience," Simone replied. "It hurts more than you can imagine. The object is to avoid it."

A Homicide detective investigating the shooting was the last to visit. He told Simone that Workman had fired six shots in the church basement. Six police officers had fired a total of fifty rounds. Simone, although his vision was clouded by blood and pain, had fired the only shot that hit Workman.

Leaning close to Simone, the detective whispered, "Jim, I need to know: Who fired the first shot?"

Simone wearily waved him away.

Lynne, also exhausted, left the hospital in the early evening, walking through the atrium, which was filled with hundreds of friends and relatives of the wounded police officers, as well as residents of the Second District and others who had heard about the shooting from news reports.

At home, she pulled on one of Simone's T-shirts. She then looked at Jim's gold chain, which she'd been handed at the hospital. She wiped away the crusted blood. The previous Christmas she had presented Jim with the chain and a medal blessed by the police chaplain. On the back of the medal, she had engraved the letters ATC. *Always Take Care.*

"Then I started crying," she said. "I was finally able to cry."

The next morning when Lynne arrived at the hospital, she was told that Simone had been moved again because of death threats. As Lynne neared his room, she was surprised to hear laughter.

"Two police officers were inside the room with Jim," said Lynn. "Back then, smoking was allowed in hospitals. As a joke, Jim had pulled the bandage away from his cheek and was puffing on a cigarette. The smoke was coming out of the bullet hole."

On the morning of November 18, Simone decided his hospital stay was over. His neurologist and other doctors argued with him, saying they needed to keep him under observation. "But they weren't doing anything at the hospital that Lynne couldn't do at home," he said.

Two days after being shot in the head, Simone was wheeled out of the hospital and into a cluster of fawning TV reporters. Any hopes he had of quashing his Supercop nickname had just ended.

Miller and Thomas would both stay in the hospital for another week. Reflecting on the Workman shooting, Miller said he was satisfied that he and the other officers had used correct tactics.

"Even if you do everything you can to minimize risk, there will always be a danger of death and injury in this profession," said Miller, who would be involved in three fatal shootings during his thirty-three-year career. "Unfortunately, there are people among us who are predators and they are going to prey on weaker people. The bad actors need to be dealt with. If we don't deal with the situation properly, innocent people will be hurt. And part of our training is preparing for the possibility of using deadly force."

Miller said most confrontations between police and civilians occur because individuals are, at some level, not compliant.

"I can't tell you how many times I've told someone to put their hands behind their back and they've complied," he said. "I slip my hand through; I put the handcuffs on; and the process is completed at no harm to them. A lack of compliance is really the causative factor behind people getting hurt."

He admitted to being bothered by the media's perceived anticop bias in recent years. While there will always be people who second-guess police procedure, Miller said the general public would be surprised at the level of pro-police sentiment, particularly in the inner city.

"The pro-police position doesn't get publicized as much, but people in distressed neighborhoods do appreciate us," he said.

Who do you think calls us when drug dealers take over their neighborhoods? The residents may not testify against criminals who prey on their communities, but they call the police. People in the inner city are afraid of criminals. They are vile people who kick in doors in the middle of the night and terrorize the elderly and the weak. The people in the inner city need our help and they thank us for being there for them.

John Thomas remembered November 16, 1983, as a "shitty gray day," gloomy with rain. "In the basement, everything happened so quickly," he said. "The gunfire was very loud. They couldn't hear me asking for help on the police radio. They brought me upstairs and I was bleeding on the sidewalk."

Thomas had lost a significant amount of blood by the time he arrived at Deaconess Hospital. "I found out that I had to have surgery. That scared me," he said. "Fortunately, a vascular surgeon just happened to be at the hospital. I was in the operating room for four hours."

Both Thomas and Brian Miller were known among their colleagues as very religious. After shooting a man who had threatened him with a gun, Miller administered first aid and prayed over the dying victim.

Thomas said he prayed for Dennis Workman, but also felt anger about the situation. "I would have helped Workman if he would have asked," he said. "At the time, we didn't have knowledge that we were dealing with an emotionally disturbed individual. We're trained to stop a threat. And we had to rely on our training that morning."

Thomas and his wife, Paula, have a large family: four daughters and two sons. Both sons followed him into public safety careers. When Thomas retired from the Cleveland Police in 2012, his badge number—687—went to his younger son, James, an officer in Cleveland's Fourth District.

While Thomas was recuperating in Deaconess, the hospital restricted children from visiting the surgical floor. So every evening, his wife Paula would have their children stand on the street below his hospital room and wave flashlights at him.

"It was a long week," Thomas said. "I missed my kids and I also missed Lady, our dog."

A German Shepherd that Thomas had brought home as a rescue, Lady was constantly by his side. "I was extremely close to that dog," he said. "She was my best friend."

Toward the end of his hospital stay, Paula called him, crying. Lady was dead. "She had died of a broken heart," Thomas said. "She must have thought I wasn't ever coming home."

When Cleveland Police officials learned that Simone was at home, they phoned him to ask if he'd mind if a few news reporters stopped by. "Just some quick comments from you to let everyone know you're okay," they told him.

Simone was tired, but agreed to a short interview. Within minutes, reporters from every Cleveland TV news station and newspaper were gathered on his front porch. As were the police department's top officers.

"The department turned it into a public relations deal for themselves," Simone said. "They talked to the media outside while I stayed in the house. Eventually, they sent the cameras inside for a few moments."

Simone told reporters that his disciplined upbringing and his military training helped him survive the confrontation with Workman. While the interview focused heavily on Simone's heroism and his seemingly miraculous recovery, a reporter asked whether it was necessary for the police to fire so many rounds at Workman. "When they saw that I was going to die, they lit the place up," replied Simone. "I'm sure that when Workman got to hell, he was looking around for me."

At home, Simone endured a difficult convalescence. Three times a day, he held his head over a sink while Lynne poured stinging doses of hydrogen peroxide into his open wounds.

In the months following the shooting, he was temporarily afflicted with extremely painful headaches and recurring seizures. "Actually, I think slamming my head against the church basement floor caused more damage to my brain than the bullet," Simone said.

He would also be left with several long-term medical issues, including partial loss of hearing and peripheral vision, as well as facial nerve damage and impairment of his salivary glands. He will take blood-thinning medication for the rest of his life to prevent blood clots, a common complication among people who have had brain injuries.

Simone could have retired on disability, but he always knew he'd go back to the job.

"As long as I'm physically able, I'm going to be a cop," he said. "Besides, trouble seems to find me, whether I'm at work or not at work, so I might as well be a cop."

During his convalescence, he walked daily for exercise, often stopping at a neighborhood doughnut shop, where the waitresses knew him.

"One day, a waitress nodded toward a customer and whispered to me that he had a gun," Simone said.

I told her to call the Second District and tell them that I was there and that I had a gun. When the customer saw she was on the phone, he quickly left. I followed him and apprehended him. He did, in fact, have a revolver in his waistband. It turned out that he was a felon, so he was arrested for illegally possessing a gun.

For Lynne, anxiety became a third wheel in her relationship with Jim. "He had survived the Workman shooting, but I was afraid that his luck would run out some day," she said.

I began worrying so much that I reached out to the wife of a policeman who had been shot and nearly killed. I learned that I had been putting all of my anxieties on Jim and he had been pushing me away because of it. As a dispatcher, I worried about all of the officers on my channel. Finally, I came to realize that there was no use in worrying. I decided to put it all in God's hands.

Two months after the shooting, Simone was permitted to rejoin the police department on an inactive basis. It would be an additional three months before he was cleared for active duty. He spent that time in the police gym, working out and chatting weekly with the police psychiatrist.

He had hoped to return to patrol duty, but his request was denied. Now, with three deadly force incidents in his file, some of his superiors didn't want him back on the street. Simone was headed back to the Homicide unit.

"A group of FBI agents came to my house while I was on medical leave," Simone said.

They wanted to know what had happened in the church basement; how three cops got shot. They were researching the incident to see if they could learn from it. I reenacted the scenario for them. I crouched down and opened the closet door with Miller and Thomas behind me, just like I had done it when I got shot. The agents tried several different approaches, but we couldn't come up with any other way to handle the situation. One officer would have always been in jeopardy. There was no way to avoid the suspect. One of us had to open the door.

Who else but Simone?

I was the guy. I'm a former combat soldier. I'm not going to panic. Gun-fights in the street are over in two seconds. How about being in a firefight with the Viet Cong for eight hours? In real life, it's very scary to have a gun pointed at you. Nobody wants to be dead. Most people scream, beg for their lives, and cry for their mothers. There is no good way to die. I don't try to put myself in danger, but I'm probably the guy you want in a scary situation.

13   A Person of Interest

December 1984: One year after the church shooting. Simone was tracking a murder suspect. He'd received a tip that the man was hiding in an abandoned house. Simone and another Homicide detective entered the boarded-up structure and searched the basement and first floor. On the second floor, Simone froze at the sight of a closet door.

"I stared at the door, afraid to touch it," he recalled. "I didn't know if I could bring myself to turn the doorknob. But I knew if I didn't overcome my fear, I was useless as a cop. My career would be over."

Simone steeled himself and motioned his partner behind him. Finger on the trigger of his gun, he took a deep breath, and then flung the door open. The closet was empty.

"Once I calmed down, I felt a sense of relief," he said. "I knew I had passed an important test. I was back in business."

A self-professed workaholic, Simone missed the frenetic activity of street patrol and the immediate gratification of cuffing criminals and calming victims. He had enjoyed the excitement of being a first responder. In the battle against crime, he wanted to be on the front line.

Working homicide cases, however, was tedious business. Simone found himself frustrated by cumbersome judicial procedures and uncooperative victims and witnesses. Even the most promising investigations sometimes ended with a whimper instead of a bang because of a legal technicality or a missing witness.

"It became very disheartening to solve a murder, but then be unable to prosecute the perpetrator because our star witness left town or died," Simone said. "We put a lot of time into cases that we had to drop."

Nevertheless, he meticulously pursued homicide leads, even spending his off-duty hours in his personal car tailing possible suspects or staking out hiding spots. At nighttime, he had a pad of paper and pen next to his bed in case he awoke with a new angle on a stubborn case.

He had a blistering run in 1984–85 when he cleared a slate of capital cases and helped send half a dozen killers to death row or life imprisonment.

A young man's dying words sent Simone after Ocie Reddick, a twenty-four-year-old Clevelander who had fled to Atlanta. The case began when a seventeen-year-old stole a Cadillac that Robert Bacote, twenty-two, planned to strip for parts.

Reddick stole the Cadillac from Bacote and stripped it himself. Bacote, angered, took the tires from the Cadillac. The men quarreled, with Reddick saying, "Rob, I gotta kill you." He then shot Bacote in the back, arm, and stomach, leaving him to die in the rear yard of a storage building.

When police asked Bacote who shot him, he used his finger to scratch "OC" in the dirt. Later, in the hospital just before he died, Bacote wrote a note that read: "Stay away from OC. He crazy."

For six months, Simone tracked Reddick, who had vanished after the shooting. A tip led Simone to Atlanta, where he found Reddick staying with relatives.

When asked why Bacote was killed, Reddick said, "He took the tires."

"So what?" said Simone. "They weren't yours. They came off a stolen car."

Reddick gave Simone a look of disbelief. "He dissed me. You understand, right?"

"You killed a man over used tires?" asked Simone, shaking his head. "No, I absolutely do not understand."

Reddick, who also shot a friend of Bacote's, was sentenced to life in prison.

Tragedy, to some degree, shaded all of Simone's homicide cases. (In his words: "somebody died; somebody's momma cried"). The murder of Mary Anne Flynn was particularly lamentable, said Simone, for its senseless brutality and the loss of a woman who was seemingly beloved by everyone who knew her.

A nurse-midwife who had delivered more than eight hundred babies, Mary Anne, thirty-three, was raped and killed in her house on August 23, 1984.

When she didn't show up for work the next day at nearby MetroHealth Hospital, a coworker called her brother, Marty. They went to Mary Anne's house, entering through a basement door. They walked upstairs to her bedroom. There, Marty saw his younger sister's battered and bruised body. She was naked, lying face down on the blood-soaked mattress. Her hands were tied behind her back with a strip of cloth. One end of a rolled-up bedsheet was tied around her neck. The other end was tied to the headboard.

She'd been struck repeatedly with a length of wood from a basement windowsill. Blood spatter stained the walls and ceiling, and slivers of wood were embedded in her torso. The back of her neck had been gouged by a sharp-edged object, possibly a hunting knife, which was never found. The autopsy determined that Mary Anne had died of strangulation. Seminal fluid was found in her mouth and vagina.

The disarray of the room indicated to detectives that she had put up a valiant battle. For Simone, who had seen hundreds of bloody corpses as a soldier and police officer, the sight of Mary Anne beaten to a pulp was disturbing. For Marty, it was unbearable.

"I went into shock," Marty recalled. "The scene somehow didn't seem real. There was a definite sense of detachment. As I ran down the stairs to call 911, I felt like I was observing myself doing that."

Marty was surprised and gratified by the response to his call. "At least a dozen cops showed up," he said. "Simone established himself very quickly as the go-to guy, the lead. I felt bad because I didn't have a lot of information to give them. But Simone said, 'Don't worry, if you have a first name, we'll go on that. If you have a description, we'll find him.'"

Simone's investigation quickly turned to Anthony Apanovitch, a handyman and truck driver who lived near Mary Anne in Cleveland's Old Brooklyn neighborhood. Earlier that summer, she had hired Apanovitch to paint a portion of her house. Soon afterwards, she had confided to friends that she was afraid of Apanovitch. She told others that "a painter" had been pestering her for a date and making her uncomfortable.

Apanovitch, twenty-nine, was tall, blonde, well built—and seemingly a complete mismatch for Mary Anne Flynn.

The well-traveled Mary Anne had grown up in comfortable circumstances, attending Beaumont, a Catholic girls' high school and then the University of Florida. After serving in the army as an obstetrics nurse, she worked as a hospital nurse in Michigan and Ohio. In the mid-1970s, she relocated to Scotland and became certified as a midwife.

Returning to Cleveland, Mary Anne bought a two-family house on Archwood Avenue in a deteriorating area that was pocked by crime. Her neighbors came to know her as generous and trusting, with some regarding her as naive. She took in unwed mothers and homeless women, prepared meals for the poor, and indiscriminately hired neighborhood hang-abouts to work on her home.

"My sister really felt like she had found her calling," said Marty, the oldest of the eight Flynn siblings. "She was delivering babies and helping women on the margins. She wanted to get mother and child off to as good a start as possible. She chose to live on Archwood because it was close to work. Compared to where she came from, it was a collision of different worlds. She picked a working-class neighborhood with a lot of good people and a few bad."

During Simone's investigation, he spoke with nearly a hundred people who knew Mary Anne. "Not one person had a bad thing to say about her," he said. "That's a rare occurrence."

Apanovitch, on the other hand, was roundly disliked. A married high school dropout who seemed to have little ambition other than bedding neighborhood women, he worked sporadically and was a fixture in local saloons.

Apanovitch was a loser in many respects. However, as a suspect in Mary Ann Flynn's murder, he was a champ. His criminal history included convictions for aggravated robbery, breaking and entering, and rape. He successfully appealed the rape conviction and pleaded guilty to a reduced charge of sexual battery.

The Flynn case was high profile and there was intense pressure on police and prosecutors to find her killer and get a conviction. Crime scene investigators and several teams of detectives combed her house, but there seemed to be very little direct evidence, such as blood, fingerprints, and hair samples, that tied Apanovitch to the crime. Although detectives theorized that the killer entered the house through a basement window, they didn't find footprints on the dusty basement floor.

The circumstantial evidence against Apanovitch, however, was compelling.

Even before detectives fingered Apanovitch as a person of interest, Simone had a prescient moment while he searched for possible suspects in the homicide unit's criminal database. At the time, the database consisted of a dented green metal cabinet filled with hundreds of 3-inch by 5-inch index cards. Simone thumbed through the cards looking for individuals who had committed violent sexual assaults in Mary Anne's Old Brooklyn neighborhood.

"I got a phone call in the middle of my search and I stopped thumbing through the cards," Simone recalled. "When I turned my attention back to the card file, my finger just happened to be resting on Anthony Apanovitch's card."

Simone learned that Apanovitch, whose wife was pregnant at the time, told friends that he thought Mary Anne was a "foxy lady," and he "wanted to get in her pants."

He also discovered that Apanovitch had asked his wife, Rosemarie, to wash the bloody clothes he had worn the night of Mary Anne's murder.

"Rosemarie claimed that she couldn't wash the blood out so she decided to burn the clothes," Simone said. "Why would she have burned the clothes?"

Apanovitch didn't help his cause either. Detectives noticed a fresh scratch on his face. When asked for an explanation, Apanovitch offered several scenarios, including helping someone fix a car and a bar fight in which he was cut with a broken beer bottle. He also couldn't provide an alibi for his whereabouts on the night Mary Anne was killed.

After he was identified as a suspect, Apanovitch asked bartenders and customers who were in the bars that night to tell police that they remembered seeing him.

"I let him tell his story and then I investigated the details," said Simone. "Nothing that Apanovitch told me matched up with what we found. I went to every bar and I couldn't find anyone who confirmed that he had been there when he claimed to be. Nobody remembered a bar fight that night. And a doctor said his scratch didn't look it was caused by broken glass."

At Apanovitch's trial, the judge prohibited any mention of his prior criminal acts. Detectives knew, however, that the circumstances of Apanovitch's previous rape case were eerily similar to the Flynn case.

"Apanovitch was a snake," said Simone. "Just about everything he told me was a lie. I believe he forced Mary Anne Flynn to have sex and then he killed her. If I hadn't been so positive that he was the killer, I would have never pursued him as strongly as I did."

In spite of his certainty about Apanovitch's guilt, Simone continued his search for a murder suspect, stopping only when the grand jury indicted Apanovitch for the crime.

Even during Mary Anne's funeral, Simone walked through the church parking lot checking the license plates of hundreds of cars. Marty Flynn asked him what he was doing.

"I'm going to run these plate numbers just in case we get a suspicious one," said Simone. "Sometimes the bad guys show up at their victims' funerals."

Apanovitch was convicted and sentenced to death. During his three decades on death row, he has launched several appeals. Apanovitch has attracted support from national antideath-penalty activists, including Death Penalty Focus, which is headed by Mike Farrell, an actor who appeared on the TV show *M*A*S*H*.

In 1993, with Apanovitch five days from execution, a federal appeals court accepted a last-minute plea for reconsideration.

At present, a Cuyahoga County judge is considering whether to grant Apanovitch a new trial, citing concerns over DNA recovered from Mary Anne Flynn's body. Apanovitch's defense attorneys say the DNA sample excludes him as the killer. Prosecutors hold that the DNA sample is a match for Apanovitch and confirms his guilt.

Marty Flynn, who is convinced that Apanovitch killed his sister, said the diligence of Simone and the other detectives has given his family a sense of comfort over the past thirty-one years.

"Simone never forgot us," he said.

He seemed to take the case personally. That was huge for us, especially for my parents. The loss of their daughter punched a hole in their hearts that never healed. Nothing can prepare a parent for the violent death of their child. Simone showed that he wasn't indifferent to the human suffering they had experienced. He wanted to make things right, keep things right, and interfere with the people who want to screw things up. As I got to know Simone, I learned that if he's with you, he's with you 100 percent. If someone had a gun to my head, I'd be praying for Jim Simone to walk around the corner.

Simone's next homicide case, the savage beating death of a young boy, would leave him with broken ribs and nightmares that would haunt him for months afterwards.

In the early evening of March 2, 1985, Mario Trevino, twelve, and a friend walked to a neighborhood delicatessen for a soda pop and to play video games. Mario never returned.

The following morning, a man walking his dog told police that a dead body was lying on a grassy hill near Cleveland's West Shoreway.

Simone and his partner were called to the scene. There, they saw the remains of Mario. He had been beaten on nearly every part of his body. His nose was broken, his ribs fractured, his liver was lacerated, and he had deep wounds around his eyes.

Calling the crime "horrific," Simone said that Mario's scalp had been ripped from his skull. "We also saw that his underwear were on backwards," he added. "Oftentimes, that indicates a sexual assault."

Simone learned that Mario's family members had been threatened by a man who had recently been released from prison. Alfred Morales, a martial arts expert who called himself the "Demon of Darkness," was angry at Mario's sister, Yolanda, because she refused to date him. He was also angry at one of Mario's brothers for not providing an alibi for Morales after he had been arrested for stealing a taxi cab. Morales was sentenced to prison for the theft.

While in prison, Morales sent letters to the Trevino family that contained drawings of skulls dripping blood and hearts pierced by a sword. The envelopes contained the initials "D.W.C.S." and "B.W.," which meant "Death Will Come Soon" and "Beware."

Simone also discovered that the Morales had been spying on the Trevino home in the weeks after he was released from prison.

The detectives interviewed Morales, noticing that his knuckles were swollen and scratched. During a search of his home, Simone found a jacket and shoes that were still wet from recently being washed.

Under questioning, Morales confessed to luring the boy from the delicatessen on the pretense of talking to him about the problems between himself and the Trevino family.

While talking to Mario about his disagreements with the Trevinos, Morales told Simone that he had "lost it." Morales, who weighed 220 pounds, put the 93-pound boy in a headlock and tore his scalp away. He then dragged him to a secluded area and punched and kicked him twenty to twenty-five times. He also said he returned to the hillside on the night of the murder to check on Mario. He saw that he was still breathing and left.

When Simone had appeared at Morales's house to arrest him, he was met by two of Mario's older brothers, Jesse and Toby. They had just broken out all of the windows in Morales's house with a baseball bat. As Simone led the handcuffed Morales to a patrol car, the Trevino brothers, both karate practitioners, aimed kicks at Morales. Simone, in an attempt to protect Morales, stepped between him and the brothers. A kick struck Simone, breaking two of his ribs.

Defense attorneys for Morales, a Shoshone Indian, told the jury that hereditary alcoholism and his fifth-grade education were to blame for his actions. One of his attorneys said that Morales had been an alcoholic since he was nine years old, typically drinking a six-pack of beer each day since dropping out of school at age eleven.

Morales was convicted of aggravated murder and kidnapping. He was sentenced to death, but a federal court threw out that sentence in 2009, ruling that he had inadequate counsel during his trial. He was resentenced to life in prison.

Mario's brothers were charged with assault for kicking Simone. When Simone learned they would miss Mario's funeral because they couldn't afford to bond themselves out of jail, he appealed to the police prosecutor to reduce each brother's bond.

Throughout his career, Simone weathered the antagonism of colleagues who resented his willingness to arrest other cops. Some police officers even regarded him as a sort of traitor who couldn't be trusted.

But every cop, even those who considered him a turncoat, knew they could always count on Simone for backup. When police officers needed help or support, Simone was promptly and solidly in their corner.

In 1985, Luis Gonzalez, the brother of police officer Andres Gonzalez, was gunned down on a sidewalk. Simone, who had partnered for several years with Andres, worked tirelessly to track and capture his killer.

Luis Gonzalez had been shot in the back in a dispute over a woman. Simone's most likely suspect was Juan Cordova, who had migrated to Cleveland from Cuba a few years earlier. Cordova had vanished after the shooting, leaving very few clues for Simone to pursue, except for a photo of Cordova with another woman.

Because Cordova and his acquaintances spoke mainly Spanish, Simone requested that Andres Gonzalez, who is bilingual, be assigned to the Homicide unit to assist in the investigation. During the daytime, they searched house by house in Cordova's neighborhood and adjacent areas on Cleveland's West Side. At nights, Simone patrolled streets in Cleveland's Hispanic communities, checking bars and clubs for any sightings of Cordova.

On January 5, 1985, the search for Cordova was stepped down when a woman attempted to hijack a Pan Am aircraft at Cleveland Hopkins International Airport. Armed with a .22-caliber revolver, Oranetta Mays shot an attendant at the ticket gate and then ran onto the jet, which was deplaning after arriving from Cincinnati. Mays fired two more shots at pursuing Cleveland Police officers.

The plane's crew members and forty passengers were able to exit the plane through the rear ventral stairs. However, Mays held five passengers, including an eight-month-old baby, as hostages. During negotiations with police, Mays demanded to be flown to Rio de Janeiro. As discussions stretched on, Mays threatened to shoot the baby. A team of FBI agents and Cleveland Police SWAT officers then stormed the plane, shooting and wounding Mays. The hostages were unharmed.

One of the SWAT officers, James Gnew, was shot by Mays. The bullet ricocheted off his body armor into his knee.

In the aftermath of the attempted hijacking, Simone and other detectives were enlisted to interview the Pan Am passengers and other witnesses. Working nearly around the clock, several of the detectives, including Simone, took catnaps on mattresses they'd brought into the Homicide unit's office.

"I would pick up fifty hamburgers at a time and bring them to the Justice Center for the guys," said Lynne Stachowiak. "They had over a hundred people to interview."

Just as the hijacking interviews were completed, Simone fielded a tip that Juan Cordova was in Youngstown, about an hour east of Cleveland. Simone and Gonzalez showed Cordova's photo to clerks at every hotel in the city. One clerk recognized the woman in the photo, saying she had just checked out.

A search of her room turned up a schedule for a Florida-bound Greyhound bus. Working through Greyhound security officers, Simone had the bus stopped in North Carolina. Cordova was found on the bus and returned to Cleveland. He pleaded guilty and served fifteen years in prison.

At the trial of Oranetta Mays, a court-appointed psychiatrist testified that she had formed a "paranoid pseudo-community" consisting of the CIA, Prince Charles, boxer Muhammad Ali, and other celebrities.

"'They were in a conspiracy, and this conspiracy was continuously harassing and raping her, and she felt that she had to get away from it,'" the psychiatrist said.

Mays would be found innocent by reason of insanity.

Simone was exhausted. He'd been grinding for seven days straight, interspersing the Pan Am witness interviews with the search for Juan Cordova. He had essentially foregone sleep during that period.

Gonzalez told reporters at the time that Cordova's capture probably would not have happened if Simone had not been on the case.

"When we were getting tips and information relative to the guy who killed Luis, Jim would drop everything and hit the road," said Gonzalez.

At one point, Jim got a promising tip while he was off-duty. Who knows where he got the tip, but he rounded up the troops and we were off. It helped that he was a fast processor. He can gather data and interpret it faster than most people. There were some people who thought Jim put extra effort into the case because I had once been his partner. But that's how he performed on a regular basis. I think he would have worked just as hard for anyone else who was suffering through pain like my family was.

Along with losing his brother, Gonzalez had faced the difficult task of breaking the news of Luis's murder to his parents. "They had lost their son," he said. "Now how do I—as a policeman, as his brother, as their son—go to them with this information?"

Gonzalez said he relied on Simone for emotional support in the days after the shooting and during the investigation. "Jim has an ability to connect with people who have been touched by crime. His level of compassion became most obvious when he was consoling and helping victims and their families. The way that he would interact and connect with victims was superior to a lot of officers. Jim did it at a higher level and perhaps that drove some cops to resent him."

While working in the Second District with Simone, Gonzalez had seen antagonism directed at him by other cops. "At times, it was tough for Jim in the locker room," he said. "It probably bothered him on a personal level, but he didn't let it impact his sense of duty. He didn't allow those things to take control of who he was and what he needed to do."

Simone's detractors were never at a loss for reasons to dislike him. Since his first day at police academy, Simone's moral absolutism had a polarizing effect on his colleagues. The officers who didn't share his rock-solid certainty of right and wrong were alienated from him. But there were others who respected his conviction and principled consistency.

"Simone had quite a few admirers or 'disciples' as I used to call them," said Ed Kovacic. "Younger cops, in particular, looked up to him."

Gonzalez, who trained under Simone as a rookie, said Simone possessed natural leadership ability.

He also had that rare "It" factor. When you have that combination, people are drawn to you. In any career, not just police work, people look towards a strong-minded, assertive personality who symbolizes success. Jim had those qualities. During our first years together, he was like an older brother to me. On my first day on the job, he gave me some simple advice: He told me to stay away from the "Three Bs: booze, broads, and bribes." It was always a point of pride for Jim to refuse a bribe.

Gonzalez, a compact, self-assured optimist, said his decision to become a police officer stemmed from a desire to help others. He knew from a young age that he was destined to enter a service field of some type. His mother and father were both pastors and they had instilled humanitarian values in their children. Gonzalez said he had always enjoyed being in a position to help people. At the age of twenty, he realized that the law enforcement profession would give him that opportunity.

As partners, Gonzalez and Simone shared a passion for justice.

We both got in this business because we wanted to make a difference. What I really, really appreciated about him was that he believed in what he was doing. He took an oath to uphold the law, no matter what the situation was. When a police officer takes that oath, it has to marry up to their personal values. For us, it did. The common bond between Jim and me was not the "thin blue line" or the "blue brotherhood." The "blue wall of silence" was not a driving force for us. What bound us, as cops, was our willingness to enforce the law even if it meant putting our lives at risk. Jim exemplified that.

Gonzalez rose to the rank of commander at the Cleveland Division of Police. He left in 2007 to become police chief of the Cuyahoga Metropolitan Housing Authority, where he oversees a staff of 135, including ninety police officers.

"What I enjoy most is bringing in new officers and administering the oath of office," he said.

I can look in their eyes and see a kid who genuinely wants to make a difference and help people. Jim used to tell me, "If you're good to this job, it will be good to you." For me, the takeaway from that was: Have pride in your job, come to work on time, stay away from corruption, and be honest. I tell my officers if they do those things, the job will reward them. For me, the reward has been the gratification in helping so many people.

When Simone closed the Cordova case, he was at the brink of collapse. He stayed in bed for two days, shaking uncontrollably and vomiting.

"When his temperature went to 104 degrees, he let us take him to the emergency room," said Lynne.

For five days, doctors ran tests on Simone. They suspected hepatitis, but were unable to come up with a conclusive diagnosis. On the sixth day, Simone woke up to find he had a new roommate. The man lit a cigarette and Simone immediately became nauseous. The doctors had confirmation: A sudden aversion to cigarette smoke can be a symptom of hepatitis.

"The doctors thought Jim might have contracted the disease from one of the dead bodies he'd handled as a homicide detective," Lynne said. "It was time to get him out of Homicide."

It would take six weeks for him to recover. He made several requests to return to patrol duty, but each was denied. One afternoon, Lynne found herself in the same elevator as the police chief. Seizing the rare opportunity, she spoke frankly and firmly to him about Simone's illness and his desire to get back on the street. Two days later, his reassignment orders came through.

He was happy to be back on patrol duty after his four-year stint in Homicide. "Jim belonged on the street," said Gonzalez. "He was an action junkie. He needed to be on that cutting edge."

Simone quickly resumed his spot as the department's top ticketer. Then in 1988, he and his partner arrested a drunk driver in the Tremont area. While the partner sat in the front seat writing the report, Simone walked the handcuffed suspect to his police cruiser. As he was placing the man in the backseat, he sensed that something was wrong.

Simone looked up and saw a car speeding toward him. "He was doing at least 30 mph.," Simone recalled. "I pushed the suspect into the backseat. As I tried to dive away, the car slammed into me. I rolled up on the hood and he continued driving for half a block with me against his windshield."

The driver made a sharp turn, throwing Simone onto the street. "The drunk guy in handcuffs ran over and asked me if I was okay. I told him to get back in the cruiser and tell my partner to call for an ambulance. I knew my leg was broken."

X-rays showed that Simone had fractured his kneecap—on the same leg that he'd injured while wrestling in high school.

"When will I be able to return to work?" Simone asked.

"Work?" said the doctor, curtly. "You're done as a policeman."

He then told him that the injury was so bad that he might never walk normally again.

14 **Angel**

Simone's fractured kneecap healed slowly. He had developed an infection that required painful debriding and intravenous antibiotics. With his doctor convinced that he could no longer perform the essential duties of his job, Simone could have cashed his ticket to a medical retirement. In copspeak, he had received a "million-dollar injury."

Simone, however, took his doctor's pronouncement as a challenge. Within days of getting the cast removed, he was in the police gym lifting weights. He was determined to return to work. But he wouldn't be content with just patrol duty. He had decided to try out for the Cleveland Police SWAT unit.

To qualify for SWAT, Simone would have to complete a grueling circuit of push-ups, pull-ups, and sit-ups. He would also have to run 1.5 miles in thirteen minutes. Not an exceedingly challenging time for candidates in their twenties and thirties, but Simone was forty years old and would be running on a knee that had undergone multiple surgeries.

With Lynne as his timekeeper, Simone ran laps at a local track every morning. During his evening dinner break, he'd jog several miles through downtown Cleveland streets, enduring the ribbing of fellow cops.

Simone qualified for SWAT—the oldest candidate to ever make the elite team—but he stayed for only five months.

"I hated the downtime," he said. "Back then, SWAT didn't serve warrants. We just waited for a call to come in. There was a lot of sitting around and playing cards. That didn't fit with my Type-A personality."

"Jim was so goal-oriented that I think he took the SWAT qualification test just to see if he could make it," said Andres Gonzalez. "But once he accomplished that goal, I sensed that he missed the true meaning of service; the true meaning of going out and making a difference in someone's life. He got bored in SWAT. He wanted to be on the road."

Simone went back to patrol duty in the Second District. Within a month of his return, he followed a hunch that led to the capture of a murderous serial rapist.

On a September evening in 1988, Simone was driving through Brookside Park in search of a fugitive when he noticed a car stopped by a baseball diamond.

"There was just something unusual about the way the car was parked," Simone recalled. "So I turned out my lights and rolled up on the vehicle."

Looking inside, Simone could see a couple engaged in sex. He rapped on the driver's window.

"A guy stepped out of the car and punched me," Simone said. "We rolled around on the baseball diamond fighting for several minutes until I could get handcuffs on him."

Simone loaded him into the backseat of his cruiser. When he returned to the man's car, a naked girl threw open the passenger door and ran into his arms.

"She kept screaming, 'Thank you, thank you, thank you,'" said Simone. "Then she said, 'Did you get the gun?' I didn't know about a gun, but I searched the car and found a revolver in the glove compartment."

The girl, who was seventeen, told Simone that the man had forced her into his car as she was walking home from a convenience store. On the way to Brookside Park, he had ordered her to disrobe and toss her clothes from the car.

"He was getting rid of evidence," Simone said. "After raping her, he was going to kill her."

Her attacker, Darryl Durr, twenty-five, would claim during his court hearing that he was having consensual sex with the girl. He was charged with rape, but released on $5,000 bail. A week later, a fourteen-year-old girl accused Durr of raping her.

After securing an arrest warrant, Simone and other officers tracked Durr to his wife's apartment, where they found him hiding in the cabinet under the kitchen sink.

Charged with raping the fourteen-year-old, Durr again professed his innocence, claiming they'd had consensual sex. Bond was set at $100,000. With Durr in jail and unlikely to post bond, his girlfriend, Deborah Mullins, eighteen, came forward with a shocking story.

She told officers that the decomposed remains of a girl found five months earlier in a ravine was her sixteen-year-old friend Angel Vincent.

Her partially naked body, which had been discovered by two boys, had been stuffed into two construction barrels laid end to end.

Mullins, who had a baby girl with Durr, said Angel had been tied up and lying in Durr's car when she last saw her nine months earlier.

Durr had been obsessed with Angel, who lived close to Mullins in Elyria, about forty-five minutes west of Cleveland. He had even convinced Mullins to name their baby Angel.

Described by her friends as pretty and nice, Angel disappeared from her parents' home on January 31, 1988, at approximately 10:50 P.M. while they were at a Super Bowl party. Just twenty minutes earlier, Angel's mother, Norma O'Nan, had phoned home to check on Angel and learned that Mullins was there and that Mullins's boyfriend, Durr, was arriving later in the evening.

In Mullins's story, Durr drove her home from Angel's home and then returned there to retrieve a pack of cigarettes. Shortly afterwards, Durr blew his car horn for Mullins to come outside. Mullins and their baby got into Durr's car. As Durr drove, Mullins heard crying from the backseat. She turned around and discovered Angel bound on the rear floorboard.

"What have you gotten yourself into?" Mullins asked Durr.

"Don't worry about it," he replied. He then told Mullins that he was going to "waste" Angel because "she would tell." According to Mullins, Durr didn't specify what Angel was going to tell.

"When I saw her in the backseat, she was crying and begging me for help, but I didn't know what to say," said Mullins.

Durr, who was married at the time, then drove Mullins and the baby home. He left, but returned three hours later. Durr told Mullins to pack her things. He then drove Mullins and the baby to his wife's apartment in Cleveland. Durr left with a duffle bag containing two shovels.

When he returned, he was wet and covered with snow. Upon entering the apartment, he placed a ring and bracelet that belonged to Angel on a coffee table. According to Mullins's police statement, Durr said he had strangled Angel with a dog chain until she "pissed, pooped, and shit and made a few gurgling sounds." Because he was unable to dig in the frozen ground, he wrapped her body in a blanket and placed it between the two barrels.

Later that day, Durr burned a bag of Angel's clothing in the basement of his wife's apartment building and asked Mullins to model the black acid-washed jeans that Angel had worn on the evening of her abduction.

Durr then drove Mullins, their baby, and his wife to Elyria, where he burned another bag of items. While driving from Cleveland to Elyria, Durr stopped at Edgewater Park and threw Angel's eyeglasses over a cliff.

In the days after Angel's disappearance, Angel's mother confronted Mullins and Durr about the whereabouts of her daughter. Durr told her, "You know how kids are, she probably ran away."

At Durr's trial, Mullins, who was the chief prosecution witness, testified that she waited nine months to report Angel's murder because Durr had threatened her and her baby's life if she told anyone. Durr and his wife, however, said that Mullins contacted police only because she was angry that Durr had broken up with her. Although Durr argued that there was no evidence to connect him to the crime, he was found guilty and sentenced to death. He was executed in April 2010.

"Darryl Durr was probably the most satisfying case of my career," said Simone. "I had a weird feeling about his car at Brookside Park. That feeling saved a girl's life and also closed the Angel Vincent case."

To the general public, cops serve a well-defined, essential role: They enforce laws, apprehend criminals, and protect the citizenry. It's expected that they be willing to risk their lives in the performance of their duties. A civilized society also expects its police officers to perform certain distasteful tasks.

"The public pays cops to see the things that they don't want to see," said Simone. "We clean up the mess. We see the bodies lying in the road after a horrible car accident. You don't want to see that on your way to work, so we take care of it."

Years of experience as a street cop haven't numbed him to the shock of encountering a traffic fatality. "I put on the Jim Simone face and pretend I don't care. I do care, but I can't show it when I'm working. I can't pull up to an accident and scream, 'Oh my God!'"

In July 1990, a gruesome auto crash tested Simone's poker face. He responded to the scene and found a dead woman lying in the street. Inside the car, the driver and a passenger in the front seat were critically injured. In the backseat, a man was bleeding profusely from his shoulder. Simone recoiled at the realization that the man's left arm had been ripped away.

He applied a tourniquet to the victim's shoulder and then looked unsuccessfully throughout the car for the missing limb.

"I looked at the dead victim in the street and guessed that she'd been sitting in the backseat on the man's left," Simone said. "I rolled her over and found the guy's arm under her. I sent it to the hospital with the ambulance crew just in case it could be reattached."

After sorting through eyewitness accounts and a statement from the driver, Simone learned that a second car driven by the dead woman's boyfriend had caused the crash.

"He saw his girlfriend in the front seat of the car and became angry. He repeatedly rammed their car at high speed. The girl in the back was frightened and she was tightly clutching her boyfriend's arm. He suffered a traumatic amputation when she was thrown from the car."

In 1992, Simone was named head traffic enforcement officer of the Second District, where he continued to lead his peers in misdemeanor and felony arrests. That same year, he was honored by the northeast Ohio chapter of MADD for leading the Cleveland Police in arrests of impaired drivers. In recognition, MADD presented Simone with a VHS-format video camera.

Nationwide, MADD was lobbying for more aggressive prosecution of drunk drivers. In conjunction with that initiative, MADD publicized statistics showing that many drunk-driving cases were dismissed or won by defendants because of a lack of evidence, particularly evidence related to the police officer's probable cause to initially stop the defendant.

MADD also found that convictions were significantly higher in jurisdictions where police used video cameras to record the entire process of stopping a suspect, conducting a field sobriety test, and executing an arrest. Beginning in the late 1980s, various MADD chapters held local fund-raisers to purchase cameras for police departments.

Simone was the first Cleveland officer to receive a video camera. While MADD intended that the camera be used for field testing of suspected drunk drivers, Simone quickly saw the value in recording all of his patrol activities. MADD had supplied him with two fifteen-minute tape cassettes. He switched to eight-hour tapes so he could record his entire shift.

Years before the public's demand for onboard dash cameras and body-mounted police cameras, Simone saw that audio/video technology could have a critical role in improving public safety and protecting the rights of civilians and police officers. He recognized that the tapes would be invaluable as supporting evidence against suspects. They would also safeguard him from unfounded citizen complaints and lawsuits.

The bulky camera was mounted in a forward-facing position on the cage that divided the front seat from the back. "It was so large that my partner and I would bang into it when we turned our heads," Simone said.

To record audio when he was out of the cruiser, Simone wore a lapel microphone connected to a tape recorder, which he synched to the video. He also wired his patrol car for sound. A sign posted on the cage warned backseat occupants that their conversations were being recorded.

When Simone returned home from work each morning, usually at 2:30 A.M., he reviewed his recording, and then duplicated the tape or burned it to a CD.

If he was scheduled to appear in court later that morning, he'd pull the portions of videotape that were relevant to his cases and spend a couple of hours preparing for his appearances. Court began at 9:30 and was typically over by noon. Afterwards, he'd catch a few hours sleep before starting his shift.

"Jimmy's cases were easy," said C. Ellen Connally, who served as a judge in Cleveland Municipal Court from 1980 to 2003. "When an attorney would claim that his client was innocent and demanded a trial, I would tell the attorney to go watch Jimmy's video. In most cases, when the attorney returned, they had reconsidered and were willing to accept the plea bargain offered by the prosecutor."

Connally recalled the case of a woman who was ticketed by Simone for illegally parking in a handicapped zone. She vehemently claimed she didn't, but Simone had the video to prove that she did.

"So then she turned into, 'He ticketed me because I'm black,'" said Connally. "Jim Simone is not a racist. Some people just don't want to take responsibility for their actions."

Connally holds the distinction of being the first African American woman elected to a judgeship in Ohio without being first appointed.

Noting that Simone had a reputation as a "hard-ass" traffic cop, Connally said she admired his consistency.

> He gave an FBI agent a speeding ticket. He gave a nun a ticket. And he gave tickets to other cops and citizens who had police courtesy cards. He'd tell them, "The law doesn't say that you can speed just because you have a courtesy card." To Jimmy, the law is the law. But he was also fair. When a defendant once argued that he had a certain model of Cadillac that had faulty brake lights, Jimmy did the research and found out the

guy was right. And he'd admit if he was having problems with his radar gun on a certain night.

In her years on the bench, Connally came to know which police officers had a tendency to not appear for a hearing or trial. "Some cops would never show up," she said.

I'd tell people to plead not guilty because the cop may not show. But if I saw badge number 387 on the ticket, I knew Simone would be there. After working all night, he'd sleep two hours and then come to court in the morning. He'd always wear his uniform and hat. The job was his whole life. His whole identity is tied up in being a cop. At home, his hobby was watching videos he'd recorded on his dash cam.

Simone didn't leave anything to chance, said Connally. "When he would put a female suspect in his car, he would call in the mileage on his car just to make sure they knew he wasn't driving the woman around."

Connally's recollections of Simone reflect the complexity of his character. Noting his leadership abilities, she said, "When he was in Vietnam, they offered him a chance to go to officer's school. It was a mistake for him not to have gone. He could have been a general."

But Simone, the combat soldier and tough cop, is also kindhearted, she said, recalling the night he phoned her to request that she set a bond for a guy he'd arrested. When Connally asked Simone why he wanted the guy held in jail on a bond, he explained that he was upset that the guy had locked his dog in the trunk of his car on a hot day. "So I called the clerk of court's office and asked if they ever lost a case file," said Connally. "When they said they didn't, I told them to lose this guy's file for four days."

Simone ended up buying the dog from the man. It wasn't uncommon for him to rescue stray and abused dogs.

"The best thing that could happen to a stray in the Second District was for me to find it," said Simone. "The dog got fed and then rode in the front seat of my cruiser until the end of my shift."

Simone wouldn't hesitate to confiscate a dog from its owner if he had evidence that it was being abused. On several occasions, he told owners that if they gave him their mistreated dogs, he would give them a good home and keep them healthy.

"If the owners didn't like that option, I'd threaten to kick their asses, arrest them for cruelty to animals, and take the dogs anyway," he said.

He also encountered dogfighters who admitted that they poured gunpowder down their dogs' throats in the mistaken belief that it would make them meaner. "In those cases, I'd remove the dogs and take them to Cleveland's dog kennel. If someone didn't adopt them in three days, they were put down. I didn't want to be responsible for the dogs dying so I'd end up taking them home."

15 A Matter of Principle

In 1990, Cleveland's police review board received 157 complaints of police misconduct. One of those complaints had been filed by James Wittine, a forty-four-year-old businessman who had accused Simone of beating and robbing him.

The complaint arose after Simone and his partner, Todd Davis, responded to an unrelated fight outside the Hot Dog Inn, a diner on a honky-tonk strip of Lorain Avenue. While Simone and Davis were separating the combatants, Wittine, who was watching from a distance, loudly jeered and taunted the officers.

When Wittine refused to leave the area, he was taken into custody and charged with disorderly conduct, resisting arrest, and carrying a concealed weapon: a pocketknife. An indignant Wittine swore at Simone and accused him of stealing $180 from his wallet.

"He told me that if I didn't release him, he'd file a complaint against me. Which he did," said Simone. The police review board investigated Wittine's complaint and found that he had spent the $180 drinking with a companion and buying drinks for patrons at several bars on Cleveland's West Side.

"I can't account for what I experienced, but I was beaten and my head slammed into a wall five times," Wittine told the *Cleveland Plain Dealer*. He added that he suspected he might have been drugged by his companion.

Based on Simone's dash-cam video and the results of the review board's investigation, Simone and Davis were cleared of wrongdoing. Angered by Wittine's fabricated complaint, the two officers lashed back and filed a lawsuit alleging defamation of character.

"He maliciously and purposely lied in public to ruin our reputations," Simone told a newspaper. The officers asked for $450,000 in compensatory and punitive damages.

The lawsuit, which was thought to be the first in the United States brought by a police officer against a citizen, triggered a shockwave among national civil rights groups.

A legal expert cautioned that Simone's unprecedented lawsuit was a "frightening proposition" that could discourage open communication between citizens and police. He theorized that citizens would be less likely to file a police misconduct report if they believed they might suffer a loss of rights and money in a subsequent lawsuit. Others, however, argued that a single lawsuit would be unlikely to deter complaints by people who genuinely believe they had been illegally wronged.

Simone was pressured to drop the case by city officials and police executives, but refused, telling them, "I don't remember giving up my civil rights when I became a cop."

The two officers settled their case with Wittine before it went to trial.

"I didn't care about the money," Simone said afterwards. "I just couldn't let him get away with lying."

For an aggressive, active cop like Simone, misconduct complaints were not uncommon. Having the ability to videotape citizen encounters protected Simone against unfounded complaints by people who were frustrated that they couldn't talk their way out of a traffic ticket or simply didn't care for what they perceived as his authoritarian manner.

The recordings also provided him with peace of mind, said Alex Zamblauskas, a former Cleveland police sergeant.

"Every time a woman said that Jim propositioned her or someone cried racism, Jim didn't have to worry about it," said Zamblauskas, now a detective in Brooklyn. "Jim always said that the purpose of his videos was not to prove what he did, but to prove what he didn't do."

As audio/video technology evolved, Simone continually upgraded his equipment. Eventually, he would amass over 24,000 hours of video. Often, his recordings would be requested by media outlets for their TV newscasts, as well as prosecutors who were seeking information about certain suspects or incidents.

While Simone's audio- and videotapes shielded him against frivolous and malicious citizen complaints, the recordings also had the unintended consequence of documenting the questionable and illegal conduct of his colleagues.

His history of arresting fellow cops had branded him as an annoyance, an odd duck, a man not to be trusted. Now, with his video camera, he was seen as an explicit threat.

For many police officers, drinking and driving on their off-duty time has traditionally been considered a privilege of the job, particularly if they get hammered in their own jurisdiction. If they are stopped by a cop, either because of a noninjury car accident or a traffic violation, they face little more repercussion than the embarrassment of being escorted home.

Unless they get stopped by Simone.

"I was tenacious about enforcing laws," he said. "If I knew someone had done something illegal or inappropriate, I couldn't walk away."

In the summer of 1993, he responded to a report of a pedestrian being hit by an impaired driver. Arriving at the scene, he learned that a pregnant woman had been in the middle of a crosswalk when she was struck by a speeding car.

Approaching the suspect vehicle, with his recording gear rolling, Simone saw his supervisor behind the wheel. "What are you going to do, Simone, arrest me?" she snarled. "Fuck you."

"She was so drunk that she could hardly stand up," he recalled. He loaded her into the back of his cruiser and took her to the Second District station to book her for drunk driving. The injured pedestrian was rushed to the emergency room, where she went into labor, delivering her baby five weeks early.

Children of police officers learn from a young age that they can leverage the professional courtesy extended to their father and mother. The words, "My dad's a cop," can typically get misbehaving youngsters out of a wide range of offenses with just a warning from responding officers, who expect the same courtesy for their family members.

In cases where young drivers are impaired, their cop parents are called to the scene to whisk them away from inquisitive news reporters or prying citizens.

"I got a call that a drunk driver had struck a police car," said Simone, recalling a 1994 case. "The driver happened to be the son of the acting police chief. He let me know several times how important his father was and he made a point of snidely calling me, 'Patrolman.'"

After the driver failed a field sobriety test, Simone arrested him and took him to the police station for booking. His father arrived minutes later and angrily confronted Simone.

"I can't believe you arrested my son," he said.

"I can't believe you would think that I wouldn't arrest him," Simone shot back.

Simone's videotape of the son's arrest would be irrefutable evidence at trial. Fearing interference from police higher-ups, Simone duplicated the tape and locked the original in his home safe. He then submitted the copy with his written report to the city prosecutor.

"On the morning of the kid's court hearing, the prosecutor's office told me that my tape was blank," Simone said. "I realized that somebody had erased it. So I made another copy and submitted that. Then the police brass demanded my original tape. When I wouldn't turn it over, they said they would get a search warrant for my house."

When a judge friend of Simone's learned of the police department's threat to seize the tape, she offered to safeguard it. "They'll never get a search warrant on me," she said.

"I was now afraid of my own police department," Simone said. "And I realized that my videotapes were my best protection against the people in the department who wanted to harm me."

Simone's supervisor pressured him to remove the video camera from his car. He resisted.

"The videos were making a lot of people nervous," he said. "They could have been devastating for a lot of reasons. Some of the tapes showed me responding to reports of shots being fired. As I'm speeding to the scenes, the tapes show cops driving in the opposite direction, away from the shootings."

Another recording showed Simone arresting a Jamaican drug dealer for a traffic infraction. He readily allowed Simone to search his car. When Simone found 7 pounds of marijuana and $5,000 in his trunk, the Jamaican offered him the cash in return for releasing him.

"Why would you think I would take a bribe?" Simone asked.

The Jamaican laughed and said, "Every other cop has."

"It broke my heart to hear that," Simone said. He added attempted bribery to the man's charges. "If I even took part of the money that I seized or was offered over the years, I'd be a millionaire. But it only takes a second to ruin a career. I'd get arrested and ruin the good name my father gave me. And then I'd go to prison and know everyone there. I put too many people behind bars. I wouldn't last a minute."

Simone also has videotape of a Cleveland Police lieutenant pulling him aside in the Second District parking lot to complain about his productivity.

"You arrest too many people," the lieutenant said. "It causes too many problems. We have to tow cars and take people to court and file paperwork. Other cars are busy backing you up instead of being on the streets."

Perplexed that he was being reproached for being too good at his job, Simone asked sarcastically, "What business management school did you go to?"

Just as Simone was being warned by his superiors to throttle back his activity, the national media was hearing about Supercop's prodigious traffic statistics and his TV-ready personality. Television journalist Connie Chung traveled to Cleveland to interview Simone for an *Eye to Eye* feature about people who drive without a valid operator's license.

Simone was then flown to Toronto, Canada, to consult on an episode of *Top Cops*, a TV show that dramatized true-life police exploits. Simone's episode focused on his 1983 church basement shooting.

While working on the show, which was executive produced by Sonny Grosso, a former New York City police detective who helped crack the French Connection heroin ring, Simone had the peculiar experience of watching an actor rehearse his near-fatal shooting a dozen times.

Good Morning America's David Hartman then did a ride-along with Simone for a series he was producing about cops throughout the United States. On the strength of Simone's appearance, Hartman invited him on a follow-up show. Hartman then expressed an interest in producing a movie about Simone's life story as well as a possible TV show. Both projects stalled, however.

Not surprisingly, the increased attention on Simone began to create tension among some of his fellow police officers. "I'd hear the grumbling," Simone said. "Usually along the lines of, 'I'm just as good a cop as Simone. Why is he getting all the publicity?'"

Others, like his partner at the time, Andres Gonzalez, weren't bothered by Simone's turn under the spotlight. Gonzalez had become accustomed to newspaper reporters referring to him simply as "Simone's partner" in articles about cases that they had worked on.

"I got a kick out of it," said Gonzalez. "At roll call, my sergeant would kid me that she saw a story about me in the morning newspaper. Then she'd read: 'Officer Simone and partner . . . '"

If Gonzalez was feeling anonymous, he would soon have company. Cleveland Mayor Michael White decided to muzzle the police department. White, who had a contentious relationship with the city's safety forces throughout his 1990–2001 tenure, forbade police from interacting directly with reporters. There would be no more Supercop headlines, no public recognition of individual officers, no more media ride-alongs with police officers, and any police-related communications would be handled by the mayor's office.

White had dimmed Simone's spotlight and he would soon be looking to pull the plug on his career.

"One day, the mayor called me into his office and told me he wanted the name of the Cleveland police officer with the most citizen complaints," recalled Ed Kovacic, who was the first of White's eight police chiefs.

"That would be Jim Simone," said Kovacic.

"I knew it!" White said. "Put him up on charges. As a matter of principle."

"I can't do that. There's no basis or policy for that," Kovacic said.

"Well, then put that policy in effect," ordered White.

Kovacic was alarmed by the implications of White's edict, but he wasn't surprised by its rashness. He considered White impetuous, even reckless at times.

At thirty-eight, White was the city's second youngest mayor (Dennis Kucinich was thirty-one when he became Cleveland's mayor) and also its second African American mayor (after Carl Stokes).

White was energetic, spontaneous, and a notorious micromanager. If he saw a pothole during his drive to work in the morning, he ordered it fixed by day's end. He personally inspected the work of maintenance employees, and he had a hand in the hiring and firing of city workers of even the lowest pay grades and positions.

Elected on a pro-business and pro-police platform, White was at the forefront of efforts to build a new stadium for the Cleveland Browns and pushed legislation that created the Gateway Complex, which houses the Cleveland Indians and Cavaliers. He elevated Cleveland's tourism appeal by promoting the construction of the Rock and Roll Hall of Fame and Museum and the Great Lakes Science Center. And he spearheaded the $1.4 billion expansion of Cleveland Hopkins International Airport.

White was relentless in his mission of building and improving Cleveland's infrastructure, but he seemed equally intent on sabotaging any semblance of a working relationship with his police force.

In the mid-1980s, a change to the city charter brought the police department's top brass, from commander up to chief, under the reins of the mayor. Ostensibly, the change was made to bring the department under civilian control. But the move was more about "political control, not civilian control," said Kovacic.

White, who was adept, although occasionally clumsy, at political maneuvering, never missed an opportunity to capitalize on the public relations currency afforded by his seventeen-hundred-member police department.

"Like most mayors, he wanted the political shine he could get from the police department," said Kovacic. "If things go good, the mayor can bask in that. If things don't go well, they can scapegoat the department."

When FBI statistics showed that violent crime was decreasing in Cleveland, White boasted that his police department was "one of the best in the country."

However, when rank-and-file cops complained that the mayor was indifferent to their concerns over broken-down, unsafe police vehicles and outdated communications equipment and safety gear, White told reporters that the complaints were merely sour grapes because he had reduced police overtime in an attempt to shore up the city's finances.

White essentially commoditized the police chief's position, appointing individuals who he believed could be leveraged for political gain, and precipitately dismissing those who objected to his interference or disagreed with him.

"When he asked me to be chief, I said, 'Only if you let me be chief,'" said Kovacic. "I told him, 'You're only putting me in charge of the police department because you don't know anything about it and you want to run it.'"

Kovacic said he fought with White from the first week of his appointment and continued butting heads throughout his three-year stint.

The nadir of White's administration may have occurred in 1999, when White called a press conference to announce that he was initiating an investigation into allegations of white-supremacist groups operating inside the Cleveland Division of Police.

When police and the media pressed for White's rationale, they were offered no hard evidence, just a hodgepodge of vague statements about officers shaving their heads, racist graffiti in locker rooms of three of the six district stations, an Elvis Presley tattoo on an officer's forearm, and another officer wearing a star-shaped pin that was supposedly symbolic of white-power movements.

The pin had initially been sighted by Gerald Goode, a generally respected sergeant who commented on the unusual pin to other black police supervisors. When none of the others said they had seen such a pin, Goode reportedly dropped the matter.

Goode's observation, however, was circulated and eventually reached White's office. White was then under attack by Cleveland's black leaders and the police union over his decision to allow the Ku Klux Klan to hold a rally in Cleveland. White further angered police when he said he was considering allowing the Klansmen to use the police garage to change into their robes.

To some observers, White's inquiry into supposed racism in the police department was little more than a ruse to counterattack the police and an attempt to regain the support of the black community. Nevertheless, in a lengthy interview with the *Plain Dealer,* White assuredly stated:

> This [investigation] is going to be a defining moment for the police de-partment. This is not just going to be an investigation of a couple of racist police officers wearing some symbols who are going to be disciplined and then we're going to go on with business as usual. I don't want to just cure what you see. I want to see if there is a way of curing what you don't see. What you don't see is the scary part.

While White had not named Goode as his source, he told reporters that a "highly ranked" officer in the Fourth District (Goode's district) had brought the information to his attention.

As reported in a *Cleveland Scene* article from May 11, 2000, Goode was now on the hot seat. According to the article's author, Jacqueline Marino:

> Although Goode was not identified by name, many in the department knew the mayor was talking about him—a devastating blow both per-sonally and professionally, friends and family say. His genuine concern for the department was now being manipulated by the mayor in his raging battle with the police unions. It upset Goode even more that some officers thought he was a mayoral snitch. Goode tried to set the record straight with officers, other supervisors, even two of the mayor's top aides. But the investigation pressed forward. And rumors that Goode was the mayor's secret informant continued to spread.

The police department's Internal Affairs division completed their in-vestigation in September 1999. White, however, waited until March 2000 to release the report, which concluded that there were no organized hate groups in the department. According to the investigators, the allegations were based on little more than innuendo and gossip.

White, instead of trumpeting the news that his police department was not racist, backpedalled on previous incendiary statements that he had made to the *Plain Dealer*. He also lambasted reporters who had implied that he was the initial source of the racism charges.

White, throughout his political career, had taken credit for every victory, but seemed unable or unwilling to accept responsibility for even the most inconsequential failures. For Goode, there was only one way that White's investigation fiasco could play out.

Several years earlier, after Goode had been disciplined by his supervisor, White had pressured police brass to suspend or terminate him. Kovacic had blocked the action, calling Goode a fine officer whom he was proud to serve with.

Now, White was seeking a scapegoat for his failed ploy. Goode, realizing that he was the logical choice, knew it was only a matter of time before City Hall leaked his name to the media. On October 29, 1999, the forty-three-year-old Goode killed himself.

When White had ordered Kovacic to bring Simone up on charges, the chief had carefully chosen his response. First he told the mayor that Simone had compiled a thick folder of commendations from supervisors and citizens.

"He has all that paperwork to back him up," Kovacic said.

But White ominously reminded him that he also had paperwork. Kovacic, per White's orders, had signed a resignation letter on the day that he accepted the position of police chief. White's message had been clear: Play ball or you're gone.

White had Kovacic in a difficult position. He wasn't ready to give up his chief's badge, but he also didn't want to see a good cop's career ended by a politician who was clearly grandstanding for votes.

"Sure, Simone is number one in complaints," argued Kovacic. "He has 120. But he's a very active cop. And not one of those complaints is justified."

"How do you know that?" White snapped.

Kovacic told him that Simone had videotape of all of his citizen encounters. So when a complaint comes in against Simone, said Kovacic, he brings a copy of the relevant videotape to the police review board. "He puts the tape on the investigator's desk, and then he says, 'Call me when you're done watching it.'"

The tapes invariably showed that the complainants were lying or grossly exaggerating.

"Jim had once shown me a videotape in which an Akron city official tried to talk him out of a ticket," said Kovacic. "Jim told the guy that it didn't matter to him that he was a public official. The guy said, 'If you don't drop this ticket, I'll accuse you of stealing $600 from me.' Jim warned the official that he was being recorded. The guy still went ahead and accused him of stealing the $600."

Kovacic reiterated that all of Simone's complaints could be refuted by video or audio or both. "So how can I possibly put charges on him?" he asked White.

The mayor was quiet for awhile. Then he asked Kovacic, "Who has the second-most complaints in the department?"

When Kovacic told him, White said, "Then put that guy up on charges."

In 1990, when the newly elected White hired Kovacic, his orders were to root out corruption and politics within the police ranks.

Kovacic quickly set to work investigating rumors of police payoffs by organizers of gambling operations. He wasn't aware, however, that the FBI was also investigating the Cleveland Police. In fact, the gambling dens, which featured casino games such as blackjack, poker, and craps, had been established and operated by undercover FBI agents.

Shortly after the agents set up their operations—one on the west side of the city and another on the east side—they were contacted by officers who offered to protect the establishments from police interference.

"We were paying police officers for protection and paying them to operate the games, to act as lookouts, and to make sure we weren't robbed or embezzled," said William Branon, who headed the FBI's Cleveland office at the time.

As part of their protection services, the corrupt police officers supplied gambling operators with information concerning investigations or impending arrests.

One group of officers accepted money to protect two separate 500-pound marijuana transactions. "The drugs went from one group of FBI undercover agents to another group, with protection supplied by police officers," Branon said.

When Kovacic was informed of the FBI's ongoing sting operation, he and his investigators joined forces with the agents.

In May 1991, thirty current or former Cleveland Police officers were indicted on federal charges that included extortion, obstruction of justice, and narcotics and gambling violations.

At a press conference announcing the indictments, White declaimed, "Bad policemen, like bad doctors, lawyers, politicians or journalists, are a cancer within their profession that must be removed."

Kovacic told reporters that he was ashamed and surprised by the scope of corruption. "It's an emotional roller-coaster. I can't put it into words," he said.

In retrospect, Kovacic says he has mixed feelings about the White administration. "At first he was good for the city, but then, as they say, absolute power corrupts absolutely. He got powerful and then he fired me. It was no big deal. It shows that I was doing a good job. People in the neighborhoods liked me and the police force liked me."

Among veteran and retired police officers, Kovacic is affectionately known as "the last good police chief," a reference to his steady rise from street patrolman through various officer positions to the top post. After Kovacic, it became standard policy for Cleveland's mayors to install chiefs based on their political usefulness rather than seniority or practical law enforcement experience.

In many cities, it's fairly common for police chiefs and deputy chiefs to serve at the discretion of mayors and city councils. While cops, in general, tend to bristle at layers of political oversight, Peter Moskos, the former Baltimore police officer, said mayoral control can provide a degree of answerability.

"We need a certain amount of politics in policing, mainly because we want democratic control of our police forces," said Moskos. "We don't want a police department with no accountability to the public."

Kovacic, however, argued that politicization wrecks a police force. "You have officers now who don't care about policing, they just want rank," he said, adding that police officers in a political environment tend to study less for promotional exams. The amount of learning throughout the department decreases, explained Kovacic, because officers know that promotions are made politically rather than by test scores and merit.

Politicization also brings a form of backbiting competitiveness that's more often seen in the corporate world, he said. "When I was chief, all of the commanders were handpicked by the mayor. The first thing that most of them did when they were appointed was to begin spying for the mayor with an eye towards taking my job."

When Kovacic was dismissed by White, he advised the mayor not to hire his new chief from outside Cleveland's police department. "He asked why and I told him that he may get great recommendations for his candidates because their employers wanted to get rid of them. But they won't live up to those recommendations. White didn't listen to me and hired someone from outside who was totally incompetent. He only lasted nine months."

White's next police chief, recruited from Washington, D.C., by a national search firm, also lasted less than a year.

White surprised his supporters in 2001 when he announced that he was retiring from public life. Four years later, the FBI announced that two of White's closest associates, Nate Gray and Ricardo Teamor, had admitted to bribery of public officials.

The FBI revealed that White may have traded construction and parking contracts at Cleveland Hopkins International Airport for bribes that were paid through Gray. Between 1995 and 2003, said federal prosecutors, Gray deposited more than $3.5 million, including $320,000 in cash, in a bank account he hid from the IRS.

Gray, who was the best man at two of White's weddings, was convicted in 2005 of racketeering, bribery, and money laundering. He was sentenced to fifteen years in federal prison.

White has not been charged with any wrongdoing. When asked by Cleveland news reporters about Gray's conviction, White said, "For public consumption, I have not made a comment and I've seen no reason to change my position. It's a Nate Gray matter, not a Mike White matter."

16 Family Plan

Mary Simone, a twenty-something attractive blonde, is chatting with friends at a nightclub in Cleveland's Flats.

Named for its flat topography, the redeveloped postindustrial area bordering the Cuyahoga River was the hub of Cleveland's downtown party scene during the 1990s.

A server arrives with an unordered drink. "From the guy at the bar," she explains. Nodding a "thank you," in his direction, Mary returns to her conversation. Two other men ask her to dance. Courteously, but firmly, she declines.

As she makes her way through the packed club to the ladies restroom, she feels a tap on her shoulder. "Are you related to Jim Simone," a man asks.

She quickly assesses him: He's tall, smiling, outfitted in black clubwear. Seems safe, she thinks. "Yes, he's my father."

Still smiling, he spits in her face.

A nearby woman gasps. Motioning toward an off-duty Cleveland Police officer who is working as club security, the woman asks if she should alert him.

"No," Mary answers. "Don't bother."

She was angry at the spitter, but also angry at herself for relaxing her guard. It wasn't the first time that she'd been targeted by someone who'd been arrested or ticketed by her father.

The man had vanished. Even if he was still in the club, Mary couldn't be certain the police officer would be sympathetic. He'd probably want a written statement from her and she was reluctant to disclose her family name. She'd had experiences over the years with cops who resented her father—for his productivity, his history of arresting other officers, or just because he was Supercop.

"There were a lot of cops who liked him, but sometimes I found out the hard way who didn't like him," she said.

Simone had given Mary and her older sisters, Michelle and Stephanie, half-size replicas of a Cleveland police badge. Customarily, these family badges, as they are known, can be displayed to evade traffic tickets or to avoid standing in line at crowded nightclubs, if a cop happens to be working the door.

"Not for us, though," said Mary. "We learned to keep our badges in our purses to eliminate any conflicts with the cops."

For anyone whose parent works in law enforcement, it's almost an expected perk to get out of the occasional traffic ticket, said Stephanie, the oldest of the sisters. "But if we get pulled over, we can't name-drop like everyone else who is related to a cop."

One evening, Michelle was stopped for speeding. In an attempt for leniency, she mentioned her father to the traffic cop.

Recognizing his name, the officer told her, "Jim Simone would probably give my daughter a ticket, so I'm going to give you one."

Michelle pointed out, however, that many cops respect his accomplishments and experience. "There are a lot of younger officers who go to him for advice," she said.

The cops who don't like him are perhaps aggravated by his prodigious traffic statistics, she theorized, explaining, "He shows them up. He's always working, so they look like slackers in comparison. He loves his job and he loves traffic duty because he's always busy. I'm like him in the sense that even if I'm sick and feeling horrible, I'll go to work. I don't like sitting around."

Mary had briefly contemplated pursuing a law enforcement career, but decided that she didn't want to cause her own children the worries that she experienced as a child.

"I was at the hospital so many times with my dad," she said. "When he was shot, he kept reassuring us that he was okay. I think he was more worried about us than himself. But I still couldn't put my kids through that experience."

Employed in the restaurant industry, Mary has declined management opportunities because of the increased time requirements.

"I remember missing my father so much when I was a kid," she said. "He was never home. When it comes to working, I think he has an addictive personality. He's not happy when he's not at work. I didn't want my kids to miss me like that."

The girls understood from a young age that their father's job took precedence over other aspects of his life. Even when he was off the clock and with his family, he was in cop mode.

"We were driving to my aunt's funeral and he recognized a suspect on the street," said Michelle. "He told us to get down on the floorboard of the car. He jumped out and chased him down. He pulled his gun and arrested the guy. Then he handcuffed him to a utility pole until a patrol car arrived. We always worried about him getting hurt or killed, but we knew the job was his life."

A consequence of growing up Simone, said Mary, "is that you become a "Popeye" yourself. A girl picked a fight with me in junior high school. She coldcocked me. When I got home from school, I told my dad about it. 'Who won?' he asked. I said I did. That's all that mattered. More recently, I was walking up a staircase at a bar. A guy came up behind me and stuck his hand up my dress. I put my hand around his throat and told him he was dead if he tried that again."

As a parent, he was strict but consistent with his discipline, recalled Stephanie.

> He never hit us. We got lectures instead. I remember an incident in ninth grade when I got caught drinking with some friends at a football game. The police called my dad to pick me up. I might have gotten a little sassy with the cops, so my dad made me apologize to them. We were always afraid to bring shame to the family name. When we got older, we understood that the media would hurt him if we got caught doing anything wrong.

And if the girls should ever get arrested? "We would rot in jail," said Stephanie. "If we do something bad, he's not going to bail us out. If we break the law, he's not going to give us any special treatment."

By the late 1990s, Simone's growing celebrity spawned exaggerated and fabricated accounts of his involvement in arrests, brawls, car chases, beat downs, and even shootings. Nearly everyone on the West Side of Cleveland, it seemed, had a story about a Supercop encounter.

Simone realized that his Supercop persona had outgrown reality on the night that he and Lynne randomly stopped into a neighborhood bar for a drink. On the stage, a local musician was performing a song he called "Fulton Road Blues" (Cleveland's Second District police station is located on Fulton Road). Sung to the melody of Johnny Cash's "Folsom Prison Blues," the lyrics cast Supercop as a crime-fighting folk hero.

Simone's notoriety occasionally became a workplace distraction. Some motorists, after being ticketed by Simone, asked to have their photographs taken with him. Others would blurt, "You're the cop who killed all those people, right?"

The police review board also saw an uptick in spurious complaints against Simone. He had become a convenient target for police haters and those seeking a quick financial settlement. In some cases, investigators discovered that Simone hadn't even been working on the day of an alleged misconduct.

"I've been in restaurants and bars where I've overheard people complaining and lying about him," said Mary. "If someone was bad-mouthing my dad because they'd been arrested by him, I'd sometimes speak up. I'd tell them that if they obeyed the law, they wouldn't have to worry about getting in trouble."

Simone doesn't doubt that there are people who hold a grudge against him. "I'm not Officer Friendly," he said. "When you've arrested as many people as I have, you're going to have enemies."

Over the years, he has received several death threats. While in a restaurant with Lynne and another family member, Simone found himself being eyeballed by three men. He recognized them as the brothers of a man that he'd sent to prison for murder. The men left the restaurant and sat on a bench near the exit.

"We had a feeling they were going to start trouble with Jim, so he walked out alone and we went in the other direction," Lynne said. "Jim didn't know what to expect from them. At that moment, a Cleveland Police car just happened to drive into the parking lot. It turned out that the officers were picking up their dinners. The three men, thinking Jim had called the police, left."

As a precaution when dining with family and friends, he always takes the outside position in a booth and he faces the door. Simone lives in a state of preparedness—relaxed but attentive—and has coached Lynne and other family members in escape strategies for nearly any perilous scenario.

Should such a situation occur, Simone is uniquely equipped to handle it, said Keith Sulzer, the commander of the Second District from 2007 to 2014.

"Jim's strong suit was that he could foresee everything before it happened," said Sulzer. "It's an instinct he has—the ability to notice the small things and then transition from sight to a split-second decision. It's almost like he has a super connection in his brain that puts things in order more quickly than most other officers. It's innate. I don't think it can really be trained, but the more situations that an officer is put in, the stronger that ability becomes."

Simone had enemies, but he also had his fans, said Sulzer. The residents on Simone's beat, particularly the seniors, the families, and the working people, recognized his appreciable impact on the area's crime rate.

"He was visible and responsive to the community," Sulzer said. "People respect and like face-to-face interaction with police officers. It humanizes them. Jim took the time to get out there and look the people in the eye."

Not only did Simone patrol the Second District, but he lived among its residents. "They all had my cell phone number. They knew they could call me if they needed help," he said. "I was doing community policing before it became a reform catchphrase."

As Second District commander, Sulzer organized numerous popular community events. "We had pancake breakfasts and we'd cook dinner for the elderly. Jim supported every event and showed the people that he cared about them. We had a dunking booth and we were able to get him to participate in that. The people loved that they could dunk a cop and then sit down and eat with him. That's what community policing is about."

The Second District, like each of Cleveland's five police districts, has a community relations committee staffed by citizens and police officers. The Second District's committee is cochaired by Bob Shores, a longtime neighborhood activist.

Shores grew up in Rocky River, an affluent Cleveland suburb. After graduating from college in the late 1970s, he found himself drawn to Ohio City, a Second District neighborhood that was then beset by poverty and crime issues.

"Ohio City was grittier and rougher back then and I loved it," said Shores. "I was rebelling against the corporate world that my family expected me to belong to. I found that I was more comfortable living in a slum and hanging out with black and Latino friends."

In the past, Shores had been the victim of several strong-arm robberies and home burglaries. When he filed police reports, the responding officers would invariably leave him parting advice along the lines of, "This is what you get when you live in the ghetto."

Put off by the unsolicited judgments, Shores said he began to question the officers' commitment to combating crime and protecting the community's residents.

When the sons of his then-girlfriend were victimized by muggers, Shores decided to look for ways to get involve in anticrime efforts. Working first as a volunteer for the local community development corporation, he organized block clubs and neighborhood safety patrols. He then took a paid position as an outreach coordinator. For a time, he worked as a crew supervisor of felons who had been sentenced to community service.

"If I had a crew of ten guys, it seemed that at least five of them would have bullet scars," Shores said. "It was a real eye-opener for me."

In the mid-2000s, Shores joined the Second District community relations committee, which is essentially a bridge-building entity among residents and police. At the time, Ohio City was gentrifying at a rapid clip, with an influx of well-heeled homeowners and the sprouting of wine bars, microbreweries, and nightclubs along West 25th Street.

"We were seeing more nice houses and more people with money," said Shores. "We also saw more crime. Burglars go where the money is. They knew there were soft targets here—people who aren't packing guns and aren't going to fight. And those people have good stuff to steal, like smartphones and computers that can be sold for quick cash."

Along with the spike in burglaries, Shores and his fellow activists were struggling with an increase in drug trafficking and prostitution.

"We were tired of it," said Shores. "We'd see a drug dealer on a corner and report him to the Second District station. The cops would come out, but they'd just drive by."

Shores said he then decided to identify Second District cops who could "make a difference" in the neighborhood. "That's when I met Jim Simone," he said. "I got to know him and I loved his commitment to law and order. He made a lot of felony arrests. I saw him as a warrior against crime; someone who could take bad guys off the streets."

Shores did periodic ride-alongs with Simone, observing numerous traffic stops. "He was smart, tenacious, and professional. I saw that he was making a tremendous difference in our neighborhood. He took thousands of drunks off the roads in the Second District. Those were people who were not only hurting other people, but also hurting themselves. He put some of them on the right track. I'd been to AA meetings where I'd hear people say they owed their sobriety to getting arrested by Simone."

Simone could also be hard-edged, said Shores, particularly when it came to holding other officers to a higher standard. "He ticketed cops, which created some problems for him. I remember speaking with him for quite awhile at a police event. I apologized for keeping him from talking to his fellow officers. He said, 'That's alright, they don't want to talk to me anyhow.'"

But Shores saw compassion in Simone—and discretion in his ticketing. He often issued warnings, rather than citations, to seniors and individuals with disabilities.

"On one of my last ride-alongs with him," said Shores, "he got a call to respond as a backup to a felony warrant arrest. He saw that a mother was being arrested, so he ran back to his patrol car to get candy for her kids to calm them down. He kept a bag of candy for just that purpose. Then he insisted that the mom not be handcuffed in front of her children. He got grandma to come to the house to take them. He was very concerned that the kids didn't see their mom in cuffs."

It was no secret to Simone's colleagues that he had a soft spot for kids and pets. "Jimmy was a gruff talker, but I've seen him save a goldfish," said Tom Evans, a police psychologist and confidant of Simone. "One night, Jim pulled a guy out of his car and arrested him. He called the tow truck to take the guy's car. Then he noticed a goldfish in a bowl on the guy's front seat. It was a cold night. He knew the fish would freeze. So he brought the fish back to his cruiser. "The fish didn't do anything wrong; I'll give it to my niece," he said.

Alex Zamblauskas, while a sergeant in the Second District, recalled the evening a social worker brought a nine-year-old girl to the station house. The social worker explained that the girl had repeatedly been raped by her father and his live-in friend.

"I didn't have exceptional officers who could talk to a little girl," said Zamblauskas.

Jimmy was a traffic guy. He wrote tickets. But he said he'd handle it. He went to the girl's house, where he collected evidence and then arrested the father. Simone brought him back to the station house and started booking him. At some point, the father told him, "Whatever that whore says is not true." Jimmy warned him not to call her a whore. "She's your daughter," he said. The father again called the girl a whore, so Simone slapped him.

At the defendant's trial, the man's attorney asked Simone if it was true that he struck his client. "There are some cops who would try to lie on the witness stand, but not Jimmy," said Zamblauskas. "He explained that the guy called his daughter a whore after being told not to, so he slapped him. Jimmy showed the jury that he was honest. When the defense attorney continued to question Simone about striking his client, the judge interrupted and said, 'Everyone in this courthouse knows that Officer Simone probably slapped the shit out of your client, but he's not on trial. If you want to file a complaint about him, do it at police headquarters.'"

The father was convicted and sentenced to twenty years in prison.

Simone's willingness to involve himself in the girl's case was not surprising to Zamblauskas, who said that Simone's enthusiasm for police work had never wavered, even during his second and third decades on the job. "No one else with twenty years of seniority would choose to work weekend nights, except Jim Simone. He preferred to work from six at night until two in the morning because those were the action hours. He was working nights and weekends even after he had thirty years in. He'd get angry if he couldn't work."

Zamblauskas noted that the surge of adrenaline experienced in a car chase or during the foot pursuit of an armed felon can be addictive. "In a cop's first few years on the job, he or she will take risks and do crazy things. They'll do it for free for the adrenaline rush. But after three or five years, they cut that out. They're still good cops, but they've matured. They have families to worry about. But Jimmy never lost that drive. He never shut it off."

The career arcs of Simone and Zamblauskas, who is twenty years younger, are markedly disparate. As Zamblauskas was rising from patrolman to sergeant and on to detective, Simone was badgering his superiors for reassignment from Homicide back to Traffic.

"Homicide detective is the most prestigious position in the department," Zamblauskas said. "Jimmy left that to return to the street. He wanted the action."

While Simone is admittedly an adrenaline junkie, his decision to remain a street cop stemmed largely from his aversion to bureaucracy and politics. "I stayed a patrolman because I didn't want 'them' to have control," he said. "As a patrolman, I only had one asshole to deal with. Myself."

While Zamblauskas said he would have liked to have been trained by Simone, he said they would have been incompatible as partners. "He ticketed cops and their family members," he explained. "That's something I wouldn't have done."

He once asked Simone to patrol a Cleveland neighborhood that had experienced a rash of drivers ignoring stop signs.

"Okay, I'll sit at a stop sign there and write tickets, but everyone is fair game," warned Simone, who knew that numerous police officers lived in the area.

"On second thought," said Zamblauskas, "I don't need you there."

Like many of Simone's colleagues, Zamblauskas took issue with his reluctance to extend professional courtesy to other cops.

"There were a lot of guys on the job who didn't like him because of that," said Zamblauskas. "But they still had a measure of respect for him. They might have been pissed off that Jim Simone arrested their daughter, but they appreciated that he was a great police officer. Whenever a cop had a question about a specific law or a procedure, they would call Simone. Even if they didn't like him, he would be the guy they'd call."

Andres Gonzalez recalled that Simone carried a laminated copy of the city's codified ordinances in his patrol car.

"If other cops called, Jim could immediately come up with the ordinance they needed," said Gonzalez.

He was so organized that other cops would emulate his system and borrow his stuff. He was always on the front end of technology. He was the first guy to have a camera in the car. When I partnered with him, we always had duct tape, scissors, extra handcuffs, first aid kit, tape recorder, and extra victim statement forms. Everything you could conceivably need in a zone car, we carried with us. It was all organized, labeled, and wrapped up.

Simone even carried a coil of rope in his trunk. He had once failed to save a man who had jumped from a bridge into the Cuyahoga River. Regretting that he didn't have a rope to throw to the man, he went out the next day and bought a 200-foot length.

To increase his ticket-writing efficiency, Simone enlisted his nephews to pretype portions of the citations.

"We had a fancy typewriter that had memory so we could program it to fill in his name and badge number and other standard lines on the tickets," said Nick Szymanski. "It would save him a few minutes each time he issued someone a citation."

Nick and his brothers, Steve, Matt, and Henry, shuttled between their home and Simone's house after their parents divorced and their father vanished from their lives. They'd come to view their Uncle Jim as a father figure.

"He was a big influence on my work ethic," said Nick.

I'm sure that got passed down to him, and then he passed it down to us. From the age of seven, he had us working on his rental properties. He would sleep four hours a night, then go to court and then work on his properties. If he ended up arresting someone at the end of his shift, he'd work another three or four hours. From him, I learned to pull my damn socks up and get the job done.

Nick, who enlisted in the Air Force after high school, said he regretted that he and his Uncle Jim didn't do more traditional activities together, like throwing a baseball around.

"But he was a workaholic," Nick said. "He loved his job and his family. He provided a solid environment for us. I have no idea how I would have ended up without that stability."

Steve, a year younger than Nick, also enlisted in the Air Force. "I wouldn't say that my Uncle Jim ordered me to join the service, but he pushed us to find direction in life and work hard. Maybe it's his generation or his upbringing, but he doesn't leave things undone. Some people think that when their work shift is over, it's okay to leave unfinished work to someone else. Not Jim. That's not his style."

Over the years, negative media coverage of Simone has disturbed his nephews, particularly when the stories seem slanted and inaccurate.

"I've seen 'hit' pieces on my uncle and articles that weren't true," said Steve, who was deployed to Afghanistan for seven months. "A lot of people don't really know him. He's one of the most honest people I know. And if any of us needed anything, he would absolutely make it happen. We moved into Jim and Lynne's home one weekend after my mom was beat up by my father. Jim went and got us new school clothes and toys so that we didn't have to go back to our house and get our things."

17   Team Spirit

On an icy December night in 1998, Simone is shooting radar from the berm of Interstate 90 West. It was his last work shift before beginning two weeks of vacation.

"I only had two hours left on my tour," Simone recalled. "I could have hung out in the station house until quitting time. But at midnight, I decided to head back out."

When his radar unit beeped, he glanced and saw a readout of 78 mph. That's strange, he thought, there's no traffic in sight. He looked again in his rearview mirror and saw a car barreling directly at him in the berm with its headlights out.

The car smashed into the rear of Simone's cruiser. The impact crushed the vehicle, pushing it 50 feet down the berm and then into the concrete median.

The car's rear seat had been driven against the front seat, pinning Simone against the steering wheel. He tried to push himself through the driver's window, but found that he couldn't move.

"I had lost the feeling in my legs," he said. "They were completely numb."

The car's radio equipment, which was mounted in the trunk, was destroyed. Simone couldn't call for help. His distress was compounded by his awareness that the model of car he was trapped in, a Ford Crown Victoria Police Interceptor, was prone to gas tank explosions in rear-end collisions. He'd read police safety bulletins warning that more than thirty cops in the United States had burned to death after their Crown Victorias were struck from the rear.

In what many engineers considered a major design flaw, Ford had placed the vehicle's gas tank behind the rear axle. As a result, in a high-speed, rear-end crash like Simone had just experienced, the tank was likely to be crushed as the car's trunk buckled. Once the gas tank was ruptured, a spark could ignite a fireball.

Simone realized that he had two grim options if his tank exploded: die in the inferno or take the quick way out with his service weapon. While he sat in the crumpled vehicle, his dash-cam recording showed that at least a hundred cars drove past.

"People were slowing down to look, but nobody stopped," he said. "Finally, a car on the other side of the highway pulled over to help me. The driver happened to be the nephew of a policeman."

Police shut down the entire highway for forty-five minutes while firefighters cut the roof off the car to extricate Simone. Second District Cdr. Greg Baeppler and other supervisors rushed to the scene, driving eastbound in the westbound lanes.

Lynne, who was working as the chief dispatcher that night, noticed that one of her dispatchers seemed upset.

"She looked frazzled, so I plugged in to help her, even though she didn't want me to hear what was going on," said Lynne. She listened to chatter about the crash, quickly realizing that Jim was involved. She immediately asked a zone car to drive her to the scene.

At the hospital, a neurologist stuck various sizes of pins into Simone's legs and feet. He had no sensation. After an MRI and CT scan, the doctors told Lynne that Jim was paralyzed from the waist down.

"In the shock of that moment, I remember praying, 'Please God, fix him or take him,'" said Lynne. "I knew that Jim would never want to live like that. He wouldn't even have been able to go to the bathroom by himself."

He was wheeled to the intensive care unit, where Lynne sat beside him until 6:30 A.M. when a nurse told her to go home and get some rest.

"At home, I took a shower and fed the dogs," she said. "Then, ten hours after he was brought to the hospital, Jim called to tell me that he wanted to come home. He had felt some tingling in his toes. The doctors said that was a sign he was going to recover."

The neurologist treating Simone suspected that his paralysis was most likely due to tissue inflammation that temporarily compressed his spinal cord. Relieved to regain the use of his legs, Simone said he survived the accident only because he had placed his car's transmission in "neutral" when he was parked on the berm.

"An old highway patrol trooper had once told me to keep it in 'neutral' when I was running radar so that the vehicle would be a moving object rather than a stationary object if anyone rear-ended me," Simone explained. "If my car had been in 'park,' the crash would have been a double fatality."

Simone learned that the man who hit him had been intoxicated. "That made me angry," he said. "A drunk had nearly crippled me."

He had enough years of service to retire. Any other cop would have considered cashing out. But not Simone. With Lynne at his side, he began walking each night around a high school track to strengthen his legs. Within a week, he was jogging. A month later, he was back at work.

Later in the year, the Ford Motor Company—after making safety upgrades to the Crown Victoria's gas tank—offered to donate a new car to the Cleveland Police. Mayor Michael White declined the offer, reportedly after learning that it was contingent on Simone appearing in a Ford television commercial.

In 1999, Lynne and Jim moved to Sheffield Village, a semirural community about 30 miles west of Cleveland. Not long afterwards, Lynne retired from her dispatcher position.

"I'm not a country girl, but Jim wanted a ranch home," Lynne said. Set on a large lot, their new home offered room for their extended family and their brood of pets. At times, up to eleven rescue dogs and twelve cats have shared their house.

Although the couple hadn't married after nearly twenty years of being together, their union continued to strengthen, despite a few rough patches.

"I had a big crisis at age thirty," Lynne said.

I had wanted to have kids. I was threatening to leave if it didn't happen. One day, Jim decided he'd had enough. He slammed the bathroom door open and told me, "If you're leaving, then just leave." I realized then that I had been putting him through a lot. I had been going out and partying until 3:00 or 4:00 in the morning. He never gave me a hard time about it. He waited me out. In the morning, he'd ask me how my night was.

After one particularly late night, Lynne came to the realization that she was hurting him. "I had a revelation," she said. From then on, she committed herself to the relationship. "We had a ritual every Friday afternoon. We'd go to our favorite restaurant and have their clam chowder and home-baked bread for lunch. We'd spend two hours just talking. Just sitting together and talking."

Since being named head traffic cop in 1992, Simone had consistently led the department in drunk-driving arrests. Each year, he was recognized by the Mothers Against Drunk Driving for his efforts in keeping Second District roads safe. In 2001, Simone again racked up department-leading statistics. That year, however, he not only distinguished himself for his number of arrests, but for the high-profile Clevelanders he'd put in handcuffs.

On November 19, 2001, the Cleveland Browns had defeated the defending Super Bowl champion Baltimore Ravens to improve their record to 5–4 and claw their way into playoff contention. In the previous two seasons, the Browns had season records of 2–14 and 3–13.

Long-suffering Browns fans finally had a reason to rally behind their beleaguered team. The night after the Ravens victory, a Cleveland patrol officer pulled over a pickup truck that had been speeding and swerving.

Inside he found Mike Sellers, a Browns fullback, and Lamar Chapman, a cornerback who had been a fifth-round draft pick the previous year. Sellers, the driver, appeared to be intoxicated.

Fearing the backlash he'd face after arresting a Brown, the patrol officer was apprehensive about taking the collar. He called Simone to the scene, knowing that he'd be willing to make the arrest. He also knew that Simone had a dash cam to record Sellers's roadside sobriety test.

The officers searched the truck, finding two bags of marijuana in the glove compartment and three burnt marijuana blunt cigars in the ashtray. Both men were charged with drug offenses while Sellers also faced a drunk-driving charge. After transporting them to the Second District station, Simone found a rolled-up dollar bill containing cocaine on the backseat of his patrol car, evidently left there by one of the handcuffed men.

While neither man was a starting player, head coach Butch Davis had predicted both would play prominent roles in the Browns' future.

As news of the arrests quickly spread, the police department and the mayor's office received calls from the media, NFL representatives, the Browns organization, and the players' agents and attorneys. Simone's supervisors, feeling pressure from above, urged him to reconsider the charges against the players.

"Everybody tried to pressure me to let them go because we were in the middle of the football season," Simone said. "One of our former police commanders had a high-level security position with the Browns. He called me and said, 'So what are we going to do about this?'"

"WE?" asked Simone. He then told him, "I am going to proceed with this case just like I would with anybody else's."

When it became clear that Simone could not be swayed, Sellers and Chapman pleaded not guilty to felony drug-abuse charges. Butch Davis suspended the players for one game, saying, "They let the team down and they let themselves down, and their families."

Eventually, prosecutors would drop charges against Sellers and reduce Chapman's charges to misdemeanor possession of drug paraphernalia.

After the players' arrest, police animosity toward Simone was writ large. Along with the many cops who were Browns fans, others earned supplemental income as part-time employees at Browns games.

Simone's conspicuous arrests became the subject of heated discussions in City Hall and police headquarters. "The city decided they wanted the camera out of my car," he said. "I was busting too many important people. I had become a liability to the politicians who ran the police department. But I told them the camera was staying."

While Simone had always strived for objectivity in his enforcement of the law, he now had to be uber-consistent. If he did anything contrary to policy, his bosses would have the leverage to dismiss him. Simone had to be even more "by the book," if that was possible. His activities were under a microscope. If he exercised his personal discretion, if he cut breaks for anyone—whether cops or civilians—he could be accused of showing favoritism and potentially face disciplinary action.

Simone had always saved copies of his written reports and videotapes. He now began storing his documents in a safe house as protection against any retaliatory action from the police department.

Not long afterward, antipathy toward Simone would ratchet to new heights after he arrested the girlfriend of one of Cleveland's most prominent businessmen.

The woman had been swerving and driving erratically when Simone stopped her. Standing at the window of her car, he noticed a strong odor of alcohol. When he asked her for her identification and registration, she informed him that her boyfriend was one of the owners of the Cleveland Indians.

Simone, recognizing her boyfriend's name, was undeterred. He realized the arrest would bring heat from every level of the police department. The lady's boyfriend was a powerful and respected real estate developer who had great influence over the city's leaders. During the past decade, he had left his mark on Cleveland's skyline and in the hearts of Indians fans. Playing in his eponymous ballpark, the Indians made it to the World Series in 1995—the first time since 1954—and again in 1997, leaving a generation of Clevelanders with lasting memories.

At the station house, Simone booked the woman, who was chatty and cooperative. As he sat at a desk typing his report, he was aware that his sergeant's office was filling with city officials and ranking police officers, all looking angry and displeased. Shortly after midnight, the lady's boyfriend marched into the office.

A supervisor approached Simone. "You do know that this guy employs more than three hundred cops as part-time security officers?" he asked.

Without looking up, Simone replied, "Well then it's a good thing I don't work part-time."

A moment later, he was tapped on the shoulder. "Jim, the sergeant would like to see you in his office."

Affecting a casual and oblivious air as if he just happened to be ambling by on his way to grab dinner, Simone stepped into the office and nodded at his peeved sergeant. "What's up?" he asked.

Despite cajoling, negotiating, and attempted bullying, Simone wouldn't budge. The drunk-driving charge stuck.

Simone had taken on his bosses—and their bosses. Typically, not a recommended career move.

"But Simone didn't care," said Margery Gerbec, a former Cleveland Police sergeant.

Jimmy wasn't going to do anything that conflicted with his ethics and integrity. He wanted to be proud of every move that he made. If a person was breaking the law, Jimmy would issue a ticket. If he saw an injustice, he acted on it, whether it was a cop or a civilian. He wasn't above busting a brother officer if the officer was no good. If he showed up and you were a cop involved in a domestic violence situation or driving drunk, he slapped the cuffs on you. He didn't give favors; he didn't acknowledge any "blue code of silence." He had that kind of self-confidence.

Gerbec, who spent several years as a patrol officer in the Second and Fourth districts, never partnered with Simone. But for one memorable night, they worked together. Gerbec and her partner at the time had responded to a 911 call from a woman who was being threatened by her ex-boyfriend. Simone overheard the radio chatter and responded also.

After receiving a tip that the ex-boyfriend was armed, the officers sped to his address. "The guy answered from the top of the steps," recalled Gerbec.

> We ordered him down; he ordered us up. So now we had an armed guy challenging us. At that point, we could have called a boss, called SWAT, or handled it ourselves. Because of the kind of cop Jimmy is, he said, "Let's go." We were halfway up the steps when the guy pulled out his gun. Jimmy charged up and grabbed the gun. I jammed my gun into the guy's throat. Jimmy was ordering the guy to drop his gun, but he wasn't complying. I had my finger on the trigger. I was ready to shoot. I knew that in a split-second, the guy could have killed us. Jimmy was finally able to wrestle the gun away from the guy without us shooting him. If it had been any other cop but Jimmy, it wouldn't have gone down like that. The guy would have been shot.

The man later told police that he had hoped to provoke the officers into shooting him. Both Simone and Gerbec were awarded the City of Cleveland's Medal of Heroism for their efforts in resolving the situation nonlethally.

Acknowledging that Simone had a reputation as a "cowboy" and a risk-taker, Gerbec said, "I had that perception of him also. But that didn't factor into it when I worked with him. Once Jimmy's foot hit that first step, I was all in. Actually, there had been times when I had pulled other cops back from similar situations. But I had ultimate confidence in Jim's experience and instincts."

Gerbec said she perhaps admired Simone's confidence all the more because she sometimes doubted her own. Candid about her background, she said she joined the police department after enduring an adolescence that she called a "self-esteem disaster."

But she was physically fit, nurturing, and could handle a gun, so Gerbec thought she might be well suited for police work.

"I'd also had some tough experiences during childhood that I figured would be good preparation for the job," she said. "My father was abusive when he drank. And my mother struggled with depression. I once saw her walk out of a bathroom in a towel that was soaked red with blood after she had slashed her wrists."

Gerbec had spent three years as a dispatcher before entering the Cleveland Police Academy. After stints as a street cop and a sex crimes detective, she was promoted to sergeant. She retired on a medical disability after injuring both knees and her back while apprehending a suspect.

"I was chasing a guy down a hill and I blew my knees out," she said. "I got up and kept running. I caught the guy in someone's backyard and held him until another officer cuffed him. As I pulled the suspect over a fence, he tried to run again. We both fell and he landed on my back."

She took the suspect to the police station and booked him, then drove herself to a hospital, where she learned that she had several herniated discs. She underwent ten hours of surgery during which doctors inserted plastic spacers between the discs.

While she had planned on making police work her career, she admittedly was becoming disillusioned with the department's politics ("If you weren't kissing the right ass, you weren't getting anywhere," she said) and its chauvinism.

"I got treated differently because I was a girl," said Gerbec. "It was a boys' club and I was at a deficit. If a male cop said something derogatory about me, I had to care because I knew I was in a club that I wasn't fully a member of."

Upset by the discriminatory treatment, Gerbec reached out to Simone for advice. "He'd shrug and say, 'Hey kid, if they're not talking about you, you're not relevant.' He never got involved in that shit. He didn't gossip or sling mud. When he asked me how I was doing, he actually waited for an answer. He took me aside and taught me things. As a woman, I don't have upper body strength, so he showed me some tricks to disarm a man."

Gerbec came to the realization that she wasn't equipped to handle the sometimes twisted environment of a police station.

"Cops are like a dysfunctional family; you're stuck with them," she said.

We would give our lives for each other, but a few cops are damaged. They beat up on each other as a coping mechanism. They are just miserable people. When civilians encounter cops who are being assholes on the street, they need to understand that those cops are being assholes to other cops also. When I blew out my knees chasing the suspect, I overheard one cop tell another, "Gerbec rolled her fat ass down the hill." That hurt my feelings and ate at my integrity.

Recalling instances of bullying and harassment by other officers, she said, "There were guys who would post my head on a picture of a naked girl and hang it in the patrolman's room."

While adding that there are "idiots and bullies in every workplace," she said that psychologically screening unfit cops would be a key step in improving relations between the community and police departments.

When you give someone the power of a badge and a gun and the right to take someone's freedom from them, it magnifies whatever their personality traits are. If a person was bullied when they were younger, a badge and gun provides them with a newfound power that they've never had. Cops are expected to go into places that nobody would imagine going, and we're expected to mediate, de-escalate, or extinguish a threat. And we're given the tools to take someone's life if necessary. That's a huge responsibility. If a person was beat up and bullied when they were younger, they might not have the appropriate respect for that responsibility.

And then there are the Simones of the world, she said, who fight for the underdog and can't stand by and watch an injustice happen.

I think I am one of those people too. I feel lucky that I had the opportunity to work side by side with Simone. I respected his ethical integrity and his bravery. He was extremely smart. He had the ability to look at people's behaviors and instantly read them. There were cops who disliked him, probably out of jealousy because he did what they didn't have the balls to do. And there were others who resented when he came to a scene because he tended to take over. But that was Jim. That's why he was involved in so many shootings. When he heard a call for assistance, he didn't sit at the station house chowing on doughnuts. When someone needed help, he went.

18   Wild Bill

As a combat soldier and police officer, Simone's courage was unquestioned. By 2001, he'd earned nearly a hundred medals and letters of commendation for valor. He'd never shied from life-or-death situations.

But he couldn't bring himself to attend any of the annual reunions of the 3/187, his unit from Vietnam. "I was a coward," he said. "I was afraid to open up those wounds."

Lynne was aware that Simone still suffered recurring nightmares of Vietnam. She believed that he would benefit emotionally by reconnecting with the men who had shared his experiences. Through Internet searches, she found various Web sites with the names of the soldiers from Charlie Company. She put him in touch with Captain Bond, Charlie Company's commanding officer. In April 2001, Bond and Simone arranged a meeting and spent the day reminiscing.

Bond, who had retired from the army as a major, had been revered by his men for his stalwart leadership and prudence.

While he was known as a field commander who "led from the front," Bond took pride in not taking unnecessary risks. "My men knew that I wouldn't waste their lives by doing anything stupid," he said.

He described Simone as a can-do soldier with a dynamic personality. "Whatever he had chosen to do after the army, I knew he would have been successful. Whenever I gave him a job to do, I knew that he'd get it done. One way or another, he'd get it done. I would have liked to have had a whole company of Simones."

Bond recalled that he had once ordered Simone and other members of Charlie Company to burn several huts in a village that had been used as a weapons cache by the Viet Cong. While the men were setting fire to the grass dwellings, a chopper carrying a U.S. news crew landed nearby.

"Without knowing the details of what was happening, a cameraman and a reporter began interfering with Simone," Bond said. "They didn't understand that the villagers provided support to our enemy. Simone grabbed the camera and removed the film. He then told off the reporter."

Simone, remembering the incident, said the reporter had become indignant when he saw the huts being burned.

"America will see what you're doing here!" the newsman screamed, while the cameraman pushed his lens within inches of Simone's face.

"We had been up all night fighting Viet Cong," said Simone. "We were exhausted. Then here comes this TV crew who had no idea of what we'd been through."

In order to back the newsman away from the blazing huts, Simone fired a rifle burst in the general direction of his feet.

An hour later, a helicopter brought two military police officers into the field to escort Simone to battalion headquarters. He was marched into a colonel's office, where he was told that the reporter he had chased away was Dan Rather, then a rising star at CBS News. Rather had accused Simone of trying to kill him.

Simone, who didn't recognize Rather's name, said, "Sir, with all due respect, if I had tried to kill him, he'd be dead."

As Simone and Bond ended their visit in 2001, Bond encouraged him to attend an upcoming 3/187 reunion. "Some of us won't be here forever," he cautioned.

Simone then told Bond that while he'd had very few regrets in his life, he'd always hoped that someday he'd have the chance to thank the helicopter pilot who medevaced him when he was wounded.

Bond informed Simone that he'd been saved by "Wild Bill" Meacham, who had written a book, *Lest We Forget,* about his Vietnam experiences. Telling Simone that the book included a section about his rescue, Bond gave him Meacham's contact information.

After a quick lesson in computer usage from Lynne, Simone sent his first-ever e-mail, a message to Meacham thanking him for saving his life. "Your courage was not wasted," he wrote. "Because of you, I have children and grandchildren. I've had a great life."

Every couple of minutes for the next hour, Simone anxiously checked his in-box. Later that night, after he still hadn't received a reply, he telephoned Meacham at his home in Shreveport, Louisiana. His wife answered and after speaking with Simone for a few moments, told him to hold while she found Meacham. When she returned, she told Simone that her husband had started crying when he learned who was calling.

Finally, Meacham took the phone. Simone, also crying, said, "I'm calling to thank you."

"Fuck you," Meacham replied.

"Pardon me?" said Simone, confused. "Did I say something to offend you?"

"If you really want to thank me, come to the reunion and shake my hand," he said.

In May 2001, Jim and Lynne flew to Oklahoma. They checked into their hotel and then walked to the nearby municipal park where the reunion was being held.

"We sat at a picnic table by ourselves because I didn't recognize anyone at first," Simone said. He surveyed the room then noticed a familiar face staring at him. It was his former platoon leader, James MacLachlan.

Suddenly, MacLachlan jumped up and screamed, "Sergeant Simone!" Then he dove at Simone, literally sliding across the top of his table to get to him.

"He was crying," recalled Simone. "He thought I had died when I was blown up by the RPG. Nobody had ever told him that I survived."

Simone had difficulty holding back his tears when he came face-to-face with Bill Meacham. "For thirty-three years, I had been waiting to thank him for risking his life to evacuate us," he said. "I found out later that Wild Bill wasn't even a medevac pilot. His primary responsibility was flying supply runs."

Meacham confessed to Simone that he had briefly considered aborting the rescue because his chopper had been loaded with too many wounded men to safely take off.

"I didn't think we were going to get off the ground, but I didn't have the heart to throw any of you guys off," he said.

Simone was surprised to see Ralph Colley, the company commander who had lost his legs and the lower half of his left arm in a booby-trap explosion. Nobody had thought he'd survive, even though he'd had the composure to ask his men to find his missing hand. "My wedding ring is on it," he'd shouted as they loaded him into the medevac.

Colley, seated in a wheelchair, was still married to his college sweetheart. After recovering from his injuries, he had returned home to Arkansas and built a successful career in the real estate industry.

Colley said he had refused to allow the loss of his limbs to hinder his life. "I just got on with it," he said. He flew his own airplane and became an expert skier, winning two gold medals at the 1992 Paralympics in France. He was also an advocate for veterans' causes. Colley served as national commander of the Disabled America Veterans (DAV) from 1984 to 1985.

At the reunion, several members of Colley's company confessed that they hadn't searched for his hand. "Nobody wanted to take the chance of getting blown up by a booby trap," one of the men said.

As Simone looked around the room and saw fellow combatants who were missing arms and legs and had suffered disfiguring injuries, he felt the swell of long-suppressed emotions.

> "Then they read the names of our guys who never made it home from Vietnam," he said.
>
> That was tough. Grown men began blubbering. We truly were a band of brothers. There is a bond among combat soldiers that is difficult to explain. It's much stronger than the police bond. As a police officer, you occasionally experience fear. On the street, when you're in a gunfight, you don't have time to think because things happen so quickly. But in combat, you have a steady diet of fear. It's protracted. You have time to think about the possibility of death. And the violence of the deaths is unimaginable.

Craig Caldwell, a Charlie Company platoon leader, said the trauma of war left its imprint on many of his men. "Within days and sometimes minutes of landing in a faraway country, you get attacked with mortars and RPGs," he explained. "One minute you can be in a well-secured perimeter, and then the artillery drops in on you. There is a feeling of dread that accompanies those memories."

The body's chemistry is not the same after a night of those experiences, said Caldwell. "So PTSD is a reality. Just like high blood pressure and diabetes."

Caldwell's tour in Vietnam was cut short when his lung was punctured by shrapnel.

> I was inside the perimeter and I thought it was a safe place to be. And then it wasn't. I was in a trench with another soldier, Lieutenant Castillo, when a mortar exploded near us. We were hit and needed bandages, so I called for a medic. I wasn't pleading at that point, but I did let them

know if they gave us a hand, it wouldn't be considered unprofessional. As I lay there, I prayed, *Please God, don't let me get wounded again.* The shelling stopped then, although I'm not sure that a miracle occurred. I think they just ran out of ammo.

Caldwell was medevaced to Long Binh and then transferred to a hospital in Okinawa. "It was the loneliest experience of my life. I had just been with a group of people that I spilled blood with. When you're plucked from a combat relationship with those individuals around you and then sent a hospital where people don't even speak English, you have no one to connect to. There was no chaplain, no psychologist, no counselor to say, 'How are you?'"

Caldwell said he has learned that a significant percentage of Charlie Company has been treated for some aspect of PTSD through the Veterans Administration. The good news, he said, is that there are solutions to PTSD.

MacLachlan, who retired from the army as a lieutenant colonel, had returned to Vietnam for a second tour after training as a Cobra helicopter pilot. "By 1971, the infantry wasn't going out and actively pursuing the enemy like we'd done previously," he said. "Instead, they began sending out Cobras in pursuit of the bad guys."

He was shot down and spent six months in a hospital. When he recovered, MacLachlan served as consultant to Gen. Maxwell Thurman during his term as vice chief of staff of the army.

MacLachlan said he was not surprised to learn that Simone had chosen law enforcement as a career. He recalled his former platoon sergeant as purposeful, well organized, disciplined, and structured. "He wasn't initially a warrior, though. He wasn't a fighter. But then he chose to become a platoon sergeant and he accepted that burden of responsibility."

During the attack on Firebase Pope, when 2nd platoon was overrun by a much larger force of NVA soldiers, Simone "took the fight to the enemy," said MacLachlan.

Noting that the intensity and stress of combat can be "unimaginable," MacLachlan said it's likely that all of the members of his unit are afflicted to some degree with PTSD. "When you're in something terrible like a bad car wreck or war, it changes you a lot. And then when you do life-threatening things for a certain amount of time, the brain gets rewired and that's PTSD."

MacLachlan, who calls himself a "damn pacifist," said he's made his peace with the Vietnam War. "For me, there wasn't anything good that came out of that war. It was brutal and horrific. It's not the way you think your life is going to end. I lost a lot of people over there. I'd almost prefer that it would have been me who was gone. Because the dead stay with you for such a long, long time."

MacLachlan said he wonders whether Simone is still trying to understand the war; still trying to get it out of his head. "I have a feeling that Jim hasn't come home yet. His war is still going on."

If the war had any upside for Simone, said MacLachlan, it's that he transferred the core values he acquired in Vietnam to his job as a police officer.

> In Vietnam, he learned how to assess risk and make split-second decisions. He learned that he couldn't show weakness and he couldn't be indecisive when someone had a gun pointed at him.
>
> Like the other soldiers I accepted into my platoon, Simone exhibited selfless service. I believe that Simone felt that it was okay if he got killed to save someone else. He had the attitude that he would go in first. Maybe as a police officer, when he's fighting back, he's trying to fix a situation. It's not like he's trying to be a hero. He's trying to prevent something bad from happening; he's trying to resolve the situation with the least risk possible.

Simone, despite his involvement in a dozen shootings, has had great success at managing risk and defusing potentially deadly confrontations. But when an armed individual seems intent on self-destruction, a police officer can often do little else but stand by and take steps to minimize casualties.

On the night of January 9, 2003, Michael Ciacchi, a troubled and depressed thirty-eight-year-old, had provoked a standoff with police in the driveway of a house on Cleveland's Stickney Avenue. Alternately waving his revolver in the air and pointing it at his own head, Ciacchi refused orders to drop the weapon. He insisted that he was going into the house, which was occupied by his roommate's wife and her daughter.

Simone, who had been one of the first officers on the scene, said, "We couldn't let him go inside the home. That could have led to a hostage situation. Or a murder-suicide."

Six hours earlier, Ciacchi had sped away from a suburban Valley View police officer who had pulled him over for speeding. The officer, suspecting Ciacchi had been drinking, asked him to step out of the car. When Ciacchi refused, the officer reached into his car to shut off the ignition. Ciacchi then drove off, dragging the officer a short distance.

The police officer chased Ciacchi in a cruiser, but lost him. Ciacchi then visited a friend, Steve Kulak, unannounced. While at Kulak's house, Ciacchi asked Kulak for a gun that he had given him to clean. Kulak turned over the firearm, a Ruger Blackhawk .357 with a 6-inch barrel.

Valley View officers, meanwhile, were hunting for Ciacchi. At 9:30 P.M., the officers saw Ciacchi's Chevy Cavalier in the parking lot of a restaurant. Ciacchi had stopped to use the outdoor payphone to call a friend and family members. When the Valley View police boxed in Ciacchi's car, he stepped out and put the handgun to his head. Returning to the car, he rammed the police cruisers and escaped.

Ciacchi then used his cell phone to call his mother to ask for his attorney's phone number. He informed her that he had run from the police after a traffic stop, but assured her that he would turn himself in to police the next morning.

At 9:50, Simone, who had been alerted to Valley View's pursuit of Ciacchi, spotted his car. He followed him to the Stickney Avenue house, where Ciacchi had recently rented a room from his longtime friend, Carl Basa.

Ciacchi sped into the driveway, stepped out of his car, and held the gun to his chin. Simone jumped from his car. "Drop your weapon! Drop your weapon!" he screamed. More police arrived and, with guns drawn, also shouted at Ciacchi.

"I'm going into the house and I'm going to turn myself in tomorrow morning," Ciacchi said.

According to a Stickney Avenue resident, one of the police officers then said, "Don't move. Your best friend's wife and daughter are in the house."

"I'll never hurt them," Ciacchi replied.

Indeed, nothing in Ciacchi's history would indicate that he was violent. Friends and relatives describe a funny, amiable, and sensitive individual. The past several years had been rough, though. He'd been injured in a trench cave-in while working in construction. The accident had left him with lingering physical issues that required pain medications, according to his older brother, Joe. He was also taking an antidepressant and medication for a persistent twitching problem.

Michael, one of four siblings, lived in his mother's home and had worked only intermittently during the past year. He'd had his truck repossessed and fell behind on bills. Two weeks before the driveway standoff, Joe and Michael had argued over money. Joe induced their mother to evict him. Michael then moved in with Basa, renting his third-floor attic space.

Joe said that his brother, who was single, loved life and loved being an uncle to his sister Diane's and brother Dean's children. But he added that Michael became confused and had difficulty functioning when he neglected to take his medications. Another family member told police that Michael drank while taking high doses of pain pills. On those occasions, Michael could be a "handful," she said.

"He had some issues," Joe acknowledged. "Our father was abusive. I fought against the abuse, but Michael internalized it. I think it really hurt him. To some extent, he was tired of being pushed around and bullied by life."

Standing in the driveway, with his gun pointed at his chin, Ciacchi seemed to be daring or baiting police to take his life.

In the house just east of Basa's, sisters Jodi Sours Grant and Jill Kekic watched the chaotic scene unfold.

"The cops looked scared," said Grant. "Their adrenaline was pumping. They didn't know what Ciacchi was going to do. He had a crazed look on his face. It was obvious, though, that whatever occurred, they were going to do what needed to be done."

On the video from Simone's dash cam, police can be heard repeatedly screaming at Ciacchi to put his weapon down.

"Every cop out there was yelling, 'Drop your weapon! Put it down!'" Kekic said.

When Ciacchi turned away from the police and moved toward the front door of the house, Simone, who was attempting to pepper spray him, yelled, "Drop the gun or I'll kill you!" Ciacchi yelled back, "Do it! Do it!" He then pointed his gun at Simone and two nearby officers.

Police opened fire, hitting Ciacchi seven times. Of the twenty-six police officers on the scene, eight fired their weapons, including Simone. During the shooting, Simone was hit by a bullet and went down. Police on the scene initially thought he was shot by Ciacchi, but investigators would discover that Ciacchi's revolver had been empty.

"When the gunfire started, it was frightening," said Kekic. "It sounded like fireworks. My dog was terrified. He was crawling along the floor. The whole scene was crazy, with the lights and sirens and the police jumping on our porch. But I don't think the police could have done anything differently."

Ciacchi was pronounced dead at MetroHealth Hospital at 10:40 P.M.

"Mike was a good-hearted person," said Joe. "He was harmless. The cops should have tried to talk to him down. They were bullying him, yelling at him. A softer touch would have helped."

When asked why his brother was brandishing the gun, Joe said, "I don't know. Maybe he felt he had security with the gun. I think he knew that if he pointed the gun at himself, it would give him time to talk. I don't think he wanted to die. He was basically saying that he needed help."

Then he added, "It was my dad's gun. It was the only thing Mike got from my dad when he passed away."

Basa, who had been friends with Ciacchi since grade school, theorized that Ciacchi's gun represented a form of power.

"He was making a statement," Basa said. "It was his last stand. He always had a problem with authority. If he was told to do something, he wouldn't listen."

At 8:45 P.M., about an hour before he was shot, Ciacchi had driven past Basa's house. Police were already there, after tracing Ciacchi's license plate. Ciacchi sped away; then left the following message on Basa's answering machine: "Well, cop cars all around. You'd think you'd be answering your phone. I guess not. Hey Carl, they pushed me, they shoved me. I'm going to miss you buddy. Bye Bye."

When police fired at Ciacchi, stray bullets struck Basa's and Kekic's houses. Both filed damage claims with the City of Cleveland, but were denied. Bullets also punctured the gas tank of Ciacchi's car. When officers noticed that gasoline was draining onto Ciacchi, who had fallen in the driveway, they dragged him away from the car onto Kekic's front lawn. The gasoline killed the grass roots, leaving a yellow silhouette of his body that is still visible twelve years later.

Simone was saved by his body armor, but suffered a bruised rib from the bullet, which came from another officer's gun.

"A supervisor asked me who shot me. I knew, but I wouldn't tell him," Simone said. "I handled it myself. Let's just say that I gave the officer a class on crossfire and target acquisition."

Police crime scene investigators spent several hours collecting evidence from Kekic's porch. Grant overheard them talking about Simone getting hit by friendly fire.

"Looks like somebody got a good angle on him," one of the investigators joked.

That night, TV news stations reported that Jim "Supercop" Simone had killed a man who was holding an unloaded gun. "That seemed a bit unfair considering that seven other officers also fired their guns," noted Simone. "In the morning, I turned on the television and watched the news ladies do their 'happy talk' thing about Supercop being involved in yet another shooting. They singled me out, just casually chatting amongst each other about the number of people I've shot. I knew then that I was at the point where my reputation had preceded me."

Saying that he "felt horrible" that they'd shot a man with an empty gun, Simone said, "I wasn't willing to gamble whether his gun was loaded or empty. I told Ciacchi nine separate times to drop his gun. I was going to pepper spray him, but then he turned and pointed the gun at us. I've been in firefights. I've been shot. I know what happens if you don't react."

Simone didn't sleep that night or the next. In the aftermath of a high-stress situation such as the Ciacchi shooting or a fatal car crash, he often turned to one of the police department's chaplains for help in coping with the stress.

Police work can be an emotional roller-coaster, said Dean Kavouras, a chaplain for the Cleveland safety forces. "It's unrealistic to expect officers to just 'suck it up' when something bad occurs. We know that the hazards of the job can take an emotional toll on them."

"Dean is my safe place," said Simone. "I know I can cry if I need to; I can open up with him and it won't go any further. Dean has done many ride-alongs, so he knows what we're going through out there."

Although a Cleveland police official told news reporters that Ciacchi's death was a "classic case of suicide by cop," the police prosecutor took four months to rule on the shooting. During that time, Simone and the seven other officers involved in the incident were relegated to gym duty. Cleveland's taxpayers footed the bill, about $125,000, for the eighty-eight days that each officer was on paid leave.

In May 2003, the city prosecutor, Sanford Watson, ruled that police had acted properly. "The officers were faced with an immediate threat of harm," Watson said. "In situations like these, things happen in a matter of seconds."

Reflecting on the incident, Simone said that it seemed clear that Ciacchi had a plan to get killed. "He knew he was facing a charge of felonious assault for dragging the Valley View police officer. He called his friends to say good-bye. When I was following him, he drove slowly and never tried to escape. Then he baited us with his gun in the driveway. Ciacchi essentially used the police to commit suicide."

Simone said that the phenomenon of suicide by cop occurs more frequently than people would imagine. Research on the subject is imprecise, partly because it's difficult to determine how many of the four hundred or so people killed each year by police actually wanted to die. Some experts say 10–15 percent of police-involved deaths can be attributed to suicide by cop, but others say the term is too often used by law enforcement agencies and police prosecutors as a justification for questionable shootings.

Arguably, three of the fatal shootings that involved Simone could be considered suicide by cop. Harley Reeser, Dennis Workman, and Ciacchi had all indicated or expressed their intent to die. Even Eugene Szejpcher, who had pointed a handgun at Simone, could be construed as scripting his own death.

"These individuals were all bent on self-destruction," said Simone. "They just didn't have the courage to do it themselves."

James J. Drylie, Ph.D., an assistant professor of criminal justice at Kean University in New Jersey, has conducted extensive research on the subject of suicide by cop (which he refers to as "copicide").

Drylie, a former police officer for twenty-five years, said three factors are typically present in a true suicide by cop scenario: The victim willingly became involved in a confrontation with police; he communicated suicidal intent (either verbally or through a gesture such as putting a gun to his head); and he acted in a threatening manner toward police.

By Drylie's definition, all of those criteria were present in the Ciacchi case.

19 The Perfect Traffic Stop

June 12, 2008. Just after 8:30 P.M. A motorcycle heading southbound on Pearl Road in Cleveland zipped in front of Simone's police cruiser. Simone noticed that the bike's rear license plate was bolted on improperly, so he followed it into a Shell gas station.

The rider, a Latino man in a white tank top and baggy denim shorts, dismounted and began to pump gas into his fuel tank. Simone approached him. His dash cam recorded their exchange:

> "Let me see your driver's license."
> "Excuse me?" said the man, somewhat nervously.
> "Let me see your driver's license, please."
> "What's wrong?"
> "First off, your plate's improperly displayed. It has to be displayed left to right, not upside down or sideways."

The man produced his driver's license. After running a check, Simone ticked off the man's violations: He wasn't licensed to operate a motorcycle; he didn't have a helmet or eye protection; and he was using a fictitious license plate that was mounted incorrectly.

> "You're setting yourself up to be arrested. Is that what you want, Ariel?"
> "No sir, I don't want that."
> "Well, Ariel, you just keep getting deeper and deeper."
> "I know, but I just got off work. I'm a school bus driver. And . . ."

Simone decided to issue the man several citations but not arrest him. He also ordered him to push his motorcycle to his home, which was a mile away on Seymour Avenue.

It had been a fairly typical traffic stop for Simone, one of an estimated 200,000 that he'd conducted during his career. Five years later, however, the man whom Simone had stopped, Ariel Castro, would be revealed as one of America's most notorious criminals.

Unbeknownst to Simone, Castro had three young women locked inside his house. The hostages—Amanda Berry, Michelle Knight, and Gina DeJesus—had been plucked off the street by Castro between 2002 and 2004.

On May 6, 2013, Amanda Berry and her six-year-old daughter escaped from the house. Knight and DeJesus were rescued shortly after. News of the women's decade-long imprisonment generated headlines around the world.

Within days, Simone received calls from news reporters who requested his video of the Castro traffic stop. The minute-long dash-cam recording would be seen by millions. Simone consented to several national TV interviews about his interaction with Castro. Some of the interviewers questioned his decision to not arrest Castro. If he had taken Castro into custody, they asserted, perhaps the women could have escaped.

"I had no idea that three women were locked in his house," Simone explained. "In retrospect, it would have been the arrest of a lifetime. But he was the perfect traffic stop: He was very, very polite and said all the right words. If I had arrested him, he might have lost his job as a school bus driver, so I cut him a break."

Simone told CNN's Piers Morgan that even if he had arrested Castro, there would have been no reason to go to his residence. "He'd have been locked up in jail and the girls would have been trapped in that house, chained up with no access to anything," he said. "The baby had just been born, so there was a small child in the house. Who would have cared for them?"

In July 2013, Castro pleaded guilty to 937 criminal counts of rape, kidnapping, and aggravated murder. He was sentenced to life in prison without the chance of parole. One month into his sentence, Castro committed suicide by hanging himself with bed sheets in his prison cell.

"The media was looking for someone to blame, so I guess I was convenient, but where were the neighbors in this?" asked Simone. He theorized that the girls had remained hidden for so long because the residents of Seymour Avenue were not diligent in noticing and reporting peculiarities at Castro's house. He added that the Castro case is a consequence of the decline of community policing.

"The day of the beat cop is over," said Simone. "It's unfortunate because there's no better communication about what is happening in a neighborhood than a cop on the street."

As a patrol officer, Simone functioned as a modern-day foot cop. After three decades in the Second District, he had come to know the usual suspects, as well as their children and grandchildren. Now in his mid-fifties, Simone was performing the same duties as when he first started. Simone had been offered opportunities for promotion, but preferred to stay on the traffic detail. It was the ideal position for a zealous cop who disliked downtime and office politics.

Executing a traffic stop is a routine task, but also one of the most dangerous duties that a police officer faces. An officer approaching a vehicle, particularly at night, has no idea what awaits.

"You ask for a driver's license. Are you going to get the license or a gun?" said Ed Kovacic. "What are the people in the backseat going to do? What if the passenger reaches under the front seat? You might think he's going for a gun, but he's going for a can of Pepsi. I'm surprised that more cops don't get hurt doing traffic stops."

"The danger is that the people we stop think we know more than we do," said Simone. "Let's say we stop a driver for a broken taillight, but he may have a kilo of drugs in his car and he's just killed someone. In his mind, he thinks we know that. So he's paranoid and willing to do anything to get away."

Simone noted that routine traffic stops often result in the arrests of fugitive murderers and other criminals. Just ninety minutes after blowing up the federal building in Oklahoma City and killing 168 people, Timothy McVeigh was stopped by a state trooper for driving without a front license plate.

Early in his career, Simone and his partner stopped a former Golden Gloves boxer for a minor infraction. With two quick punches, the man knocked out Simone's partner. He then tried to take Simone's gun. Simone absorbed numerous body blows, but held onto his weapon until two officers driving by stopped and arrested the man.

Later, while acknowledging that losing his gun could have been catastrophic, he recited another of his Simone-isms: "I never run, never beg, never kneel, and never give up my weapon."

Every few years, Simone would compile videos of his most interesting arrests and car chases into a CD highlight reel of sorts. The recordings graphically reveal the daily abuse endured by traffic cops, particularly by inebriated drivers. Simone has been punched, kicked, cursed, spit at, accused of brutality and racism, and had his job and his life threatened by men and women of every occupation and age.

Despite the obscenities and insults spewed at him, Simone manages to remain unperturbed. "They aren't saying anything I haven't heard one thousand times before," he explained. Simone is a frequent instructor and speaker at police academies, where he advises new officers to emotionally detach themselves from the verbal attack. "Words cannot hurt you," he tells them. "They can curse your mother, brother, and father, but why would you get upset about that?"

He added that there's an element of artistry in handling backseat abuse. "One of my favorite methods is to turn it around on them," he said. "For example, I'll say, 'It's hard to believe that someone as smart as you is using that kind of language.'"

Tom O'Grady, who spent twenty-two years as a police officer in Lakewood, Ohio, said it's not uncommon for arrested drunk drivers to become argumentative and combative. "Usually, they are angry that they got caught," he said. "We're seeing them at their worst. They wouldn't act like that in front of anyone else but us."

Critics of strict DUI enforcement say that police and cities are more interested in generating revenue than keeping roads safe. O'Grady, however, said that such criticism is levied by those who haven't seen the casualties caused by drunk driving.

O'Grady, who trained as a paramedic, was a first responder to numerous alcohol-related car crashes. "I've had to lie on top of people who had broken necks to keep them still while rescue crews cut them out of their cars," he said.

O'Grady has also rung doorbells in the middle of the night to inform families that they lost loved ones. "It's a horrendous thing to have to wake someone up to tell them that their son or daughter has died in a car crash. Sometimes the family members became so emotionally distraught that they attacked me."

Simone said that doctors, attorneys, and other professionals would often decide to contest their drunk-driving charges in court. Arriving at their initial court hearing with their lawyer and a fictional story about

Simone's improper conduct, they were far removed from the intoxicated belligerence that had been recorded on his dash cam.

"No matter what they accused me of, the videos saved me every time," Simone said. "It's a mistaken belief that where there's smoke, there's fire. The defendants' lawyers would watch my tapes and realize they couldn't poke holes in my arrests. They didn't want a jury to see the embarrassing behavior of their clients so they would plead out instead of fighting it."

Along with capturing illegal activity, Simone's dash-cam tapes would also prove advantageous in solidifying domestic violence cases.

Noting that battered women often withdraw their complaints against their abusers, Simone said, "There are a lot of reasons why they change their stories. Most often, the batterer convinces the victim that he's sorry and the abuse will never happen again. But of course it does. The woman also realizes that if the man goes to jail, his income stops."

To ensure that victims followed through on their complaints and their abusers faced consequences, Simone would wear a microphone when he initially spoke to battered women. "Then I had them on record and she couldn't recant," he said.

In the mid-2000s, he found himself drawn into a domestic violence case after issuing a speeding citation to a young woman. "You're giving me a ticket?" she had asked. "Where were you guys when my husband was beating the hell out of me?"

Surprised, Simone questioned her about the domestic violence she'd experienced. She was initially reluctant to confide in him, saying, "It doesn't matter. My husband is a cop. The police don't help me when I file complaints against him."

Simone had no obligation to directly involve himself in her case. He could have reported it to a supervisor, who would have assigned it to an investigator. Nevertheless, Simone showed up at the bar where her husband worked part-time as a security guard.

"Hey Jimmy, what's up?" the man asked.

"Turn around and face the wall," Simone said, slipping handcuffs over his wrists.

The arrest would have serious career implications for the man. Because federal law bans access to firearms by people convicted of domestic violence, he couldn't be a police officer anymore. In a twist of irony, his wife, after divorcing him, went through the Cleveland Police Academy and became a patrol officer.

"She went on to have the career that he lost," said Simone. "There should be higher standards for us. I don't think it was too much to ask him or any other police officer to uphold the law in their personal lives."

Whether through chance or divine providence, Simone had often found himself encountering circumstances that dictated his interdiction. On three separate occasions, he had unknowingly entered banks while they were being robbed. The third occasion, July 9, 2008, ended in Simone's fifth deadly shooting.

After spending the morning in court, Simone stopped by his neighborhood bank on Memphis Avenue in Old Brooklyn to deposit his paycheck. He eschewed direct deposit and ATMs, preferring instead to banter with the tellers every two weeks. He also had a routine of picking up $10 in pennies every payday, which he split up among his grandchildren's piggybanks.

Simone, who was off duty, removed his police uniform shirt before entering the bank so that he didn't cause concern among the customers. He also removed his gun belt and cell phone, hiding them under his shirt on the front seat of his pickup truck.

He stuck his Glock 9mm service weapon in his waistband, draped his T-shirt over it, and walked into the bank through the rear exit. The tellers, who all knew Simone, knew that he showed up every two weeks to get his pennies. He was accustomed to a warm greeting.

"I got 15 feet inside and I realized that it was awfully quiet," recalled Simone. "And then I noticed that the tellers weren't smiling. I could tell by their strained facial expressions that something was wrong."

Intuiting that he had stepped into a robbery in progress, Simone scanned the teller cages and saw a male customer push a packet of bills into his pocket.

The man, perhaps following the teller's eyes, turned to look at Simone. He hurriedly grabbed a few more packets of bills off the counter and pivoted to leave.

"He was walking towards me, but I had decided that he wasn't going to get past me," Simone said. When Simone moved sideways to block his path, the robber stuck his hand in his jacket pocket and pointed the bulge at Simone, implying that it was a gun.

Simone, in turn, lifted his shirt and drew his Glock.

"Police!" he yelled.

The robber turned and ran toward the opposite door.

"There was a sensor inside the frame of the exit door," said Simone. "One of the packets of bills given to him by the teller contained a dye pack that contained a transmitter. When he ran through the door, the sensor detected the dye pack and it exploded. I could see smoke coming from his pants pocket."

Instructing the tellers to call police, Simone chased the robber through the parking lot and onto a side street. "At sixty years of age, I was jumping over the hoods of parked cars like T. J. Hooker," he said.

Suddenly, a woman driving a Jeep pulled up next to Simone. Recognizing him, she told him that the bank had just been robbed. "I know!" he yelled, "I'm chasing him."

"Hop in," said the woman, an off-duty nurse.

They followed the robber for a block until he climbed into a truck parked on a side street. The woman then did the unexpected: She screeched to a halt directly beside the robber's truck.

"God bless her for helping, but she wasn't tactically trained," said Simone. "She dumped me right in front of the guy. I had nowhere to hide in case he started shooting."

Simone jumped from the jeep and onto the running board of the truck. "Show me your hands!" he screamed.

The man gave Simone a surprised look. Ignoring several commands to freeze, he reached down toward his pants pocket. Simone—afraid that he was reaching for a gun—fired one round through the door of the truck. The bullet struck the man in his left side and went through his chest. The truck rolled forward and struck a telephone pole. Simone pulled the man from the vehicle and laid him in the street.

Identified as Robert Hackworth, thirty-five, he died before the ambulance arrived. Internal Affairs and the shooting investigation team came to the scene. Over the next several hours, they reviewed bank surveillance video and questioned Simone about his actions. They learned that Hackworth had been arrested thirty times since turning sixteen years of age. He had ten felony charges and had served prison time for theft, drug, and weapons offenses. Several of his arrests involved failure to comply with police orders.

On the morning of the shooting, Hackworth had stolen the truck from an auto dealership on the pretext of taking it for a test drive. Investigators were unable to find a gun in Hackworth's pocket or in the truck. They theorized that when Simone saw Hackworth reach toward his pants, he may have been reaching into his pocket to pull out the dye pack that had exploded and was undoubtedly burning his skin.

Hackworth's long criminal record and his feigned use of a gun during the bank robbery didn't mitigate Simone's sorrow over his death.

"I felt bad for his family," he said.

Unfortunately, he created the scenario that caused his own death. If he would have raised his hands when he was told, there wouldn't have been a shooting. When I walked in on two previous bank robberies, I was able to arrest both guys without a problem. But Hackworth fooled the tellers into thinking he had a gun. And he baited me into shooting him. He made a lot of bad decisions that day and he paid for it with his life. But that didn't change the fact that I felt very bad about what had happened.

In the minutes after the shooting, Simone's blood pressure skyrocketed. The Second District commander at the time, Keith Sulzer, encouraged him to go to the hospital, but Simone stayed on the scene and helped investigators gather data for their report.

"Other cops asked why I had to shoot him," Simone recalled. "They said it was 'just money.' That was upsetting to me because I believed he had a gun. Internal Affairs asked me why I didn't just walk away from the situation. What would it have looked like if I walked away? Was I supposed to call 911? I'm a cop—I *am* 911."

That night, Hackworth's girlfriend, who had recently given birth to his baby, told TV reporters that he had been turning his life around, that he was getting his GED, and that they planned to marry.

"Did that cop really need to kill him over money?" she asked tearfully. Three weeks later, she herself was dead of a heroin overdose.

Internal Affairs and the police shooting team cleared Simone of wrongdoing. Legally, Simone seemed to be within his rights. According to the so-called fleeing felon rule, U.S. courts have ruled it acceptable for police officers to use deadly force against a fleeing suspect who poses a significant threat to the officer or others.

Cleveland's prosecutor, Victor Perez, however, declined to rule the Hackworth shooting justifiable, leading to speculation that he would be sending the case to the Cuyahoga County grand jury.

Several weeks after the shooting, Perez encountered Simone in the Justice Center. "You used bad tactics," he told him.

Simone, in reply, said, "I don't remember you being there."

On February 18, 2009, Perez announced to Cleveland's news media that he was sending the Hackworth case to the grand jury. Simone was now facing the possibility of a felony indictment and an ignominious end to his thirty-six-year career.

20 Regina's Ride-along

Cleveland police officer Jim Simone has an alarming record of killing people. If anyone else gunned down five people, we'd call him a serial killer. Folks are calling Simone a supercop. If only they knew what that truly is. . . .

So began *Plain Dealer* columnist Regina Brett in a piece published a week after Simone shot Robert Hackworth.

Brett, who had never met Simone and didn't attempt to interview him about the circumstances of his shootings, wrote:

[S]ome worry that he's a trigger-happy cop out of control.

Which is he: Cleveland's Dirty Harry or our Jack Kevorkian? . . .

Killing five suspects doesn't mean he's a great cop.

It means he's a good aim.

Just because you can fire your service revolver doesn't mean you should. Most cops don't and never will in their entire careers.

Those are the true supercops—the men and women who rely on their wit and wisdom more than their 9 millimeters. . . .

They don't hand out death sentences. That's not their job. They issue citations. . . .

They scoop up children whose bodies and spirits have been crushed by abusive parents.

They rescue women from rapists, drivers from burning vehicles, seniors from scam artists.

They save people perched on the brink of despair and risk life and limb to pull them back, to give them hope. . . .

The real supercops never fire their guns, or if they must, decline to talk about it. . . .

They remain unnamed and unknown except to fellow officers. You rarely see them named in the news, unless they make the ultimate sacrifice. . . .

Brett called for an independent inquiry of Simone, arguing that a review of the Hackworth shooting by Cleveland detectives wouldn't be adequate. In her words, "We need something more. We need another eye on Simone. We need a citizen review board and an investigation by law enforcement officers outside of Cleveland."

Brett, however, had misgauged Clevelanders' sentiment toward Simone. Within hours of the column's publication, Simone's supporters deluged Brett and the *Plain Dealer* with angry phone calls, e-mails, online posts, and threats of cancelled subscriptions.

In a follow-up column, Brett acknowledged the pro-Simone backlash, stating: "As you might have guessed, hundreds have bombarded me with calls and e-mails. I stopped counting at 500."

About two-thirds of readers disagreed with her scathing commentary, she admitted. Many said she was ill-informed about police procedure and some demanded that she apologize to Simone. One reader wrote: "Regina Brett, you should be ashamed of this column. I'd like to see you approach a vehicle without knowledge of who is in the car, what weapon they are carrying and make a decision of life and death in a second. That's all it takes."

Another noted that Brett was too quick to judge the actions of an inner-city police officer from the relative safety of her suburban home. "Walk a little bit in someone else's shoes before writing," the reader counseled.

While taking a conciliatory tone in her rollback, Brett didn't fully capitulate to the pro-Simone camp. As she put it, "Of the dozens of readers who said they know Simone, half said he's the world's hardest-working cop; the other half said he is a brute and a bully. Many readers thanked me for the column. Blacks, in particular, said they are too familiar with cops who abuse their power."

Brett's original column even spurred a rebuttal of sorts from a colleague, *Plain Dealer* columnist Phillip Morris. He wrote: "There are some who wonder why Cleveland police officer Jim Simone, who has killed more civilians than possibly any officer in the city's history, is being hailed as a hero in some quarters. The answer is really quite simple. He is a hero."

As a community, we can't have things both ways, stated Morris, telling readers: "We can't continue to handcuff police officers and then expect them to perform safety miracles in a dangerous, crumbling city. We can't eviscerate the thug culture that greases Greater Cleveland's slide into chaos and then decry an officer like Jim Simone, who has continuously drawn a courageous line against crime."

Noting that Simone has consistently evidenced a willingness to die in service of a dying city, Morris wrote: "So now this is the thanks he gets for stopping a resistant bank robber. He is denigrated as a serial murderer and a bully. It would seem a bit more fitting, however, that we recognize his valor and thank him for his proven willingness to make the ultimate sacrifice."

Simone, meanwhile, was stung by Brett's column. "I walked into the Justice Center and everybody was walking up to me and telling me that she had called me a serial killer with a badge," he said. "I have kids and grandkids. What are they going to think? These newspaper columnists live in suburbia. They have no idea what life is like in the 'hood, where there's gunfire every night."

Simone contemplated suing Brett for defaming him, but instead telephoned her. He told her that he agreed with her right to criticize him. "But I wish I'd had the opportunity to talk to you earlier," he said. "I've saved thousands of lives in my career. No one remembers the ones I *didn't* shoot. There are probably one thousand times I took the other route."

Simone told Brett that when Hackworth reached down as if to draw a weapon, he had a split-second to make a decision on the use of force. "I never thought that I *shouldn't* chase him. This is a bank robber. It wasn't the money that got him killed. I thought he was armed. If you put me in jeopardy, whether that jeopardy is real or imagined, I have to defend myself."

They concluded their conversation with Simone inviting Brett to ride with him. "See what the police really do," he said.

In mid-September, the City of Cleveland cleared Simone to return to work, although his case was still scheduled to be heard by the grand jury.

Brett heard that he was back on the road and phoned him to arrange her ride-along. Not missing an opportunity to inject anticipatory drama, she told readers that the city would require her to wear a bulletproof vest and be covered by at least $1 million of liability insurance.

"My friends and family think I'm crazy," she wrote. "They keep ask-ing, 'You sure you want to do this?' No, but I'm going to."

In the first of two columns about her ride-along, she described her initial encounter with Simone:

> Officer Simone greets me at the door, scans me up and down.
>
> "You're taller than I expected," he says. . . .
>
> He's 60, short, but solid muscle tucked into navy cargo pants, black boots and a shiny black shirt. He has dark brown eyes, closely cropped, gray spiky hair and Bruce Willis' nose and tough-guy demeanor.
>
> He hands me a fistful of blue gloves and a hand cleaner. He gives me the extra set of keys to the squad car—"In case anything happens to me," he says.
>
> Is he joking? I look at the keys. The gold metal tag reads SIMONE. He's serious. Dead serious. I clip them to my belt loop. My heart beats so fast my bulletproof vest is doing pushups. . . .
>
> He straps on his vest plus 16 pounds of handcuffs, pepper spray, ammo, Taser, radio, steel pipe, flashlight and gun.
>
> We walk to Car 266. He checks the trunk. Crime scene tape, stuffed toys for kids, blankets to cover the dead.

Riding with Simone from 7 P.M. to 3 A.M., Brett listened to his stories ("enough to fill a book," she noted) and recorded her observations as he chatted with citizens, made several arrests, and conducted a handful of traffic stops.

In her October 7, 2008, column, which she titled, "The night I wore a bulletproof vest," she wrote:

> **7:47 p.m.**
>
> Jim . . . runs plates on a red GMC truck. *License suspended.* He pulls it over and taps on the window. "Anything on you that could hurt me, a knife, a gun?" he asks.
>
> Jim takes the keys and pats him down. "By any stretch of the imagina-tion do you have insurance?" No. "So what happens if you hit someone? What happens to them?"
>
> He tells the guy he could put him in jail but won't.
>
> "You're getting a ticket. I'm getting the car. If you have the misfortune of meeting me again, you will go to jail. Start walking." . . .

1:17 a.m.

The radio crackles: *Stabbing. Victim at hospital. Suspect at house.* We fly to West 41st. Jim hops out of the cruiser with gun drawn. Three other cops join him. He and one officer run up the dark side of the house. Two officers run up the porch steps.

"On your knees!" Jim screams. The suspect drops. "We got the stabber!" Jim yells. . . .

At the end of Brett's seemingly transformative night, she had asked Simone what he was feeling when he drew his gun at the West 41st stabbing scene.

"You gotta control the fear," Jim says.

How do you control it?

"By belief in what you do. The belief I'm gonna win. I expect I'll survive," he says. "My obligation to the public should override the fear. See, even if I don't like you, I have to be willing to exchange my life for yours."

Just four months later, Simone would, in fact, risk his life to save another's. On the night of January 10, 2009, twenty-six-year-old Kelly Bane and her younger sister, Kara, were drinking at a bar in Cleveland's Flats.

At 11:45 P.M., the women left the bar and began walking to Kelly's apartment on East Ninth Street about a mile away. As they made their way toward a bridge to cross the Cuyahoga River, Kara realized that her sister was floundering in the frigid water. Unable to reach her from the riverbank, which was 8 feet above the water, Kara used her cell phone to dial 911.

Simone, who was writing traffic tickets on Fulton Avenue, heard the call on the police radio. He told dispatchers that he had rescue gear in his cruiser, including 200 feet of rope. He arrived on the scene and joined a half-dozen other officers who had begun rescue attempts. The officers had found a life-preserver ring on the banks of the river and were lowering it to Kelly, who was desperately flapping her arms.

"She grabbed the device, but her hands were so cold that she was unable to close her fingers around it," Simone said. "So she hooked her arm in the ring."

The officers pulled her from the water, but she lost her grip and fell back into the river, disappearing below the surface. The officers tried once more, but Kelly again lost her grip on the ring and dropped into the water.

"Each time she fell she went below the ice line," said Simone. "I was afraid that she was going to come up in a different spot. She had been in the water for fifteen minutes. It was obvious that she was hypothermic and was not going to be able to hold out much longer."

At that, Simone, who was sixty-one and had a history of heart problems, began removing his shirt.

"What are you doing?" a sergeant asked him.

Simone explained that he'd been in SWAT and had been trained in rappelling. The sergeant agreed to let Simone attempt the rescue. He quickly pulled off his body armor, gun belt, radio, and Taser. He then stepped into his rappelling harness and was lowered near Kelly, who was clearly in distress. Simone reached out to her, but she was unable to lift her arms and began sinking.

Simone had no choice now but to jump into the water ("It was astoundingly cold," he recalled). He grabbed Kelly by her belt and jeans and helped her hook her elbow into the life ring to keep her head up above the water. A firefighter in a dry suit then entered the river and helped lift her to safety.

"At that point, I was so cold that I was unable to move," said Simone. "My legs went numb. I was in the water for five minutes and I couldn't bend my fingers. They were frozen solid. I called out for help and the firefighters pulled me out."

Kelly and Simone were both taken to MetroHealth Medical Center and treated for hypothermia. Kara Bane told police that she didn't know how her sister ended up in the water, but officers theorized that Kelly may have tried to walk across the frozen river as a shortcut home.

"I don't think she realized that ice near the riverbank is always thinner because of the warmth of the land," Simone said.

Just before his hospital discharge, Kelly visited Simone. They exchanged introductions and then she asked, "Do you know me?"

"No," replied Simone, surprised by the question.

"Then why would you risk your life for me?"

Simone explained that he couldn't allow himself to watch her die. "What would I tell your parents?" he told her. "I have a family myself. I would never throw my life away, but I would gladly exchange it for yours."

She nodded and left his room. "I don't think she got it," Simone said. "But it doesn't matter. If we took this job to be appreciated, we would be so disappointed."

Simone's river rescue occasioned another column from Regina Brett, who wrote:

Even heroes need help.

Cleveland police officer Jim Simone has finally thawed out enough to talk about the heroes who saved him. . . .

Simone and I are buds. Last year, I blasted him for killing five suspects in his 30-year career as a cop. Then I rode with him one Saturday from 7 P.M. to 3 A.M. Since then, we've grown to like and respect each other.

When I heard that a cop jumped into the icy Cuyahoga River over the weekend to save a drowning woman in the Flats, I knew it was Simone. When I called him, he wanted to talk about the EMS workers, police and firefighters who helped save him and the woman.

Each of Brett's columns about Simone generated hundreds of reader comments on Cleveland.com, the online affiliate of the *Plain Dealer*. Many of the posters were generous in their praise of both Simone and Brett. Others, cloaked in anonymity and competing for distinctiveness, took exaggerated positions in their criticism, particularly of Simone, whom they labeled sociopathic, corrupt, and reckless.

To Simone, it seemed that he was taking shots from every individual he'd ever ticketed. Whether the online commenters truly had personal involvement with Simone or were indulging in confirmation bias, they were free to fabricate lies and publicly disparage his character with no obligation to substantiate their claims.

In February 2009, Brett would write her sixth column about Simone, this time addressing the possibility that he could be indicted by the grand jury for the Hackworth shooting.

Conceding that her ride-along with Simone had "opened her eyes," Brett wrote:

Is Simone a brute? A bully? A tyrant who abuses his power? Sometimes.

Is Simone a hero? A guardian angel who possesses superhuman power? Sometimes.

There's a fine line that separates the two. Simone walks on both sides of it—sometimes during the same shift. . . .

Let's hope the grand jury comes back with no charges for Simone's sake and for ours—and for every police officer on duty who straddles that fine line.

They patrol a black and white world of good guys and bad guys, where cops have to choose fast if they want to come home alive.

Brett seemed to be hedging her grand jury bet, but she had neverthe-less undergone an undeniable conversion in her view of Simone. Six months earlier, she had likened Simone to a serial killer and called for him to be investigated. Now, she was essentially appealing to the grand jury to find no criminality in his shooting of Hackworth.

Some Cleveland journalists, however, were not so inclined to absolve Simone of wrongdoing. Mansfield Frazier, an activist and writer who has contributed to the *Daily Beast*, questioned how any police officer could be involved in a dozen shootings and still be on active duty.

"If you're a pretty good cop, you never have to fire your gun," said Frazier.

> If you're a real good cop, you never even have to pull it. Nobody's luck could be so bad that he's involved in that many shootings. I think Simone was looking for opportunities to pull his gun. There is always a lesser way of handling deadly force situations—wait for backup, lob in tear gas, use a Taser, try other non-lethal tactics. After a couple of shootings, someone in police headquarters should have said, "This guy is bad news. Maybe we need to put him where he can't hurt anyone."

Frazier discounted Simone's life-saving heroics, saying his courage is born of recklessness.

> Did he save lives? Yes. Like a boxer who doesn't duck anyone, Simone is fearless. He's fearlessly foolish—a junkie for excitement. He does not value life, even his own. Who would jump in a freezing river or run into a burning building? Simone would jump in front of a moving train to save someone. But he thinks that because he puts his life on the line, he can do that with other people's lives.

Comparing Simone to Wyatt Earp, John Wayne, and Dirty Harry, Frazier said he fits squarely within the "American zeitgeist" of a stolid lawman exacting extralegal justice through violence. Simone conforms to the pattern of law enforcement behavior that is considered justifiable, conceded Frazier, adding, "He just does it more often than other cops."

Frazier does not personally know Simone, but is familiar with his Vietnam service. He theorized that Simone may have been indelibly impacted by his combat experiences.

"If you see that kind of death up close, it imprints on you," he said. "He may have been psychologically damaged from Vietnam. That's the type of person who should be screened out from police departments. But they saw him as a tough guy. And Americans love their tough guys."

Frazier, who is black, acknowledged Simone's consistency. "The positive about Simone is that he's not a racist," he noted, with broad-stroke cynicism. "He's the furthest thing from a racist. He gets points for applying the law equally. He's a prick to everyone."

On March 5, 2009, the Cuyahoga County grand jury convened to determine whether Simone should face charges for shooting Robert Hackworth. Against the advice of his attorney, Robert Ducatman, Simone took the rare step of voluntarily testifying before the grand jury. Attorneys generally don't like their clients to testify because their statements can be used against them if criminal charges are filed.

"I had nothing to hide," Simone said. "The prosecutor asked me if I was sure that I wanted to testify. I said I was absolutely sure. I'd done nothing wrong. Besides, who could tell the story of what happened better than me?"

Simone's straightforward, direct manner was viewed favorably by the grand jury, which declined to issue charges against him.

Following Simone's grand jury appearance, Ducatman said it was "worthwhile" for him to testify. "And I believe that it was the testimony of an honest policeman that helped to exonerate him," he said.

Ducatman, a partner with the Jones Day law firm in Cleveland, credited Simone's "impeccable" character, saying, "There was no basis to indict Simone. There was no probable cause. Police officers are sometimes maligned and considered trigger-happy. We always read about the bad events. But you don't hear about the thousands of officers who protect and serve every day. Jim Simone is one of them."

Police officers and citizens cheered in the Justice Center when they heard that Simone had been cleared. "I had so many people stopping me to shake my hand that I couldn't get to work," Simone said.

Ed Gallek, a veteran TV newsman in Cleveland, was not surprised that Simone had elected to speak to the grand jury.

"It's part of Jimmy's character to be forthcoming and sure of himself," said Gallek, a reporter with WJW, a Fox affiliate. "In his heart of hearts, he always felt that he did the right thing and he had a reason for what he did. Simone was never afraid to explain his actions, whether to the media or his superiors. He felt that if he was going to be questioned, he wanted to man up and deal with it. He knew that he would be able to defend himself best in his own words."

On patrol, Simone admittedly presented an intimidating figure. "My mouth would get me into trouble," he said. "I'd tell suspects things like, 'If you move, your birth certificate will be a worthless piece of paper.' But those first few seconds of interaction with a bad guy are critical. If they think they can intimidate you, they will. On the streets, it's important to speak the language of the lion, not the mouse."

That bravado rubbed some people the wrong way, Gallek said. "Some saw him as cocky. Jimmy just sees it as self-confidence. It's his nature to go towards danger, not away from it. I think the reason that he was involved in so many shootings is because he considers it his duty to confront danger."

Gallek is not a fan of Simone's Supercop nickname. "Jimmy stands out as a police officer, but whoever named him Supercop minimized the hard work of other officers who also risk their lives regularly," he said.

Nevertheless, said Gallek, "When you come home late at night and your security alarm is going off. Your front door is open and you don't want to go in the house. Who do you want with you? It's going to be Jim Simone. At its base level, what's so bad about that?"

Throughout 2009, Simone collected a dozen plaques, medallions, and commendations for his part in rescuing Kelly Bane. *PARADE* magazine, in conjunction with the International Association of Chiefs of Police, named him one of America's top police officers. He was honored by national women's organizations and the U.S. Congress.

At a Cleveland City Council meeting, he was presented with a dry suit. Simone downplayed his heroics, saying, "I don't consider myself a hero. Any one of the police officers on the scene would have gone in after her. I was just the first."

In January 2010, he was named Cleveland's Patrol Officer of the Year. He had received the same award in 1980, and is the only multiple recipient in the city's history.

Less than a month after his grand jury appearance, Simone responded to reports of a man sitting on a bridge railing 100 feet above a roadway. He parked his car on the shoulder and edged to within a few feet of the man.

"If you jump, you're going to be hurting my family," Simone told him.

"How's that?" the man asked.

"Because I'm going to grab you and probably get pulled off this bridge with you," Simone said. "My kids and grandkids are going to be very sad that I'm gone."

The man considered Simone's words for a moment, then backed away from the railing.

21   **Terms of Retirement**

In January 1973, on Jim Simone's employment application for the Cleveland Police, he wrote: "I believe being a Cleveland Patrolman would be a rewarding and interesting occupation."

For thirty-eight years, it had been every bit of that. On March 21, 2011, his sixty-third birthday, the time had come to hang up badge 387.

Although Simone wasn't ready to join the civilian world, Ohio's pension regulations required him to take his retirement.

"God's been good to me—he's spared my life so many times," he told the *Plain Dealer*. "It's time to retire and on my terms. I've had a great career. If they knew how much fun I had, they would have made me pay them."

Simone had happily spent the majority of his career as a patrol officer, continually declining opportunities for promotion.

"Just because you're the best salesman doesn't mean you'd make the best sales manager," he explained. "I'd be a terrible boss. My expectations are high, and not everyone would work as hard as I do, so I'd be miserable as a supervisor."

It's probable that Simone's five lethal shootings will constitute a significant part of his legacy, but he said he would prefer to "dwell on the many lives he saved by arresting drunk drivers who are potential killers behind a wheel, or talking people from jumping from bridges, or performing rescues when the opportunities arose."

Rabbi Sruly Wolf, a chaplain with the Cleveland Police since 1972, spent many hours in Simone's cruiser on ride-alongs. Describing him as a workaholic who didn't take breaks, Wolf said, "Jim would respond to every call. He was always in the right place at the wrong time. I believe in my heart that Simone only fired his weapon when he felt he had no other option."

He added that he was present at several threatening situations in which Simone managed to disarm men who were brandishing guns and knives.

"In those situations, I myself might have shot," said Wolf, who has attended police academy and worked in law enforcement.

Wolf said it seemed that most cops, at their retirement, are forgotten the minute they walk out of the police station. "Simone, however, will long be remembered by the storeowners and the residents on his beat. They loved him. He looked out for them and they appreciated that."

Simone's retirement party attracted more than six hundred people, including many Second District residents, who thanked him for keeping their neighborhoods safe.

He took his turn at the microphone, but managed only a few sentences before choking up. "I'm the son of Anthony Angelo Simone . . . My father is very proud of me today," he told the crowd.

Predictably, Simone's retirement didn't last long. He missed the excitement and busyness of police work.

"Besides that," he said, "I knew there was a shelf life on police officers. When they retire, they sit at home waiting for the angel of death."

Simone took a position as a part-time patrol officer in Grand River, a village of 398 in Lake County, Ohio. The community's slow pace of life and paucity of offenders contrasted sharply with his Second District beat, which perennially had one of the nation's highest violent crime rates.

However, as in Cleveland, a great many of Grand River's offenses involved substance abuse. "If it wasn't for drugs and alcohol, I would have never had a career," he said.

In a July 11, 2012, *Plain Dealer* column, Phillip Morris asked Simone about his transition to small-town policing. "'It's like working in Mayberry without Otis,' Simone quipped. 'People here smile and wave at you using all of their fingers, not just the one in the middle.'"

Michael Jenovic, also a part-time Grand River police officer, said Simone's hiring was controversial because he was viewed as a "hot potato" by some of the village's residents.

"But it's a learning experience to patrol with Jimmy," said Jenovic. "He shares a lot of knowledge with the younger officers. He's a great cop and he's compassionate, although not always politically correct."

In his first few weeks on the job, Simone was gently reproached by a female officer after he had used salty language on an intoxicated man who was disruptive in a restaurant. "We don't talk to people like that here," she told Simone. "It's different than being in Cleveland."

"They don't make many cops like Simone anymore," wrote Morris in his column. "Perhaps that's a good thing. It's difficult to be a crime-fighting maverick in a culture of hyper-conformity, political correctness and systemic laziness."

Simone lamented the decline of old-school policing, telling Morris:

> I'd rather smack a kid in the back of his head or carefully get the attention of a disorderly than slap them with a felony arrest that may follow them and ruin their lives. But we're not allowed to do that anymore.
>
> Police work has changed. Politicians run the department. We're not allowed to use the fear of heavy-handed policing to try and influence behavior.

Simone's observation is worth understanding, said Morris, writing: "Does nonlethal, extra-judicial punishment lead to a more just and orderly society? That's an untested thesis. But perhaps stronger policing once created an alternative to needless felonies: Deal with the long arm of the law on the streets rather than in the courts."

Simone took an additional part-time patrol job in Sheffield Lake, where police chief Tony Campo said he was pleased to have an officer with thirty-eight years of police experience. But he added that the upscale town of nine thousand residents required a different type of policing than the urban environment that Simone had been accustomed to.

Agreeing with Campo, Simone said,

> I'm still protecting and serving, but the emphasis is now on "serve." The residents here have money and a position of importance, imagined or real. They like their cops kinder and gentler. I miss the adrenaline rush of speeding from one crime scene to another when I was in Cleveland. Out here, they call us if their power goes out or they need their flat tire changed. There is crime here, but it's a smaller scale. In suburbia, people are in bed by 11 P.M. In Cleveland, at that hour, they are going out for their second pass.

Four decades of fighting crime have damaged his body and left him in chronic pain. He's suffered multiple heart attacks. His hips and knees hurt from car accidents, too many parachute jumps, and from running too many miles. The 1983 church shooting permanently affected his hearing and facial nerves. His back aches, he has arthritis, and both rotator cuffs are torn.

"I can only hit someone with an uppercut now," he said, cracking a rare smile. "My shoulders hurt too much to throw an overhand punch."

Simone's departure from the Cleveland Police was providential in its timing. Over the next three years, Cleveland officers would be involved in several deadly force incidents that would thrust the city into the national spotlight.

On November 29, 2012, Timothy Russell and Malissa Williams, a homeless couple who had met at a shelter, were driving through an area of Cleveland notorious for drug sales. A police officer observed Russell commit a traffic violation and tried to pull him over. But Russell sped away, driving past two police officers standing outside the Cuyahoga County Justice Center. The officers heard a loud bang that they believed was a gunshot from Russell's car.

The two officers reported that they were fired upon, triggering a twenty-minute chase that exceeded speeds of 120 mph and involved up to sixty-two police cars and one hundred officers from three cities, as well as the Cuyahoga Sheriff's department and the Ohio State Highway Patrol. During the 22-mile pursuit, Russell ignored more than one hundred stop signs and red lights.

Eventually, police trapped Russell's 1979 Chevy Malibu in a school parking lot in East Cleveland. Officers surrounded the vehicle, with several screaming that they saw one of the occupants holding a gun. Others believed that Russell was attempting to run them over. One officer opened fire and others joined. Later they'd tell investigators that they believed that someone inside the car had fired at them.

At least 137 shots were fired into the car by a dozen police officers. Russell, forty-three, was hit by twenty-three bullets, while Wilson, thirty, was struck twenty-four times. The couple, who were both black, died at the scene. No gun was found in the car. Investigators concluded that the sound of gunshots heard outside the Justice Center was backfiring from the Malibu's exhaust system.

Five Cleveland police supervisors were charged with misdemeanors for their oversight of the case, while one officer, Michael Brelo, was charged with two counts of manslaughter. Brelo shot forty-nine times at the car, continuing to shoot after most other officers stopped. At one point, he jumped on the hood of the Malibu and shot directly into the car.

"I've never been so afraid in my life," Brelo told investigators after the shooting. "I thought my partner and I would be shot and that we were going to be killed."

In May 2015, a Cuyahoga County judge acquitted Brelo, saying that while he did fire lethal shots at the victims, other officers did also. Judge John P. O'Donnell concluded that Brelo was legally justified in his use of deadly force because he and other officers believed that Russell and Williams had a gun and had fired shots.

The judge's verdict sparked protests in Cleveland that resulted in more than seventy arrests. Many in the black community—already angered by the August 2014 Michael Brown shooting in Ferguson, Missouri—believed that the acquittal of Brelo, who is white, had racial overtones. Even before Brelo's trial, the City of Cleveland paid a total of $3 million to the families of Russell and Williams to settle a federal civil rights lawsuit.

Two years later, on November 22, 2014, a white Cleveland police officer shot and killed a black youth, twelve-year-old Tamir Rice, after responding to reports of a person waving a gun outside a recreation center on the city's West Side.

Tamir had been sitting on a table holding an Airsoft-type replica pistol. The gun's orange tip, a safety feature required by federal law to indicate the gun is fake, had been removed. Surveillance videotape showed that a patrol car driven by officer Frank Garmback pulled directly in front of the 5-foot 7-inch, 195-pound Tamir, who had placed the gun in his waistband. Officer Timothy Loehmann jumped from the passenger seat and almost immediately shot Tamir.

Loehmann, who had joined the Cleveland Police just seven months earlier, told investigators that he fired because he believed Tamir was reaching for his gun.

The death of Tamir Rice led to a week of demonstrations in Cleveland and added fire to the national Black Lives Matter movement, which has called for prosecutors to bring charges against Loehmann.

Asked to deconstruct the shootings of Russell, Williams, and Tamir Rice, Simone said the incidents, like nearly all deadly force scenarios, were the culmination of a series of unfortunate actions by the victims and sometimes the police.

Simone has listened to the police tapes of the Russell-Williams chase. The pursuit itself was warranted, he said, explaining, "If I think you have a gun, I'm going to chase you until I run out of gas or I burn the tires off my car or I catch you."

He said, however, that he would have attempted to "terminate the thing" as quickly as possible using a PIT (precision immobilization technique) maneuver in which a police car taps the rear of a suspect's car, causing it to turn abruptly and stop. Because the pursuit went on for as long as it did, he said, the officers became increasingly adrenalized and angry at the suspects, whose reckless driving was putting civilians at risk as well as the police.

> In a high-speed pursuit, the longer the suspects run, the more you want them. You develop tunnel vision. And, in the officers' minds, there was no doubt that Russell and Williams had a gun because they had been told that they did. Brelo's tactics may have been askew, but his adrenaline had been running for twenty-five minutes. He reacted to what he believed. Unfortunately, everybody responds differently to stress and fear.

Noting that fear spreads "like wildfire," Simone said it's not uncommon for cops to follow suit when one starts firing.

> We're all policemen. If someone else shoots, I'm shooting also. When you have a situation where multiple cops are firing their guns, it can seem like overkill to the public and the media. But the bottom line is that people oftentimes take actions that precipitate their deaths. If you don't want to be hurt, don't put yourself in a position to be hurt. No cop wants to be involved in a deadly force situation. Russell and Williams should have stopped their car when they were told. Every Sunday in every church, the pastor should be telling parishioners to comply with the police.

Shortly after the Tamir Rice shooting, Simone analyzed the incident for a Cleveland TV station. He attributed the shooting, in part, to bad communications and unfortunate proximity.

Because 99 percent of suspects run when police arrive, the officers assumed that Tamir would also, he said, explaining that it's standard procedure to pull up close in order to block someone from escaping. "But in this case, he didn't run," Simone said.

When the officers sped toward Tamir, their car slid on the snowy grass. "The vehicle stopped right in front of Tamir, putting Loehmann dead in the line of fire."

When seen through the lens of hindsight, the public and media may perceive Loehmann as the killer of an unarmed boy.

But Simone said it's likely that Loehmann, a rookie officer, was truly afraid. That's evidenced by the fact that both officers ran behind their cruiser after the shooting, he said. "These policemen were responding to an assignment of a male with a gun. And they have that male with a gun. After the shot, they were seeking cover in case the shot didn't stop him."

He noted that critical mistakes were made by the police dispatcher. The 911 caller who initially reported that a male was scaring people with his gun also said that he was "probably a kid" and that the gun was "probably fake." But that information was never relayed to the responding officers. After the shooting, the dispatcher refused to tell investigators why she didn't provide the information. She then resigned from her job.

It would be unrealistic to expect an officer to instantly discern whether a gun is real or fake, or loaded or unloaded, said former police officer Peter Moskos.

"In the Tamir Rice case, the gun turned out to be fake, but I wouldn't have been willing to roll the dice and bet that it wasn't real," Moskos said. "It's a tragedy for everyone. It's almost a cliché to say this, but cops don't go out trying to kill someone. Even a justifiable shooting is not good for a police officer."

When faced with a deadly situation, every cop hopes that they'll do the right thing, said Simone. "But every incident is different and every person reacts differently to fear. Unless you've been in a situation where you truly believed that your life could be over in a couple of seconds, then you don't know how you're going to react."

Despite what Hollywood depicts, said Simone, suspects do not automatically drop their weapons when police tell them to.

"In real life, a deadly force incident happens very, very quickly," he said. "And in circumstances that are chaotic and confusing. When you're out on the streets, you only have a fraction of a second to make a decision that will stay with you the rest of your life. Or maybe die if you're wrong."

Ed Gallek, who has spent two decades reporting on crime, has seen firsthand the emotional aftermath of a police shooting.

"At the scene, you see the human element of the officers who were intimately involved," he said. "You see them genuinely upset. And you see other officers at the scene scrambling to figure out what happened."

In comparison to the number of arrests made each year by Cleveland's police, Gallek said the cases of misconduct constitute a very small percentage. "Whenever the cops put a hand on someone, there's a news conference and attorneys involved. But when two young teens shoot each other, virtually no one says a word or blinks an eye. Where are the protests over that? Police complain that people are killing each other in the streets a lot more often than cops are involved in use of force incidents, but nobody seems to get upset about it."

Simone said that deadly force incidents very often become media events and then racial scenarios.

"It's not about color until the media makes it about color," he said. "It's too easy to blame it on race. When I shot Robert Hackworth, the Reverend Al Sharpton put in a request for my personnel file. When he found out that Hackworth was white, he dropped the request."

Moskos agreed that the media has a role in ascribing racial motivations to police shootings. "I think the media has a lot to do with promoting the perceived national epidemic of cops shooting blacks," he said. "But there is no real data to show that cops are gunning for minorities. If you want to reduce cops shooting black people, you have to reduce cops shooting any people. To say that cops are targeting blacks is a red herring. People may think that cops don't use deadly force against white people, but they do."

Because the stakes are so high in the criminal justice system, police are particularly susceptible to criticism and second-guessing by journalists and commentators, said Kathleen Sutula, a Cuyahoga County Common Pleas judge.

Noting that society today is highly influenced by agenda-driven mainstream media, Sutula said, "It's very easy for a deskbound writer who lives in suburbia to second-guess cops. It sells papers and they don't even have to be right. To me, it seems unfair because the second-guessers typically have no experience in law enforcement. So they are the least qualified to second-guess, but they are the most heard."

In Simone's view, the media has used its influence to turn the profession of policing into a war of "us versus them." One of the problems of being a cop, he said, is that "people don't really want us to act like policemen. Everyone wants the law enforced except when it's against them. And then when one cop does something bad, the whole department gets dumped on. People see the badge, not the badge number."

Certainly there are officers who shouldn't be on the street, said Simone, either because they are lazy or afraid.

"Unfortunately, there are no perfect policemen, but if an officer can't be the person he promised to be when he took the badge and gun, then he needs to find a different line of work."

A proponent of dash cams and body cams, Simone said all police should be recording their activities.

"First off, let's document everything we do," he said. "We need more accountability. Let's put cameras in every car and on every cop. It never bothered me when people were using their phones to record me. I had a camera in my car because I wanted everyone to know what I was doing eight hours a day."

While it may not be feasible for cash-strapped big cities to expand their police departments, Simone said he'd like to see a larger police presence in high-crime areas. At the very least, he suggested, readjust staffing so that more cops are on streets at night when crimes typically occur, rather than in the office during the daytime.

"In general, we need more cops and better-trained cops," he said. "And we need to spend more time being professional police officers."

Simone said the best cops are those who want to be a part of the community that they patrol.

> I don't want cops who are going to run out to their homes in suburbia and then come back each day like an invading army. I think you're a better police officer if you're a part of the community. It builds trust among residents when cops interact with the people they are responsible for policing. I was never afraid to live in the Second District. I've sometimes heard cops say to Cleveland residents, "If you don't like the crime in the city, then move out." I disagree with that perspective. It's our job to make their neighborhoods safer.

Would he like to see one hundred Jim Simones working the streets?

"No," he replied, "there wouldn't be enough jail space for all the people they'd arrest."

Attorney Daniel Chaplin represented Edward Henderson, who was beaten by Cleveland police in 2011 after a pursuit. Henderson had stopped his van during the pursuit and surrendered to police by lying face down with his arms outstretched. After he was cuffed, officers kicked him in the head several times. He suffered a fracture of his eye socket and permanent vision impairment. The attack was captured on video by a police helicopter overhead.

No charges were brought against the involved officers because none would tell investigators how Henderson had received his injuries. The City of Cleveland paid $600,000 in a lawsuit settlement to Henderson, who had a history of mental illness.

Chaplin said the Henderson case and the Russell-Williams shootings are indicative that the Cleveland Police have systemic issues regarding discipline, crisis training, and use of force.

"On the night of the Russell and Williams chase, sixty-two police cars were involved, which is more than a third of the Cleveland police force that was on duty," said Chaplin. "At the time, there had been a general police directive that only two cars should be involved. So when a third of your police force goes rogue, the man responsible is the man on top. The police chief should have been sacked the next day. But instead he was promoted to safety director."

Within the rank and file, said Chaplin, a good cop will always be reluctant to out a bad cop. "Every good cop out there knows they themselves are human and subject to emotion and can make mistakes," he said.

Good cops can see themselves in that bad cop's shoes if things suddenly spin out of control. That's why good cops support bad cops in a union setting. That's Jim Simone's dilemma with other cops. If he catches a cop or a cop's kid driving drunk, that's a no-brainer arrest for him. But if a cop is all amped up and discharging his weapon into a car numerous times, it depends how easily Simone can imagine himself in that situation. Sadly, not all cops get training in de-escalation. But Simone received a lot of training from his mother in good sense and going to church and when you need to amp up and then bring things down. Military experience also helped him to handle pressure.

Because Simone didn't automatically do favors for other cops, he knew he was on his own, said Chaplin. "There was always the possibility that other cops wouldn't come and help him when he needed backup. Cops have guns and cars running around. If they don't trust Simone, things could get scary for him. They might be a danger to him or just not show up when he needs them to."

Simone was relieved that he had left the Cleveland Police before the national scrutiny of the Russell-Williams and Tamir Rice shootings. But one year after his retirement, he would face a life-or-death battle of his own.

22 The Wall

After surviving five heart attacks since 2004, Simone was hospitalized in September 2012 to have a stent implanted in a coronary artery. The procedure was successful, but he experienced a bad reaction coming out of general anesthesia. For several harrowing hours, he hallucinated that he was back in Vietnam as a twenty-year-old platoon sergeant.

His family realized that he was experiencing a flashback episode when he barked commands at police officers who were visiting him, apparently believing they were members of his platoon.

"He kept reciting his rank and serial number," recalled Lynne. "Then he became paranoid and ordered people out of his room. In order to calm him, we all had to pretend that we were military people. He thought I was an army nurse and when our nephews came to visit, we told him that they were new soldiers in his unit."

His brother, then sixty-six, walked into the room. Simone looked at him, expecting to see a man in his twenties, and said, "Joe, you got old."

When he asked Joe for coffee with a shot of whiskey and a cigarette, which had been his daily ritual in Vietnam, Joe told him there was no smoking in the hospital. "Since when?" he asked.

"Then he wanted to know where our Uncle Tom was," said Joe. "When I told him that he had passed away, he started to cry. The whole episode was frightening. It's like he had been hypnotized. Even the hospital nurses were freaked out."

At times, Simone clutched his neck and screamed, "Where are my men!"

To his daughter, Michelle, it was clear that he was reliving the grenade explosion that had punctured his carotid artery and nearly killed him.

"I'd always known how bad Vietnam was for my father," said Michelle. "He always cried when he talked about it. To see him relive the experience was scary. It was very difficult to witness. I fully believed then that he had PTSD."

Jon Jakeway, who had served in Charlie Company with Simone, wasn't surprised to hear that he'd suffered a severe flashback. Noting that Vietnam was generally a nightmarish experience, Jakeway said:

When we first got to Vietnam, we were excited to be there. But we didn't know what was in store for us. I had always been the type of person who rode a motorcycle and skydived. If I couldn't get killed doing something, I wasn't interested in doing it. But in Vietnam, we all got much more than we bargained for. It became really, really scary for us when we realized that there was a very good chance that our lives could end at any second. The army can't train you to handle that level of fear. And it can get quite bad.

Despite the ever-present danger, there were times when the soldiers were too utterly exhausted to care, said Jakeway. "As infantrymen, we spent most of our time in the field. There was always the chance of an ambush or mortar attack, so we rarely slept for more than a few minutes. After a while, we got good at gauging how far away the enemy was. We'd hear the enemy rifle fire and grenade explosions getting closer and we'd know how many more minutes of sleep we could get until they were within shooting range."

If they survived the surreal horror of war, the soldiers were abruptly dumped back into civilian life with very little out-processing. Shortly after Jakeway arrived back in the United States, a young woman asked him if the army provided therapists for returning veterans. "I laughed so hard that I nearly fell over," he said. "There was nothing ever done for our mental wellness."

With Simone still trapped in his Vietnam flashback, doctors were planning to treat him with Haldol, an antipsychotic drug that is commonly used to reduce confusion.

Lynne, however, suspected that the drug would only exacerbate his hallucinations. She instructed the doctors not to begin the Haldol. A half-hour later, Simone woke up with no memory of his flashback.

Reflecting on his three-hour nightmare, Simone said the episode, while frightening to observers, may have been therapeutic for him.

"My life was turned upside down at age nineteen when I saw death all around me," he explained. "I not only saw death, but as a platoon leader, I sent young men to their death. When I got home, I repressed a lot of those experiences. Maybe the hallucinations were a way of finally letting go of those memories."

Simone wasn't out of the jungle yet. He underwent heart bypass surgery a month later. After a violent coughing jag, he broke open the metal wires used to tie his sternum together. Titanium bolts were used to close the surgical wound. He then contracted sepsis, which led doctors to keep him in an induced coma for twenty days to help his body fight the life-threatening condition.

It would take Simone nine months to recover from the bypass complications. As soon as he was medically released, he resumed working as a part-time patrol officer.

He even accepted a third part-time job serving warrants for Cleveland's Housing Court. He told people that he was enjoying retirement, joking that he had cut back his work schedule to six days a week. "But at least I don't have to jump fences anymore to arrest people," he said.

Carole Deighton Gentile, the daughter of his old friend, Bob Deighton, questioned why he was working so hard in his older years.

"They need me," Simone answered glibly.

"Or do you need them?" asked Gentile.

Simone is financially comfortable, with a large portfolio of rental properties and a secure pension. His near-compulsion for work seems puzzling to some. When the question is put to him, he says, with characteristic brevity, "What else would I do?"

To probe Simone's psyche, to search for his essence, reveals a determinism that invariably circles back on itself. He offers an uncomplicated explanation of himself: "I'm the son of my parents. I am who my father and mother made me."

Simone enjoys police work and is good at it. But the activity of work might also serve a protective function for him, said Lynne.

"He can't handle being idle," she said. "It's all about keeping his mind busy, trying to clog his brain to keep out the memories. Jim can talk about his feelings, but he can't watch war movies, especially movies about Vietnam."

Simone offers curt acknowledgment of his PTSD affliction. "We probably all had it," he said. "Our fathers who served in World War II probably had it too. But they went to work."

Whether or not Simone stays busy as a way of self-medicating his PTSD, police work has unquestionably been his raison d'être.

"People think it's unusual that I'm still chasing bad guys at age sixty-seven," he said. "But in life there are sheepdogs, sheep, and wolves. As long as I'm able, I'm going to make sure that no wolves bother the sheep. For me, being a cop is not just what I do, it's who I am."

By 2013, Lynne and Jim had been together for thirty-two years. They were so close that some of their younger family members had thought they were husband and wife. But on Christmas Eve of that year, Simone, in front of their extended family, asked Lynne to marry him.

"He had actually bought an engagement ring twenty years earlier," Lynne said. "He'd wanted to get married for years and eventually it was just time for me to say yes."

Both are traditionalists, with Simone wanting assurance that she was going to take his last name and Lynne insisting that they include the phrase, "To love, honor, and obey" in their wedding vows.

Opting for a casual, outdoor celebration, they married in August 2014 at her brother's home in front of nearly six hundred guests. "I figured that this would be my one and only wedding, so I didn't want to cut anyone out of the celebration," she said.

One month after their wedding, the couple traveled to Arlington National Cemetery for the internment of Bill Meacham, who had died six months earlier.

After the ceremony, they arranged to meet Jon Jakeway at the Vietnam Veterans Memorial Wall. It would be Simone's first visit to the memorial and he was, admittedly, nervous.

"I knew so many of those guys whose names are inscribed on the wall," he said.

I fought with them, slept in ditches with them, ate with them. And then, in a second, they were gone. We were eighteen- and nineteen-year-old kids, with a lot of potential, in the best shape of our lives. We left a lot of blood in the soil—ours and theirs. A lot of things happened in combat that we can never talk about. When we were there, it seemed appropriate. Later on, it didn't seem so right. Ultimately, I'll answer to God. He'll make the final decision on whether I did the correct thing.

Under a leaden sky that threatened rain, Simone approached the black granite wall, anxiously searching for the names of his fallen friends: Philip "Zeke" Zeleski, Ron Rondo, and Kenny Kotyluk. "They weren't just names to me; they were guys I knew. Seeing Rondo's and Zeke's inscriptions brought back a lot of memories. Rondo only had eight more hours on his tour when he was injured. He would have been leaving Vietnam the next morning. I had just told Zeke to treat Rondo when the grenade landed near us. Zeke took the blast and died instead of me."

Lynne, Jakeway, and Jim then found Kotyluk's inscription, located on a lower section of the wall. "We knew he wanted to be alone, so Jon and I stepped away," said Lynne.

Jim knelt on one knee and placed his hand against the wall, touching Kotyluk's name. He thought about the call he'd made several years ago to Kenny's mother to let her know that her son was thinking of her in his last moments. She had cried when he told her that Kenny had served bravely and died peacefully. A week later, he'd unexpectedly received a check from her. "Reimbursement for your long distance call," she'd written in a note. *War,* thought Jim, *is tougher on mothers than soldiers.*

He recalled his own mother. After he'd returned from Vietnam, his father told him that she had cried every single day that he was gone.

It's not true that time heals all wounds, thought Jim.

Long-resisted memories swelled and settled. He pressed his forehead against the wall and said a prayer for the dead.

Notes

In writing this book, I conducted dozens of interviews with Jim Simone, his family members, the soldiers and law enforcement professionals who served with him, and various experts in the fields of criminology and criminal justice. Source information was also gathered from Cleveland Police reports, U.S. Army records, court documents, and published news accounts from the *Plain Dealer, Cleveland Press,* Associated Press, *Cleveland Scene Magazine, Point of View,* CNN, WOIO-TV, Fox 8-TV, and others. In addition, I utilized information from William C. Meacham's book, *Lest We Forget: The Kingsmen, 101st Aviation Battalion, 1968* (New York: Ballantine Publishing Group, 1999) and James E. Bond and Robert L. Aylor's book, *Rakkasans: A History and Collection of Personal Narratives from Members of the 3rd Battalion, 187th Infantry, 101st Airborne Division* (Baltimore: Gateway Press, Inc., 2008).

The following notes indicate the sources I used in writing each chapter of the book. Conversations and actions by multiple participants are based on interviews with at least one of the participants. Unless noted otherwise, all information about Jim Simone and quotes attributed to him were provided by Simone during my interviews with him from March 2014 through December 2015.

Introduction
Jim Simone, interviewed by author, March 2014–December 2015.
Ed Kovacic, interviewed by author, August 22, 2015.

1. No Exit
Aftermath of church shooting: Cleveland Division of Police incident report, November 16, 1983; "3 Policemen Shot, Gunman Is Killed," *Plain Dealer,* November 17, 1983, 1-A, 7-A.
Ernestine Buckley and Donald Buckley at Lincoln-West High School: Ernestine Buckley, interviewed by author, June 1, 2015.
Interaction of Dennis Workman and Carla Giganti in school: Cleveland Division of Police report, November 17, 1983.

Marriage and activities of Rita Workman and Dennis Workman: Rita Workman, interviewed by author, May 6, 2015.

Dennis Workman seeking psychiatric help: Rita Workman, interviewed by author, May 6, 2015; Case files, Cuyahoga County Common Pleas Court, July 8, 1987; Bob Becker, "Shootout Widow Sues CPI, Metro General," *Plain Dealer,* July 9, 1987, 2-B.

Pastor Fred Yearsley, interviewed by author, May 8, 2015.

John Thomas, interviewed by author, March 14, 2015.

Brian Miller, interviewed by author, June 8, 2015.

Greg Baeppler, interviewed by author, June 24, 2014.

2. Friendly Fire

Account of Jim Simone's childhood: Joe Simone, interviewed by author, June 2, 2015.

Background information about the 3/187, C Company: James E. Bond and Robert L. Aylor, *Rakkasans* (Baltimore: Gateway Press, Inc., 2008), 7–12.

James MacLachlan, interviewed by author, July 8, 2015, and July 10, 2015.

Craig Caldwell, interviewed by author, May 11, 2015.

James E. Bond, interviewed by author, July 8, 2015.

Circumstances of Ken Kotyluk's death: Bond and Aylor, *Rakkasans,* 87–94.

3. Firebase Pope

Joe Simone, interviewed by author, June 2, 2015.

Dave Grossman, interviewed by author, August 26, 2015.

Mike Roberts, interviewed by author, May 26, 2015.

Account of Ralph "Chad" Colley wounding: Bond and Aylor, *Rakkasans,* 137–41; Jim Simone, interviewed by author, March 2014–December 2015.

Battle of Song Be: Bond and Aylor, *Rakkasans,* 37–46.

The attack on Firebase Pope: James MacLachlan, interviewed by author, July 8, 2015, and July 10, 2015; Bond and Aylor, *Rakkasans,* 264–95.

4. Homecoming

Simone's rescue: William Meacham, *Lest We Forget* (New York: Ballantine Publishing Group, 1999), 210–15; Jim Simone, interviewed by author, March 2014–December 2015.

Convalescing at Walter Reed hospital: Jon Jakeway, interviewed by author, May 3, 2015.

5. Transition

Information about Fort Indiantown Gap: Pennsylvania National Guard Military Museum.

Account of My Lai Massacre: Seymour Hersh, "My Lai 4: A Report on the Massacre and Its Aftermath," Dispatch News Service, November 12, 1969.

James MacLachlan, interviewed by author, July 8, 2015, and July 10, 2015.

Jon Jakeway, interviewed by author, May 3, 2015.

Carole Deighton, interviewed by author, June 14, 2015.

6. Back on Patrol

Joe Paskvan, interviewed by author, March 6, 2015.

Peter Moskos, interviewed by author, May 27, 2015.

The Hough Riots and 1970s racial tension in Cleveland: Mike Roberts, interviewed by author, May 26, 2015.

The Glenville Shootout: Louis H. Masotti and Jerome R. Corsi, "The Glenville Shootout and the Trial of Fred Ahmed Evans," the Cleveland Memory Project.

Joe Simone, interviewed by author, June 2, 2015.

7. The Crooked Line

Cleveland Police corruption: Ed Kovacic, interviewed by author, August 22, 2015.

Cleveland Demographics: Mike Roberts, "Cleveland in the 1970s," Teaching Cleveland Digital.

8. "You Never Get Away from 213A"

Cleveland Police spy: Ed Kovacic, interviewed by author, August 22, 2015.

Harley Reeser Jr. shooting: Mary Jane Woge, "Police Kill Burglary Suspect after Chase across Rooftops," *Plain Dealer,* October 18, 1977, 13-A.

Terry Murray captured in crawl space: *Plain Dealer,* May 17, 1980, 12-A.

Capture of rapists: "Kidnap, Rape Charges Filed against Brothers," *Plain Dealer,* February 1, 1981, 1-B.

Convenience store robbery: "Two Officers Halt Holdup at Lawson's—for 5th Time," *Cleveland Press,* March 20, 1981, 5-A.

Simone in burning house: John P. Coyne, "Policeman Saved from Fire, Recovers to Arrest Gunman," *Plain Dealer,* September 20, 1980, 18-A; "Policeman Saved from Arsonist's Blaze," *Cleveland Press,* September 20, 1980, 3-A.

9. Split-Second

Eugene Szejpcher shooting: Maxine L. Lynch, "Police Slaying of Gunman Ruled Self-Defense," *Plain Dealer,* February 27, 1981, 3-B.

Joe Paskvan, interviewed by author, March 6, 2015.

Criticism of Paskvan shootings: Roldo Bartimole, *Point of View,* March 12, 1983, 1, 4.

Dave Grossman, interviewed by author, August 26, 2015.

Baltimore Police backlash: Justin George and Luke Broadwater, "Mayor Tells Baltimore Police Officers to Do Their Jobs," *Baltimore Sun*, June 17, 2015.

10. Homicide

Michael S. Scott, interviewed by author, May 5, 2015.

Tom Evans, interviewed by author, March 28, 2015.

Simone disarming attackers: "Policeman Cut in Fight on West Side," *Plain Dealer*, January 7, 1981, 4-A.

Cleveland's Supercop: James Neff, "A Policeman's Lot," *Plain Dealer*, May 1, 1982, 1-C, 24-C, 25-C.

Simone publicity: Maxine L. Lynch and John P. Coyne, "A Policeman's Policeman," *Plain Dealer*, November 17, 1983, 1-C, 3-C.

Lynne Stachowiak-Simone, interviewed by author, March 2014– December 2015.

11. Dimple, Lola, and Curly

Podborny murder: Jerry Masek and Jerry Kvet, "Dimple Podborny, Others Get Life," *Cleveland Press*, October 11, 1981, 1-A; Walter Johns Jr. and Thom Cole, *Cleveland Press*, March 28, 1981, 3-A; Maxine L. Lynch, "6 Indicted for Chicagoan's Murder," *Plain Dealer*, March 28, 1981, 1-A, 25-A.

Cleveland mob wars: Ed Kovacic, interviewed by author, August 22, 2015; Mike Roberts, interviewed by author, May 26, 2015; Edward P. Whelan, "The Life and Hard Times of Cleveland's Mafia: How Danny Greene's Murder Exploded the Godfather Myth," *Cleveland Magazine*, August 1978.

Stephen Jones case: W. C. Miller, "West Sider, 3 Others Face Sex Charges," *Plain Dealer*, November 15, 1983, 1-A, 6-A.

12. Through and Through

Radio transcript of church shooting: Cleveland Division of Police, November 16, 1983.

Lynne Stachowiak-Simone, interviewed by author, March 2014–December 2015.

Greg Baeppler, interviewed by author, June 24, 2014.

John Thomas, interviewed by author, March 14, 2015.

Brian Miller, interviewed by author, June 8, 2015.

Sumskis interview at hospital: *Plain Dealer*, November 16, 1983, 7-A.

13. A Person of Interest

Ocie Reddick case: John F. Hagan, "Fatal Shooting over Stolen Car Means Life Term," *Plain Dealer*, August 10, 1985, 20-A.

Mary Anne Flynn murder: John P. Coyne, "Midwife to over 800 Is Found Beaten, Slain," *Plain Dealer,* August 25, 1984, 1-A; John F. Hagan, "Slayer of Nurse-Midwife Sentenced to Electric Chair," *Plain Dealer,* January 9, 1985, 1-B, 3-B; Jim Nichols, "Test Links Inmate to Murder," *Plain Dealer,* September 29, 2006, 5-B; John Caniglia, "Judge Throws out 1985 Murder Conviction of Death Row Inmate Anthony Apanovitch; Prosecutor Plans to Appeal," *Plain Dealer,* February 12, 2015, 3-A; Jacqueline Marino, "Bound to Die," *Cleveland Scene,* February 10, 2000.

Marty Flynn, interviewed by author, September 15, 2015.

Mario Trevino murder: John F. Hagan, "Alcoholic Guilty in Youth's Murder," *Plain Dealer,* December 19, 1985, 1-A, 6-A.

Simone injured during arrest: Dell M. Mosley, "Detective's Ribs Broken by Kick," *Plain Dealer,* March 6, 1985, 1-B.

Cleveland Airport airplane hijacking: "SWAT Team Storms Jetliner in Cleveland," United Press International, January 5, 1985.

Andres Gonzalez, interviewed by author, June 11, 2015.

14. Angel

Andres Gonzalez, interviewed by author, June 11, 2015.

Gruesome auto crash: Pat Galbincea, "2 Die as Car Is Rammed in Ohio City; Driver Held," *Plain Dealer,* July 24, 1990, 12-A.

Darryl Durr case: Dell M. Mosley, "Neighbor Charged with Slaying of Elyria Teen," *Plain Dealer,* April 15, 1988, 1-B; Karen Farkas, "Jury Convicts Elyria Man of Slaying Girl," *Plain Dealer,* December 6, 1988, 17-A.

Simone commended for drunk-driving arrests: Northeast Ohio chapter of MADD.

C. Ellen Connally, interviewed by author, May 20, 2015.

15. A Matter of Principle

Police misconduct cases/James Wittine lawsuit: Dell M. Mosley, "Cleared Policemen Suing for Defamation," *Plain Dealer,* December 11, 1990, 4-B; Case files, Cuyahoga County Common Pleas Court, December 4, 1991.

Alex Zamblauskas, interviewed by author, June 14, 2015.

Andres Gonzalez, interviewed by author, June 11, 2015.

Ed Kovacic, interviewed by author, August 22, 2015.

Gerald Goode case: Jacqueline Marino, "Tangled up in Blue," *Cleveland Scene,* May 11, 2000.

Background on Michael White: Mike Roberts, "Cleveland in the 1990s," Teaching Cleveland Digital.

16. Family Plan

Mary Simone, interviewed by author, June 15, 2015.

Stephanie Simone-Berardinelli, interviewed by author, June 6, 2015.

Michelle Simone, interviewed by author, June 6, 2015.

Lynne Stachowiak-Simone, interviewed by author, March 2014–December 2015.

Keith Sulzer, interviewed by author, April 13, 2015.

Bob Shores, interviewed by author, April 15, 2015.

Alex Zamblauskas, interviewed by author, June 14, 2015.

Tom Evans, interviewed by author, March 28, 2015.

Andres Gonzalez, interviewed by author, June 11, 2015.

Nick Szymanski, interviewed by author, September 14, 2015.

Steve Szymanski, interviewed by author, September 20, 2015.

17. Team Spirit

Collision danger of Ford police cruisers: Maggi Martin, "Crown Victoria Police Cars Still Draw Worries about Fires," *Plain Dealer,* October 27, 2007, 1-A.

Lynne Stachowiak-Simone, interviewed by author, March 2014–December 2015.

Margery Gerbec, interviewed by author, April 3, 2015.

18. Wild Bill

James E. Bond, interviewed by author, July 8, 2015.

Lynne Stachowiak-Simone, interviewed by author, March 2014–December 2015.

Craig Caldwell, interviewed by author, May 11, 2015.

James MacLachlan, interviewed by author, July 8, 2015, and July 10, 2015.

Michael Ciacchi case: Tom Beres, "Cleveland Officer Reportedly Shot; Suspect Killed," WKYC-TV, January 13, 2003; Lila Mills, "Police Who Shot and Killed Man Acted Properly, Prosecutor Says," *Plain Dealer,* July 4, 2003, 4-B.

Joe Ciacchi, interviewed by author, May 29, 2015.

Michael Ciacchi's last hours: Carl Basa, interviewed by author, May 26, 2015.

Jill Kekic, interviewed by author, May 26, 2015.

Jodi Sours Grant, interviewed by author, May 26, 2015.

Dean Kavouras, interviewed by author, June 7, 2015.

Suicide by cop phenomenon: James J. Drylie, *Suicide by Cop: Scripted Behavior Resulting in Police Deadly Force* (Saarbrücken, Germany: VDM Verlag Dr. Müller, 2008).

19. The Perfect Traffic Stop

Dash-cam video of Ariel Castro: Recorded by Jim Simone, June 12, 2008.

CNN interview of Simone: *Piers Morgan Live,* May 9, 2013.

Ed Kovacic, interviewed by author, August 22, 2015.

Ariel Castro kidnappings: Henry J. Gomez, "The Rescue of Amanda Berry, Gina DeJesus and Michelle Knight," *Plain Dealer*, May 10, 2013, 1-A, 3-A; "New Secrets Revealed in Ariel Castro Case," WOIO-TV, May 5, 2014.

Tom O'Grady, interviewed by author, July 12, 2015.

Robert Hackworth shooting: John C. Kuehner, "Cleveland Cop Shoots and Kills Man Suspected of Robbing Bank," *Plain Dealer*, July 9, 2008, 1-B; Jim Nichols, "Supercop Jim Simone Braces for Criticism after Wednesday Shooting," *Plain Dealer*, July 10, 2008, 1-A.

Prosecutor's ruling on Hackworth case: Mark Puente, "Simone Case Goes before a Grand Jury," *Plain Dealer*, February 19, 2009, 1-B, 3-B.

20. Regina's Ride-along

Regina Brett's *Plain Dealer* columns about Simone: July 16, 2008: July 17, 2008; July 24, 2008; October 5, 2008; October 7, 2008.

Rebuttal to Brett: Phillip Morris, "Officer Simone and His Gun Are Making Cleveland Safer," *Plain Dealer*, July 15, 2008, 1-B, 6-B.

Retrospective of Simone career: Regina Brett, "Story of Cleveland Police Officer Jim Simone's Life: Not on My Watch," *Plain Dealer*, January 14, 2009, 1-B, 3-B.

Robert Ducatman, interviewed by author, May 27, 2015.

Simone's grand jury appearance: Mike Tobin, "Grand Jury Clears 'Supercop' James Simone in Fatal Shooting," *Plain Dealer*, March 5, 2009, 1-B.

Ed Gallek, interviewed by author, April 14, 2015.

Simone's river rescue: Brie Zeltner, "Woman Falls through River Ice, Is Rescued by 'Supercop' Jim Simone," *Plain Dealer*, January 11, 2009, 1-A, 5-A.

Simone honored: Gabriel Baird, "'Supercop' Gets Drysuit for Next Water Rescue," *Plain Dealer*, January 27, 2009, 3-B; Mark Puente, "*PARADE* Magazine to Recognize Local Policeman's Bravery," *Plain Dealer*, September 28, 2009, 3-B; "America's Top Police Officers," *PARADE* magazine," October 4, 2009, 14.

Criticism of Simone's tactics: Mansfield Frazier, interviewed by author, May 20, 2015.

21. Terms of Retirement

Rabbi Sruly Wolf, interviewed by author, March 20, 2015.

Simone's retirement: Phillip Morris, "Cleveland's Retired 'Supercop' Is Now Patrolling 'Mayberry,'" *Plain Dealer*, July 11, 2012, 1-B.

Michael Jenovic, interviewed by author, March 19, 2015.

Tony Campo, interviewed by author, September 4, 2015.

Michael Brelo case: Peggy Gallek, "Six Officers Charged in Deadly Police Chase and Shooting," Fox 8-TV, May 30, 2014; "Cleveland Cop Michael Brelo to Stand Trial for Voluntary Manslaughter," NBC News, April 6,

2015; Ida Lieszkovszky, "Why the Judge Found Cleveland Police Officer Michael Brelo Not Guilty," Cleveland.com, May 23, 2015.

Tamir Rice case: Cory Shaffer, "Cleveland Police Officer Shoots 12-Year-Old Boy Carrying BB Gun," Cleveland.com, November 22, 2014; Timothy Williams and Mitch Smith, "Cleveland Officer Will Not Face Charges in Tamir Rice Shooting Death," *New York Times,* December 28, 2015, 1-A.

Kathleen Sutula, interviewed by author, June 7, 2015.

Ed Gallek, interviewed by author, April 14, 2015.

Peter Moskos, interviewed by author, May 27, 2015.

Daniel Chaplin, interviewed by author, May 13, 2015.

22. The Wall

Simone's Vietnam flashbacks: Lynne Stachowiak-Simone, interviewed by author, March 2014–December 2015.

Joe Simone, interviewed by author, June 2, 2015.

Michelle Simone, interviewed by author, June 6, 2015.

Jon Jakeway, interviewed by author, May 3, 2015.

Carole Deighton Gentile, interviewed by author, June 14, 2015.

Made in United States
North Haven, CT
15 July 2023

39104165R00148